Global Competitive Strategy

Globalization fundamentally changes the game of business. Strategic frameworks developed for the analysis of purely domestic business necessarily fall short in the international business context. Managers and business students require new approaches to understand and cope with these far-reaching changes. We must learn to think globally in order to succeed. *Global Competitive Strategy* shows how we can do this by providing a unique set of strategic tools for international business. Such tools include the "Star Analysis" that allows strategy makers to integrate geographic information with market information about the global business environment. Also introduced is the "global value connection," that shows managers how to account for the gains and costs of trade. Aimed at MBA students taking courses in international strategy, consultants and managers with responsibility for strategic development, this book offers a comprehensive strategic framework for gaining competitive advantage in the global market place.

Daniel F. Spulber is the Elinor Hobbs Distinguished Professor of International Business and Professor of Management Strategy at the Kellogg School of Management, Northwestern University. He is the founder of Kellogg's International Business and Markets Program.

Global
Competitive Strategy

Daniel F. Spulber

Northwestern University

CAMBRIDGE
UNIVERSITY PRESS

CAMBRIDGE UNIVERSITY PRESS

Cambridge, New York, Melbourne, Madrid, Cape Town, Singapore, São Paulo

Cambridge University Press
The Edinburgh Building, Cambridge CB2 8RU, UK

Published in the United States of America by Cambridge University Press,
New York

www.cambridge.org
Information on this title: www.cambridge.org/9780521880817

First published 2007

Printed in the United States of America

ISBN 978-0-521-88081-7 hardback

Companion website: www.cambridge.org/spulber

Contents

Figures

Tables

Preface

Globalization promises ever greater competitive challenges to business. Competitors are likely to be radically different than your company, since they may have huge cost advantages and offer customers unexpected product features. Managers must be ready to design competitive strategies that will succeed against global rivals. This book introduces techniques for strategic analysis and strategy making in a global market.

Top managers need to conduct an effective analysis of the global market place. The sheer size and complexity of global markets can be overwhelming, and the business manager seeking global competitive advantage must be able to address both the forces of global scale and the differences between countries. The manager will also require new tools for handling a vast flood of new information. To form a coherent competitive strategy, the manager will need a clear and comprehensive framework. This book presents just such a method of strategic analysis.

This book introduces the "Star Analysis" framework for evaluating the country context of the international business environment. The manager uses country-level data to evaluate country features and the implications for the firm's home base, suppliers, customers, partners, and competitors. Using information revealed by the "Star Analysis," the manager formulates global competitive strategies.

Traditional competitive strategy took place at the level of the industry. The industry still matters, of course, but the business manager must compete in the global market place. Suppliers, customers, partners, and competitors differ across countries. In putting together a global competitive strategy, the business manager must understand the country components that make up the global market place.

Countries matter a great deal in global business because borders are "sticky." Global businesses face high costs of crossing borders, and these costs of trade reinforce the economic differences between countries. The result is a global mosaic with tremendous cross-country variations in income, prices, wages, and innovations.

The global business manager must gather information about these key country differences: the country context includes cultural, social, and historical differences. National economies differ in terms of prices, products, resources, and technologies. Companies face different currencies, laws, regulations, and government policies.

The book gives managers tools for translating such international information into competitive strategy. As business has evolved from domestic to regional to global, it faces a strategic dilemma. The firm must compete in a global industry but, at the same time, it must address the different needs of country-level markets. Handling this dual challenge requires innovative competitive strategies.

To achieve competitive advantage in a worldwide industry, the firm needs to have world-class economies of scale and outstanding product quality. At the same time, however, to achieve competitive advantage in country-level markets, the firm must adjust to the local context in its customer service, supplier procurement, partnership arrangements, and competitive strategies.

The toolkit in this book draws from the economics of international trade and the economics of transaction costs. To structure the best transactions across country borders, the manager must develop an understanding of the gains from trade between national economies. The manager can then create a global value connection between many countries.

In the process, business will, as we have seen, encounter "sticky" borders. This means that the manager must also understand the costs of trade that arise when crossing national borders. Not only are there costs of communication and transportation, there are substantial government costs from tariffs and other barriers to trade. To compete in global markets, the firm creates global added value, and chooses its strategies to maximize net gains from international trade.

The book presents strategies for creating and capturing global added value. The discussion draws on the important concept of gains from trade in international economic analysis. The firm's global added value equals net gains from trade – that is, gains from trade minus the costs of trade. The firm that creates the greatest added value as compared to its competitors achieves global competitive advantage.

The discussion examines five key global competitive strategies, referred to as the "G5 strategies":

- G1 is the Global Platform Strategy, which is a method of achieving economies of scale while offering product variety to international customers.
- G2 is the Global Network Strategy, which is a method of coordinating sup-

plier and buyer networks to achieve competitive advantage.

- G3 is the Global Intermediary Strategy, in which the company provides matchmaking and market making services on a global scale.
- G4 is the Global Entrepreneur Strategy, in which the firm creates new combinations of buyers and sellers that cross international borders.
- The Global Investment Strategy (G5) guides decisions for establishing distribution and manufacturing facilities abroad. The G5 strategy emphasizes the fact that the firm must make the best mix of transactions, contracts, and vertical integration to enter new markets and develop existing ones.

The book also examines the design of the global business organization. The discussion looks at how the manager should determine the divisions of a global business organization to effectively carry out the company's strategy. It considers how the international business organization has evolved over time. The book also examines how to incorporate international geographic divisions in a market-based organization.

The book presents four business cases that provide a diverse set of international situations in which to apply critical parts of the strategic framework. The Lenovo case (chapter 7) examines how China's leading computer company decided to become a global company. The case provides insights into the influence of the features of the company's home country. The Cemex case (chapter 8) looks at the Mexican cement company's role as an international market maker, and provides insights into the globalization of a manufacturing company with particular emphasis on its supplier countries. The Dairy Farm case (chapter 9) studies the regional strategy of an Asian retailer facing global competition, and emphasizes management decisions concerning the choice of customer countries. The case study of Europe's diversified food company Danone (chapter 10) looks at the organizational structure of a growing global business, and considers how managers design the organization to carry out the company's global competitive strategy

This book is intended for MBA courses on International Business Strategy and should also prove highly valuable as a guide for global business executives. The book can be used for Economics courses that introduce students to international economics and business strategy, and can be supplemented by additional case studies that correspond to the content of each chapter.

Geography matters for global competitive advantage: globalization is tearing down barriers between countries but borders will remain "sticky" for a long time to come. Managers can apply the economic insights and international business tools presented here in designing their strategies for global competitive advantage.

Acknowledgments

This book is dedicated to my wife, Sue. I thank Sue for her patience, consideration, insights, and helpful discussions, and for believing so much in this project. This book would not have been written without her enthusiasm and understanding. I also thank Rachelle, Aaron, and Ben Spulber for being great supporters of this book and for providing comments and insights. Aaron provided valuable help with the Lenovo case.

I thank Dipak Jain, Dean of the Kellogg School of Management at Northwestern University, for his support for this work. I thank my international business students at the Kellogg School of Management for their feedback and discussions that have enhanced the present work and increased its value in the classroom. I thank my colleague Alberto Salvo for his highly helpful comments and suggestions and for coauthoring the Cemex case. I also thank Donald Lessard, Ramon Casadesus-Masanell, and Yoshiro Miwa for their valuable comments, that significantly improved the presentation.

This book draws upon some previously published work:

Daniel F. Spulber, 2005, "Lenovo: The Leading Chinese Computer Company Enters Global Competition," *Journal of Strategic Management Education*, 2(1), Senate Hall Academic Publishing.

Alberto Salvo and Daniel F. Spulber, 2006, "Cemex: International Market Maker," *Journal of Strategic Management Education*, 3(1), Senate Hall Academic Publishing.

Daniel F. Spulber
January 2007

Introduction: the global challenge

The global market place is the World Cup. It definitely is not one big level playing field. Many top teams vie for supremacy, with the best talent scattered around the world. Teams from many countries bring different traditions and diverse playing styles. Every football team brings a different mix of athletic skills and their competitive strategies vary widely. No competitor can count on home-field advantages. Success requires sufficient endurance and versatility to overcome many teams. Winning requires beating multiple challengers from across the globe.

Gaining the World Cup requires world-class competitive advantage – and global competitive advantage is what your company must have to make it in the global market place. This book provides a new method for strategic analysis that accounts for variations in business environments across countries. It explores novel competitive strategies that can help your company to win worldwide. The discussion further considers global investment strategies and the design of the international business organization. The analysis offers managers a comprehensive framework for gaining global competitive advantage.

Global competition

Globalization changes everything! Before globalization, a firm's competitive advantage was likely to be little more than a critical edge – just a subtle distinction between rival firms. In the global market place, companies can have spectacular differences. Firms with a global competitive advantage will overwhelm rivals who are not prepared.

Before globalization, your main competitor likely was located in the same country, the same city, even on the same street! Your company and its competitors fought for the same customers. Your firm and its rivals drew from the same labor force, with similar wage and benefit costs and comparable skills. Managers in your firm and its rivals shared the same outlook and cultural

1

background, often coming from the same business schools, ethnic groups, and perhaps even the same family. Your firm and its rivals often had the same costs of capital, resources, energy, equipment, parts, and technology. Your company and its competitors faced the same legal, regulatory, and public policy constraints.

In this cozy environment, competitive advantage was at best the result of luck, talent, and clever management maneuver. Some firms expected to deter rivals just by outspending them on capital investment. Strategy recommendations were tailored to this environment, urging companies to gain the upper hand through pricing techniques, marketing gimmicks, bundles of product features, or frequent model changes.

Companies could afford complacency. They could go to market with similar products, relying on customer inertia or traditional sales channels. Firms could depend on brand image and marketing messages to drive home a competitive wedge. They could even prosper while offering uninspired designs and planned obsolescence, relying on rebates and end-of-season sales to move merchandise. Companies could dictate styles and trends to their customers and hope for the best. They could tolerate inflated labor costs and workplace inefficiencies, secure in the knowledge that their competitors faced the same problems. Survival was possible even with poor performance, uneven service, bureaucratic organizations, and sluggish responses to market forces.

With rapidly increasing globalization, such safe strategies are no longer sustainable. Managers cannot hope to stay within their comfort zone. The global market place requires managers to go beyond their familiar surroundings. Their companies face intense competitive challenges from around the world.

Managers must think globally to succeed. They need a global strategy framework because of the complexities of the international market place. Those frameworks developed for the analysis of purely domestic business strategy necessarily fall short in the international business context. Suppliers, customers, partners, and competitors likely are located abroad. Competitors have vastly different costs, products, technologies, and strategies. It is only by understanding – and, indeed, harnessing – the forces of globalization, that managers can develop global competitive advantage.

With globalization, competitive advantages become earth-shattering chasms. A competitor's costs may be a tiny fraction of your company's costs because their products are made in low-cost countries. Robert "Steve" Miller, chief executive officer (CEO) of the world's largest auto-parts maker, Delphi, noted that: "Globalization is a fact of life these days."[1] Delphi declared bankruptcy in its US operations where its labor costs were $65 per hour while comparable labor costs in China were only $3 per hour. Miller further observed that:

Behind all this financial drama are the lives and livelihoods of thousands of our loyal and dedicated workers. These are honest, hard-working human beings who played by the rules and cannot be blamed for pursuing the American dream by taking a job at General Motors Corp. or Delphi. They expected us to live up to our promises, but have been caught by fast-changing global economics.

Looking ahead, your company is more likely to face a competitor with extremely innovative products and world-class brands. US auto makers GM and Ford struggled with considerable effort but experienced declining market share competing against global brands such as Toyota, Honda, BMW, Audi, and MercedesBenz. Brock Yates, the editor at large of *Car and Driver* magazine, worried about the chances for GM's survival, its only hope being in "revamped, reformed, and re-energized design studios and engineering spaces."[2] With Toyota headed for the top slot in world markets, both GM and Ford considered an Alliance with Renault–Nissan.

The classic generic competitive strategies of cost leadership and product differentiation, while useful, offer limited guidance with globalization. New strategies must address the vast differences in costs, capabilities, and products that exist in world markets. Companies need to understand how global competitors devise dazzling business deals that cross international borders. Firms require strategies that create advantage from new international combinations of buyers and sellers.

Before globalization, you often knew your competitors intimately; their strategy and tactics were all too predictable. As globalization unfolds, your competitor is not only coming from half-way around the world, its very identity may be previously unknown to your company. Global competitors may follow innovative and original strategies. Your greatest competitor may turn out to be an aggressive entrepreneurial firm from an emerging market rather than a familiar stodgy conglomerate from a developed economy. The element of surprise heightens the new entrant's competitive advantages.

Before globalization, your target markets were familiar, as well. With increasing globalization, keeping up with competitors means that you must expand your reach to distant countries. Getting close to your customers requires adapting to many distinct national environments. This requires managers and employees that are familiar with local languages, customs, cultures, and business practices.

The global market place is not only a matter of competitive challenges. It also represents an expansion of opportunities. Global firms choose target countries to select from 6.5 billion potential consumers in over 190 countries. Countries with large populations such as China and India offer diverse internal markets. Emerging markets are just that – opportunities to serve new consumers. Emerging markets offer faster growth rates for consumption than in developed economies, as consumers there have not had the best choices of goods and services.

The global market place offers firms vast new labor forces. Many emerging markets suffer from unemployment and underemployment, and there are significant opportunities to increase productivity in such markets through infusions of capital, technology, and training. As the impact of globalization expands, there are opportunities to increase productivity in developed countries, as well. Global competition will require companies in the developed world to streamline organizations and change wasteful work patterns. Companies in developed economies must increase innovation and productive efficiency to stay in the game.

Achieving global competitive advantage cannot be done in a domestic fortress. Lobbying governments to erect barriers to trade has limited value: better or cheaper goods find their way into even the most closed markets. Trade barriers merely postpone the inevitable and provide a false sense of security. Companies cannot resist the forces of globalization for very long: success goes to those companies that actively address the global challenge and seize global opportunities.

Global competitors use the international market place to transcend the limits of their home market – on both the demand side and supply side of the business. Companies seek incremental revenue from targeting customers abroad. Companies also must go global to lower their costs, improve their products, and find innovative suppliers and partners. Innovative business strategies are those that embrace globalization.

What is globalization?

Christopher Columbus was right. The world is round, not flat. In fact, the world is very bumpy! The countries of the world differ greatly, with some at the highest peaks of industrialization and technology, others on the hillsides of economic development, and emerging markets roaring out of the economic valleys. It is this great diversity that provides opportunities for trade.

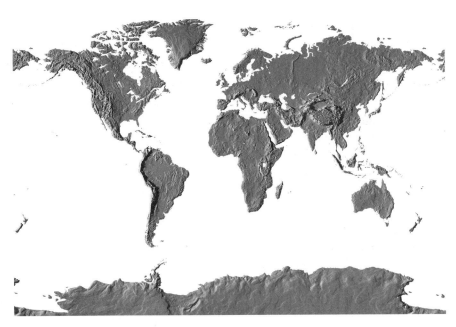

Fig. I.1   The world is bumpy! Managers need to read the contours
Source: Digital Wisdom, Inc.

Just like the physical topography shown on a globe, the map of the economic world is *contoured*, see Figure I.1. In each area of the world, there are many different levels of economic development. The uneven distribution of income, technology, human capital, and infrastructure creates a contoured world, and the manager must understand how to adjust strategy to the ups and downs of the world's contours.

Why is the world so bumpy? The Internet was supposed to eliminate all frictions. Video teleconferencing and software fostered collaboration across borders. Mobile computing and advances in telecommunications made it possible for people to be constantly in touch. Improvements in express shipping led the shift to just-in-time (JIT) production. Jet-age advances in transportation allowed people to meet customers and suppliers anywhere and anytime.

Shrinking distances should have begun to erode economic differences between countries. In a frictionless world, the playing field was level, and this would stimulate enough competition to even things out around the world. Yet there was an apparent puzzle – many of the "peaks" and "valleys" remained.

What could explain the persistent economic differences between countries? What made country borders into barriers? The answer to the puzzle is the costs of trade, costs that decline only at a measured pace.

Globalization is the gradual reduction in the costs of trade. Economic distances are indeed shrinking, but they will not disappear overnight. Globalization is neither an origin nor a destination. It is a journey, and a long and difficult one at that. Contrary to what many believe, we are not there yet.[3] The effects of globalization are earth-shattering because even small changes in the costs of trade can have spectacular effects. These extreme effects do not imply that we live in a borderless world, they are only an indicator of changes to come. Managers need to understand the challenges that lie ahead and prepare for the changing environment.

What makes borders so "sticky"? Global businesses face four types of trade costs or barriers. I refer to these trade costs as "the four Ts":
• Transaction costs
• Tariff and non-tariff costs
• Transportation costs
• Time costs.

These are the costs of doing business across international borders. They preserve the economic contours of the world.

Transaction costs result from the difficulties of doing business across borders. The international business encounters different cultures, customs, traditions, and societies: a handshake can mean something different from place to place. Social relationships form the backdrop of business and the international manager must account for social networks. Business practices and marketing methods are likely to differ substantially. Managers and employees must transact in different languages. They must search for customers and suppliers in unknown markets. Contracts are negotiated and honored in different ways. Customer preferences and incomes are likely to vary considerably.

Government trade barriers are an important source of "sticky" borders. The online virtual universe has opened new channels for international competition and collaboration. Yet, here on earth, the massive tangle of regulations has only begun a slow process of unraveling. Countries are not about to give up their national sovereignty. The nation-state is here to stay. Even in the European Union (EU), with a common market and a central parliament, governments jealously guard their political power. Around the world, trade protectionism continues to erect roadblocks to imports and investment. Economic nationalism defends domestic employment, manufacturing methods, cultural traditions, and local ownership of companies.

Goods, services, and investments do not move perfectly freely. Tariff and non-tariff costs imposed by governments are everywhere. All countries restrict the movement of goods and services to some extent: they charge tariffs at the border, they limit imports with quotas, and they use all kinds of health, safety, and other rules. Even the Internet has barriers, as governments control access and censor content. In addition, governments restrict foreign investment. For example, the US turned back a Chinese oil company, CNOOC, bidding to buy UNOCAL, and blocked Dubai Ports World from managing terminals in US ports. The French government arranged a merger of water and energy utility Suez SA with natural gas utility Gaz de France to head off a bid for Suez by Italy's largest electric company, Enel SpA.

Location and distance still matter a lot. Transportation costs necessarily remain a barrier to trade. The international business not only pays the freight to move parts, components, energy, and final products around the world. It also bears the costs of the complicated logistics needed to coordinate far-flung supply chains and distribution networks. A manufacturer must finely tune its systems to adjust inventories and achieve JIT manufacturing. A retailer or wholesaler must have final products arrive where and when they are needed in response to market demand. Only some international business is virtual; software and services are only a small slice of the pie. Many deals may be online, but the goods still have to reach their destination somehow.

Finally, there is the cost of time. Doing international business simply takes longer than doing business in one's own backyard. Distribution and supply chains are geographically dispersed, leading to longer cycle times. Managers must travel abroad and do business in unfamiliar business environments. Companies must handle government bureaucracies that can impose unexpectedly long delays. Managers need to form new relationships with foreign suppliers and customers and learn about new countries. Adapting to new environments and learning about unfamiliar customers necessarily take more time than testing home markets, and companies can incur increased investment and inventory costs as a result of these delays.

Reaction time is slower in international business. Managers must find ways to adapt more quickly as they compete with many established competitors and creative entrants. Dispersed distribution and manufacturing facilities slow down bureaucratic organizations. Properly deployed and managed, decentralized operations offer faster local response to changing market conditions.

How can we explain globalization? Some barriers to trade are being dismantled by governments. Institutions such as the World Bank aid economic development and the International Monetary Fund (IMF) helps to stabilize currencies and country economies. Countries reduce barriers to trade either unilaterally or through bilateral and multilateral agreements with other countries.

After the Second World War, the General Agreement on Tariffs and Trade (GATT) began a process of trade liberalization, with eight trade rounds over the next fifty years. The final GATT negotiation round, known as the Uruguay Round, developed rules, procedures, and protocols that served as the foundation for the World Trade Organization (WTO). The WTO agreement on Trade Related Aspects of Intellectual Property Rights (TRIPS) established rules for global intellectual property (IP), including copyrights, trademarks, and patents. The Dispute Settlement Understanding (DSU) established a trade dispute system designed to allow countries to bring violations of WTO law before an international ruling body and to provide countries with a way to appeal WTO resolutions. Countries supplement the WTO with multilateral trade agreements such as the North American Free Trade Agreement (NAFTA), between the US, Canada, and Mexico.

It is important to emphasize that the process of reducing trade barriers is not a straight line. Governments sometimes add new barriers as fast as they dismantle the old ones. Tariff reductions may be replaced by import quotas; trade liberalization in one sector may be matched by tightening elsewhere in the economy. For example, while joining in lowering trade barriers within the EU, France established stricter limits on foreign investment.

The political side of globalization captures headlines and attracts heated protests but, contrary to popular belief, it is only one of the forces moving globalization. Perhaps the most important source of globalization is the fact that international business has many incentives to overcome trade barriers. International trade often has grown steadily despite rather than because of reduced barriers. Businesses increasingly find ways to circumvent or adjust to government trade restrictions. For example, they move manufacturing and assembly to countries that face lower trade restrictions from countries where final customers are located. The growth of international transactions itself fosters the learning and trust that helps business to reduce contracting costs.

International businesses also find other ways to overcome the trade barriers associated with costly transactions. Technological change in computers and communications are driving new international business; the Internet lowers transaction costs between buyers and sellers, and has only begun to be harnessed as a means of lowering international transaction costs. Outsourcing of customer call centers and software services is due in large part to the lower costs of communication online.

Technological change also offers ways to lower transport costs. The application of information technology (IT) to logistics has brought substantial

growth in international business. There are substantial complexities in dealing with several million international shippers and over 40,000 freight for-
warders;[4] the introduction of freight containers has allowed better integration
and coordination of trucking, rail, and ocean transport.

To summarize, globalization is the process of reducing the costs of transactions, tariffs and non-tariff barriers, transportation, and time. These
changes are very difficult to observe directly. The hidden underlying forces of
world change manifest themselves in the growth of world trade and investment. It is much easier to see the effects of globalization.

Since the Second World War, the pace of change has been steady. First and
foremost, world trade is growing faster than world output – the ratio of world
trade to world output is growing at almost 3 percent per year. The world
factory is growing, with inputs and final goods crossing borders, so that the
ratio of manufactured goods trade to total manufactured output is growing at
well over 3.5 percent per year.[5] Capital is crossing borders, with business and
portfolio investment growing faster than the world economy itself.

The size of the global market place is simply staggering. International trade
surpassed the $10 trillion mark some years ago – but the global market is not
just international trade. It is the sum total of the domestic markets of over 190
countries. Scale economies offered by world markets exceed anything ever
achieved in a home-country market. Efficient supply chains stretch across
continents. Sources of product innovation are more diverse and imaginative
than any single Silicon Valley. International transactions are more complex
and creative than deals confined within national borders.

Globalization reaches into the details of our everyday life. What we eat
and drink, what we wear, what we drive, and what we use to heat our homes
are likely to come from different countries around the world. More fundamentally, our occupations and those of our children are determined by
whether our skills and wages are competitive with other people around the
world. Managers who adapt to these trends can benefit from a profusion of
opportunities.

Global opportunities

Many people feel that the promise of globalization already has been achieved.
Some fear that globalization will have devastating effects on their jobs and
lifestyles. Others worry about the increasing intensity of competition in world
markets. But globalization is a story of increasing opportunity.

To understand what lies ahead, consider some of the differences between countries. There are vast disparities between household incomes in the developed economies and those in emerging and less developed economies. Education levels, standards of health care, nutrition, and housing differ greatly around the world. The historian David Landes has observed that: "Now the big challenge and threat is the gap in wealth and health that separates rich and poor . . . Here is the greatest single problem and danger facing the world of the Third Millennium."[6]

These differences in income between countries will not be eliminated soon. The emergence of a middle class in China and India is a welcome development, yet significant structural changes still are needed for a poor villager in these countries, or in many areas of Asia, Africa, and Latin America, to achieve similar prosperity. It is apparent that wage differences will persist.

Countries differ substantially in technology, whether for manufacturing, agriculture, communications, or information processing. Technical knowledge and research and development (R&D) activities are distributed unevenly across countries. Significant changes in societies, improvements in education and training, and diffusion of innovations must occur before technologies converge. The technological differences that underlie the comparative advantages of nations will continue for a long time to come.

The business environment differs across countries. Legal and political factors join with cultural and social underpinnings to create disparities in the business climate. The organization Transparency International ranks individual countries on the basis of surveys of popular perceptions of corruption, with political parties, legislatures, police, the judiciary, business, and tax authorities among the most corrupt institutions worldwide.[7] The reform necessary to harmonize the business climate across the world is a necessarily slow process, hampered by social differences and by human nature itself.

Training of managers and expertise in business also vary across countries. Regulations and government red tape impact the time needed to establish and develop private businesses. It takes a long time to make the investments needed to improve the transportation and communications infrastructure, so critical to doing business. These differences between countries are likely to continue.

All of these inter-country differences represent vast opportunities. The populations of emerging markets are the untapped consumers of the future. Nigeria has become the third-largest customer country for Guinness beer, behind Ireland and the UK, reflecting a growing market for consumer goods and luxury brands throughout Africa.[8]

Emerging markets offer huge potential for growth, with populations that are underemployed in traditional agriculture, handicrafts, and labor-intensive manufacturing. Moreover, emerging markets have the potential to launch creative new businesses, as already shown by Mexico's cement giant Cemex or China's Lenovo computer company.

Emerging markets are not the only source of global opportunities. As emerging markets provide and purchase new products, developed countries also undergo significant change. When faced with competition from imports, enterprises in developed economies must move up the value chain, providing novel product designs, new types of services, innovations in production processes, and management expertise. These structural changes in the developed economies create economic value, and the global business can benefit from such economic transformations.

The greatest potential lies in business between countries. Throughout the world, barriers to trade cause companies to do much more business within countries than they do between countries. Huge profits from business across borders come from *arbitrage* opportunities. Price differences between countries signal opportunities to provide products, services, and investments, moving them from low-price sources to high-price markets. Myriad new businesses profit by serving underserved markets with new products: little wonder that business growth is coming from deals that cross borders.

Global analysis and strategy

The companies we work for will not be around for long unless they are successful in the global market. Managers cannot venture out into global markets with guidance from traditional strategies or from concepts and case studies better suited to closed national markets.

Managers already know the generic concepts of cost advantage and product differentiation. International business managers already understand product life cycles and the possibility that product availability may vary across countries. They are already familiar with the need to coordinate their many international operations. International managers already understand the need to distribute knowledge across the international organization.

Managers are increasingly sophisticated when it comes to international business. Most managers have traveled and often studied abroad. They attend business programs where students from many countries extensively interact. Many have worked for international businesses. They follow business news from around the world. Managers' greater knowledge about international business provides them with a solid foundation. What remains to be added is a conceptual framework suited specifically to international business.

Globalization requires that managers develop business strategies for the new world market place. Many companies already have many customers, suppliers, partners, and competitors located abroad. Many business transactions of necessity already cross international borders. Businesses already are operating or planning to establish facilities in many countries. Businesses already know that many of their customers and some of their competitors are located abroad. Dealing with globalization requires a comprehensive system for achieving global competitive advantage.

This book presents a framework for global business strategy. That framework has four main parts: competitive analysis, determination of the company's added value, competitive strategy formulation, and design of organizational structure.

The discussion begins with a method of global market analysis for competitive advantage. The manager gathers country-level and regional-level data. Using this information, he or she applies the "Star Analysis" to the company's actual and potential markets. The "Star Analysis" has five main components:

1 The features of the company's *home country*
2 The features of the company's *supplier countries*
3 The features of the company's *customer countries*
4 The features of the company's *partner countries*
5 The features of the company's *competitor countries.*

The competitor countries are the home, supplier, customer, and partner countries of the company's competitors, see figure I.2.

By explicitly addressing country differences, the "Star Analysis" helps the manager to pull together a *global strategy*, which systematically incorporates the essential geographic and business information needed to identify opportunities and threats in global markets. The method of analysis provides a consistent way to process the country information needed for strategy formulation. The "Star Analysis" framework guides the international business manager in formulating strategies to achieve competitive advantage in the global market place.

The manager must then examine the company's *global added value*. The global company's value proposition results from business that crosses national borders. Value for the international business is generated by gains from trade that crosses borders, a value offset by the high costs of doing business across

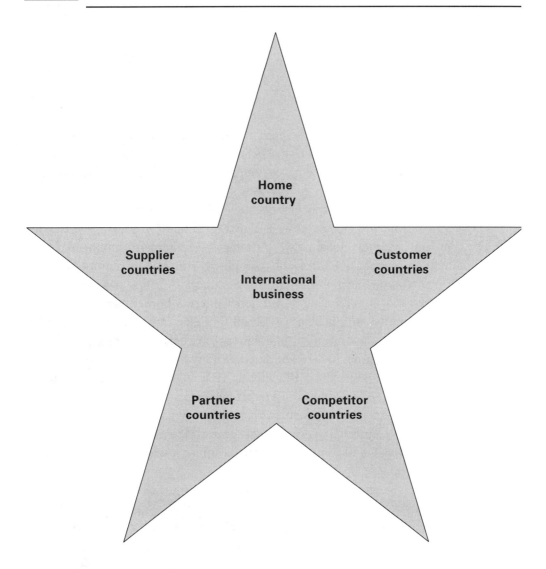

Fig. I.2   The international business strategy "Star Analysis" for global competitive advantage

borders. The value created by the international business therefore equals the net gains from trade – that is, the gains from trade minus the costs of trade.

The profitability of the international business depends on how much it can capture of the value that it creates. Capturing value is based on the company's *global competitive advantage*, which is reflected directly in the company's *global value connection* between countries. The greater the company's added value relative to that of its competitors, the greater will be its profit.

I next present a set of five global competitive strategies, the "G5 strategies":

- Global platform strategy
- Global network strategy
- Global intermediary strategy
- Global entrepreneur strategy
- Global investment strategy.

The analysis highlights how the manager can examine the company's strengths and weaknesses. The discussion shows how best to match company strengths with international market opportunities to achieve global competitive advantage.

The global platform strategy helps the firm decide what activities to standardize around the globe and what activities to tailor to local markets. The company using the global network strategy harnesses large numbers of customers and suppliers to form global supplier chains and distribution systems. The firm follows the global intermediary strategy by acting as a matchmaker or market maker, increasing the efficiency of cross-border transactions. As a global entrepreneur, the company establishes new combinations of supplier and customer relationships in international markets. The global investment strategy distinguishes between horizontal and vertical forms of foreign direct investment (FDI). It covers the alternative modes of entry that the international business can follow in its target markets.

These strategies allow the company to achieve global competitive advantage in ways that transcend traditional cost and differentiation advantages. The company creates and captures value by creating greater net gains from trade than its competitors.

The manager finally considers how to structure the firm as a global business organization. The organization must provide sufficient flexibility to respond to changing global market conditions, while generating the information necessary to implement the firm's global strategy. Following the "Star Analysis," the company establishes *global market-based divisions*. These divisions have global market responsibilities and are best able to identify and profit from the opportunities generated by the net gains from trade across country borders. The discussion examines the structure and prospects of conglomerates that traditionally have played an important role in international business and considers whether they will be able to adapt to changes in the global market.

Overview

Global competitive strategy requires managers to understand the contours of the global market place. These contours create opportunities for those businesses that make creative connections across borders. The rising tide of globalization is only just beginning to cover some "peaks" and "valleys." Although trade barriers are falling continually, international borders will continue to be "sticky."

Country differences at the same time pose problems and create economic opportunities. By processing information about country differences through the "Star Analysis," managers can formulate global competitive strategies. The firm must recognize and adapt to the features of its home country, and those of its suppliers, customers, partners, and competitors.

Global competitive advantage requires superior performance in comparison to both international and local rivals. Global business must achieve world-class cost efficiencies, product quality, and innovation, while tailoring its offerings to local preferences and needs. International competitive strategy is designed to integrate these dual requirements. The successful global business will turn the diversity and strengths of global markets to its own advantage.

1   The global mosaic

The world is a colorful mosaic. Each country contributes a tile with a distinct shape and texture to the global picture. The panoply of economic differences between countries creates many opportunities for international business, and global business strategy necessarily recognizes the geographic dimensions of world markets.

Country economies differ substantially in the extent of their industrialization and overall economic development. Economic differences across countries primarily show up as variations in prices and wages. Different standards of living translate into inequalities in health care, longevity, nutrition, housing, child care, and education. Gaps in R&D and scientific knowledge are apparent.

Why do countries differ? This question has been a major subject of public debate for a long time.[1] In 1776, Adam Smith published his famous book that addressed this very question: *An Inquiry Into the Nature and Causes of the Wealth of Nations*. He found that: "The greatest improvement in the productive powers of labour, and the greater part of the skill, dexterity, and judgment with which it is anywhere directed, or applied, seem to have been the effects of the division of labour." When cities, regions, and even countries specialize in different activities, their individual expertise improves and overall productivity grows.

Smith observed that those countries with the greatest wealth were those that engaged in international trade and took advantage of the division of labor. Countries that traded with other countries were able to specialize in particular types of agriculture, manufacturing, and other productive activities. The greater the extent of the market, the greater would be the prosperity of individuals: "the number of people of whose industry a part, though but a small part, has been employed in procuring him this accommodation, exceeds all computation."[2] The more that a country participates in trade and commerce, both within its own borders and together with other countries, the better off will be its economy. For a business, the more it participates in the world economy, the greater will be its economic opportunities.

Joining the world economy is easier said than done. Businesses must deal with "sticky" borders. The high costs of trade make it difficult for businesses to transact between countries, and these limits on trade can freeze the economic differences between countries. Globalization makes borders less "sticky" and creates arbitrage opportunities. The dynamics of international trade modifies the economic differences between countries. The global mosaic changes continually.

The four costs of trade

International borders are "sticky" – both for products coming into countries and for products leaving them. The international business faces many costs of crossing national borders. Trade costs are an important driver of international business decisions; Anderson and van Wincoop estimate that on average the combined costs of trade act like a staggering markup of 170 percent! The markup is the difference between the final delivered price and the initial price that was paid before crossing international borders.[3] Despite such high costs, there is still a very large volume of international trade. The persistent growth of international trade suggests that many opportunities remain to be discovered. As the costs of trade continue to fall, global business will experience significant additional growth.

Cost of trade: 1 – transaction costs

Transaction costs are intrinsic to the organization of business and the scope of the firm. The Nobel prize winner Ronald H. Coase was among the first to notice that there are costs to using markets. Transaction costs can be high: as a rough measure, the activities of retail, wholesale, and financial intermediaries account for over one-quarter of the net output of the US economy.[4]

Domestic transaction costs are high, but transaction costs between countries are likely to be much higher. In its supplier countries and customer countries, the international business faces very different environments. The firm must adapt to different business contexts, including languages, cultures, social customs, business practices, and political, legal, and regulatory climates.

The international business deals with different local suppliers and different customer groups in its various locations that may require adjustment of its business methods. The international manager must develop knowledge and relationships in the local market in which the company is operating. In each context, the international business may need to vary its prices, products, sales, service, contracts, purchasing, hiring, and management practices. These critical issues are discussed extensively in the field of international management.

There are even more daunting problems than just operating in multiple countries. The international business must transact *across* borders, which brings to bear a host of unique transaction costs. The costs of cross-border trade are often greater than transactions within countries.

The cross-border transactions of the international business are bridges between national economies. The global business operates as an international intermediary, as it simultaneously buys and sells in many different countries. The global business searches for customers in one country, finds suppliers in other countries, and matches their demands and supplies. This means that a customer in a given country does not have to search for a supplier in a distant country, relying instead on the international business to make the necessary connections behind the scenes. The customer of a retail store is often unaware that the goods in his or her market basket represent an assortment of products carefully assembled around the world. The buyer of a computer or appliance often does not know that the manufacturer obtained the best combination of parts from a global supply chain that stretches across many countries.

The global business deals with each supplier and customer in their own locations, languages, and cultures. It must operate seamlessly in multiple time zones, making suppliers and customers comfortable in their own time zone. A global logistics provider such as UPS helps companies move information, products, and funds around the world. For example, the company operates a network of 650 locations worldwide to provide delivery of critical parts in one, two, or four hours. The company states that: "We don't just synchronize deliveries. We synchronize trade across borders" (www.ups.com).

The international business must handle multiple currencies, subjecting itself to all the risks that come from fluctuating exchange rates and bearing the costs of hedging those risks. This allows each of the company's customers and suppliers to deal with the international business in their own local currency.

The global firm juggles many different types of purchasing and sales contracts, making them work effectively in combination. For example, the international business handles many procurement contracts in the different countries that make up its supply chain. These contracts have to be managed effectively to make sure that the final product is delivered to the right place, at the right time, and with the desired quality.

Sporting goods company Adidas Salomon AG introduces as many as 10,000 new apparel items and 4,000 new footwear items every three months.[5]

According to UPS: "Many retailers are implementing a just-in-time delivery cycle, requiring more orders more often as opposed to bulk shipments. The team orders filled by Adidas are also highly variable, ranging from as few as 50 shipments to as many as 2,500. A high percentage of the units shipped by Adidas are for priority requests, which must be received within one or two days." UPS provides a single-source logistics solution to handle the millions of shipments of clothes, footwear, and sporting goods to retailers, reducing the transaction costs of dealing with multiple logistics providers for cross-border distribution.[6]

Transaction costs present opportunities for international business. The business that is able to create innovative transactions that reduce these costs can find major untapped business opportunities. Some of these will take the form of international arbitrage. Others will involve the creation of entirely new forms of business, such as outsourcing of business services from the US and Europe to Indian firms. Through novel business methods, applications of IT, and superior knowledge of multiple country markets, some international businesses will gain competitive advantage by lowering cross-border transaction costs.

Cost of trade: 2 – tariff and non-tariff costs

Although many government-created barriers are falling, roadblocks to trade and investment remain. Governments are not eager to give up their national sovereignty, even within close associations of countries such as the EU. Restrictions on trade and investment are instruments of national policy used by every country to achieve domestic and international objectives, and are not easily dismantled.

All governments impose various types of tariff and non-tariff barriers to trade. These include such things as import quotas, product standards, subsidies, voluntary export restraints, and licensing. Countries use trade and investment regulations to protect and promote particular industries, to encourage employment in particular sectors, to benefit domestic political friends, to collect tariff revenues, and to pursue national security objectives. Countries also use trade and investment agreements for geopolitical purposes, rewarding countries that are allies and penalizing opponents. Managers must make their cross-border deals with a clear view of trade alliances and regulations.

Trade barriers, as we have seen, preserve many of the economic differences that make up the global mosaic. Every country imposes a complex set of trade regulations, and global managers should explore carefully the trade costs of alternative strategies. Advances in computers and communications have brought the virtual world closer together, but goods and services must still travel through the real world.

Trade barriers make the world very bumpy. Governments restrict trade and investment using various types of tariff and non-tariff barriers. Non-tariff barriers include such things as import quotas, product standards, subsidies, voluntary export restraints, and licensing. There are also barriers in the form of product standards, including domestic content, technical compatibility, quality, health, safety, packaging, and labeling. Investment regulations include domestic ownership requirements and limits on foreign investment.

A World Bank Study offers the following vignette:

Moussa, a shirt maker in Damascus, exports to Italy. For each shipment he needs a license and a certificate of origin from the Ministry of Trade. Every box of shirts is inspected before being loaded into a container. Customs is cleared twice, in Damascus and at the Syrian port of Latakia. It takes 49 days, 12 documents and 19 signatures from the moment the shirts leave Moussa's factory to the time they are on the ship to Naples.[7]

This story illustrates how governments can limit exports through domestic regulations.

Government policies shape the business climate in each host country. The World Bank finds that physical infrastructure, such as port and terminal handling and inland transport, accounts for only one-quarter of trade delays. Much more important are process costs such as prearrival document preparation, customs, and inspections, which account for the other three-quarters of trade delays.[8] The time required to import goods varies substantially across countries, with developing countries often the least efficient (see table 1.1).

The importing delays are caused by bureaucracy, corruption, and myriad regulations. Many delays result from the need to obtain signatures and from cargo inspections at ports (see table 1.2). The number of signatures needed to import goods and the documents that are required usually are very few for developed countries. Developing countries, in contrast, tend to require the most signatures and documents. See table 1.3 for some of the countries with the most red tape for importers.

Every host country has its own legal system, with different rules for handling property rights, contracts, and torts. An international business usually operates subject to the jurisdiction of the host countries and must adapt to local procedures. In addition, manufacturing locally requires conforming to

Table 1.1. Number of days needed to import goods, including prearrival documents, port and terminal handling, customs, and inspections

Region	Total time (days)
OECD high income	14
East Asia & Pacific	28
Latin America & Caribbean	36
Middle East & North Africa	43
Eastern Europe & Central Asia	43
South Asia	47
Sub-Saharan Africa	59
World	39

Source: Doing Business 2006, p. 54.

Table 1.2. Cargo inspections, by region

Region	% of imported cargo inspected at the port
OECD high income	5
Eastern Europe & Central Asia	18
East Asia & Pacific	31
Latin America & Caribbean	51
Middle East & North Africa	63
Sub-Saharan Africa	67
South Asia	69

Source: Doing Business 2006, p. 57.

Table 1.3. Documents and signatures needed for import restrictions for selected countries with export restrictions

Country	No. of documents	Country	No. of signatures
Azerbaijan	18	Congo, Rep.	51
Kazakhstan	18	Niger	52
Kyrgyz Republic	18	Azerbaijan	55
Syria	18	Burundi	55
Uzbekistan	18	Afghanistan	57
Burundi	19	Mali	60
Iraq	19	Nigeria	71
Niger	19	Central African Rep.	75
Rwanda	19	Iraq	75
Zambia	19	Congo, Dem. Rep.	80

Source: Doing Business 2006, p. 57.

land use regulations, environmental standards, workplace health and safety rules, and labor laws. Products must conform to local standards of quality, safety, and labeling. These costs must be weighed by managers in determining the best countries from which to obtain goods and services, and the best target countries for international sales growth.

Trade and investment barriers result in high costs for the international business. Managers should take into account these costly trade barriers in structuring cross-border deals, and in location decisions. The international manager also needs to be aware of continual changes in trade regulations and their effect on international trade flows. For example, the dispersal of textile manufacturing was to some extent an artifact of the Multifiber Agreement (MFA) that imposed quotas on imports to the US and Europe. With the phaseout of the MFA, there were shifts in the types of clothing produced by many developing countries, and even changes in clothing fashions in developed countries.

Government-created trade barriers restrict the entry of international firms to local markets and restrict importing by domestic firms. These trade restrictions are market entry barriers that protect firms from some types of international competition. As these entry barriers are reduced, competition intensifies. With ongoing trade negotiations through the WTO and bilateral and regional trade agreements, trade barriers are continually changing and generally falling. An important way that the international business manager can achieve global competitive advantage is by discovering new business opportunities presented by falling trade barriers.

The Indian government altered its investment regulations to allow foreign companies to own 51 percent of a retailer that sold products bearing a single brand. Companies such as Gap, Zara, Timex, and United Colors of Benetton signaled their intention to enter the Indian retail market.[9] Restrictions on general retailers such as Carrefour and Wal-Mart continued to restrict their entry into the market. Relaxed investment rules in China after its admission to the WTO brought major market entry by Carrefour, Wal-Mart, and Tesco with additional entry planned by many others such as Metro Group of Germany, Best Buy of the US, and furniture retailer Ikea of Sweden.[10]

Government regulations are the rules of the global game, and the impact of rule changes can be dramatic. Noreen M. Culhane, executive vice president of the New York Stock Exchange (NYSE), pointing to new financial regulations in the US, said: "it's pretty irrefutable that there's been a sea change." She observed that twenty-three out of twenty-four firms seeking to raise more than a billion dollars in capital chose to list outside the US.[11] The next effect was the NYSE's bid to acquire Euronext, which operates stock markets in Amsterdam, Brussels, Lisbon, and Paris and a futures exchange in London. John A. Thain, the NYSE CEO observed: "The challenge is to build the best marketplace in the world."[12]

Seeking to mitigate the impact of US financial regulations, most notably the reporting requirements imposed on corporations by the Sarbanes–Oxley law, the NYSE–Euronext merger would create the largest publicly traded exchange in the world. The proposed deal ran into political opposition in Europe over concerns that US regulations also would apply there. Euronext's CEO, Jean-François Theodore, responded by suggesting that the merged company would be structured to prevent this from happening. The Chair of the US Securities and Exchange Commission (SEC), Christopher Cox, flew off to meet with British, Dutch, French, and Spanish regulators. Cox said that the proposed merger had set off "a[n] . . . acceleration in our collaboration."[13]

Cost of trade: 3 – transportation costs

One of the major issues that depends on "the four Ts" is whether to locate production close to the customer, or whether to find the best location for production based on local manufacturing costs. When transportation costs are high relative to the cost savings from finding a low-cost supplier country, the international business will tend to locate production close to the customer. As transportation costs fall through improvements in freight technology, production tends to disperse globally.

The international business gains competitive advantage by using improvements in transportation to craft innovative international business transactions. An example is the expanding role of transportation firms into the field of logistics. These firms apply a combination of transportation options and computer technology to organize international supply chains and to help firms reduce inventories through international JIT deliveries. As developing countries improve their transportation and communications infrastructure, new procurement and production possibilities arise. This changes the international business landscape and opens up new supplier and customer countries for international business firms.

Transportation costs are falling continually. An important technological change is the creation of links between different modes of transportation. What made this possible was the standardization of shipping through the development of the "big box." The shipping container can be loaded easily onto a truck, a rail car, and a "box boat," all without unpacking and repacking its contents. The container remains packed from the moment it leaves the factory to its arrival at the ultimate destination. Each transfer happens quickly through mechanized loading and unloading. The box can be tracked readily, just as a package is tracked in the mail. The "big box" made possible the integration of trucking, rail transport, and ocean shipping.

Another key development, closely related to the "big box", is the integration of logistics. UPS, for example, "provides consolidation of international freight, air, ocean and ground transportation, customs clearance, and direct delivery to multiple addresses within a destination country – all through a single source." UPS "will pick up or receive your shipments, provide consolidation, transport your shipment to the destination country, provide customs clearance, deconsolidate into individual shipments, drop them into either the UPS package or less-than-truckload (LTL) network and deliver them directly to your customers" (www.ups.com).

Cost of trade: 4 – time costs

Time is money, and international business takes time. Some of these time costs show up in the form of transportation delays and transaction costs of doing business in multiple countries. However, there are also delays in cross-border transactions that do not fit neatly into other categories. Setting up a production facility or negotiating a procurement contract in another country just takes more time. Some delays are caused by travel time while others are caused by the costs of learning about doing business in an unfamiliar environment.

In addition, in many developing countries there are substantial delays in establishing a business caused by government regulations or problems of corruption. These delays are compounded by the need for the international business to establish a presence in multiple countries. There are also delays that are imposed by a host country on foreign companies that are not experienced by domestic companies. These delays entail direct costs as well as indirect costs through delayed earnings.

Globalization is speeding up international business. As international businesses set up shop in a particular country, later entrants may find that they can become established more quickly. They can learn from the experience of the early arrivals and can take advantage of institutions and suppliers established to help the earlier entrants.

The economic landscape: economic differences between countries

The key differences between countries, from a strategic perspective, are differences between national economies. Although global integration is greater than at any time in economic history, the process has only just begun. The evidence that global integration still has a long way to go is contained in these highly visible economic differences.

Economic differences between countries reflect underlying differences in population size, density, education, and health. In turn, economic variations in income and wealth impact demographic trends, affecting population growth, education choices, and the quality of health care. The international business manager must factor in detailed demographic information. Each country's population has a different set of vital statistics, and these are the elements of the global mosaic that drive strategic decisions.

Economic differences are preserved by country borders, which are highly resistant to globalization. Some commentators predicted the end of the nation-state and argued that business would operate in a borderless world.[14] As globalization increases in force, premature predictions of the demise of the nation-state are likely to continue, but countries continue to matter a great deal. The international business manager structures the best deals in a global market place, while still recognizing national differences and the need to leap over the hurdles of country borders. Managers should not expect to conduct their business effectively in Brazil, China, or India without recognizing the importance of policy making by the host governments.

When economic distances between countries are large, international business faces roadblocks, which preserve economic differences between countries. The many observed differences between economies in the world show the effect of these roadblocks. International businesses can nonetheless seize opportunities for cross-border arbitrage.

The place to start in observing country differences is gross domestic product (GDP). Contrary to its name, this is a *net* number, like profit: it is the difference between a country's revenues and its costs. GDP is approximately a measure of a country's total annual income. Of course, differences across countries are vast, with the EU accounting for more than one-third of world GDP, the US a bit less than one-third, and the rest of the countries of the world making up the remaining third.

Comparing countries' GDP levels is a good rule-of-thumb indicator of the relative size of their markets. All other things equal, a country with twice as

Table 1.4. GDP *per capita* rankings, selected countries, in US dollars at current prices

Selected countries above $35,000

Luxembourg	Denmark	UK
Norway	Sweden	Japan
Switzerland	US	France
Ireland	Austria	Germany
Iceland	Finland	Canada

Selected countries between $4,000 and $7,000

Mexico	Malaysia	Argentina
Chile	Turkey	Brazil
Russia	Venezuela	Uruguay
Libya	Panama	Kazakhstan
Gabon	South Africa	Romania

Selected countries below $500

Bangladesh	Niger	Malawi
Togo	Nepal	Myanmar
Tanzania	Rwanda	Ethiopia
Uganda	Sierra Leone	Dem. Republic of Congo
Madagascar	Eritrea	Burundi

Source: Based on data from the IMF, World Economic Outlook Database, April 2005, www.imf.org, hereafter, IMF/WEO 2005.

much GDP as another country should offer twice as much in sales. But this rule can be much too simple. The next step is to look at GDP on a per person basis, which is referred to as *per capita* GDP. This is a highly useful measure of income per person per year.

GDP *per capita* indicates a lot about a country's wealth or poverty. It is a good indicator of purchasing power at world prices, although not necessarily at prices within the country. GDP *per capita*, since it is income per person, also is a good quick indicator of labor costs within the country. Table 1.4 lists some selected countries based on GDP *per capita*. The persistent differences in income per person illustrate the global mosaic.

Some caveats are in order. Some countries have rapidly increasing GDP *per capita*. Emerging markets, such as Brazil, China, and India, are in that group. Some countries have significant internal income disparities. An unequal distribution of income can indicate rapid but uneven economic development with opportunities for future growth, or it can foretell social unrest and government instability. Even countries with low GDP *per capita*,

India being a case in point, can have a large often urban middle class that seeks consumer goods. Other countries, such as China, have geographic inequalities, with coastal China having higher GDP *per capita* than those parts of inland China that are still largely rural. These geographic inequalities can change rapidly, however. Many parts of China have experienced substantial rural to urban migration and rapid growth of cities.

Because countries with lower GDP *per capita* also tend to have lower prices, for some types of goods and services, it is possible to adjust the GDP *per capita* measure to account for this. In evaluating GDP, the relative values of currencies of different countries can be adjusted statistically to reflect different local prices. This equalization is called *purchasing power parity* (PPP). Such an adjustment gives a GDP *per capita* that reduces some of the cross-country inequalities. The price adjustment uses an average over a basket of local goods selected to indicate standards of living. These adjusted numbers are readily available and provide a guide to managers concerning consumer purchasing power and worker wages. For example, after adjusting for PPP, Brazil's GDP *per capita* is $9,132 (versus $4,368), China's is $6,760 (versus $1,554), and India's is about $3,500 (versus $726).

The international manager next considers price differences across the globe. A survey conducted by A. C. Nielsen compared retail prices for consumer items in France, Germany, the UK, and the US. For example, compared with the UK, prices for ground coffee were more than 30 percent less expensive in Germany, France, and the US. Prices for chocolate chip cookies as compared to the UK were 60 percent higher in Germany, 16 percent higher in France, and 35 percent higher in the US. Milk prices were comparable in the UK, France, and the US but 25 percent less in Germany.[15]

The Economist Intelligence Unit surveyed international price differences and found substantial variation for internationally traded, branded consumer goods. Comparing retail prices in France, Germany, Sweden, the UK, and the US, they found that a CD recording of Verdi by the operatic singer Andrea Bocelli was most expensive in the UK and 33 percent less expensive in the cheapest country, Germany. A CD by the rock group U2, whose lead singer Bono is known for his concerns about international income inequality, was 22 percent less expensive in the US and France than in the UK. As compared to the UK, an Ikea sofa costs 30 percent less in Sweden, the company's home country, but 15 percent more in the US.[16] The Economist Intelligence Unit explained the price differences as being caused by the variation in countries' level of development, wealth, land prices, market size, exchange rates, degree of competition, distribution costs, customer preferences, tax rates and excise duties, and Internet usage.[17]

When traded goods are involved, price differences between countries generally reflect the height of trade barriers. Otherwise, the forces of business arbitrage would seize the profit opportunities and cause a narrowing of the gap. These price differences can be particularly high when comparing developed countries with emerging markets. For traded goods originating in developed economies, trade barriers can push prices for branded goods significantly higher in emerging markets. Conversely, for domestically produced, non-traded goods such as services – say, a haircut or a meal at a restaurant – prices in emerging markets will be much lower. In between these extremes are prices of different goods that are made locally by competing producers. India's Tata Motors planned a "People's Car" for India to sell for around $2,200 to appeal to those with annual incomes over twice that amount.[18] Low-cost cars made by foreign auto manufacturers in China powered a rapid increase in auto sales there.

Another important aspect of the global mosaic is the cost of labor. Wages and salaries vary significantly around the world. Immigration restrictions and the difficulty of relocating to distant and unfamiliar countries limit labor mobility. Trade barriers that constrain the movement of goods also have an impact. For goods produced with labor-intensive methods in developing countries, such as clothing and agricultural products, trade barriers translate into lower labor earnings. Some indication of differences in labor costs is given by the hourly compensation rates shown in table 1.5.

Wage rates differ significantly across countries. Table 1.6 shows the considerable variation in hourly wage rates for comparable jobs at McDonald's in different countries. The last column of table 1.6 also shows the wage rate divided by the price of a "Big Mac." This gives a rough indicator of hourly productivity if the main output of the restaurant is "Big Macs."[19]

Another important difference between countries is their scientific and technological knowledge. This type of knowledge is shared around the world through scientific and technical publications, conferences, trade exhibitions, and educational institutions. Technology diffuses around the world through markets and through investment abroad by international businesses. Personnel take ideas and information when they leave a firm to work for another, or to start their own new firm. There also is technological diffusion through copying, reverse engineering, and industrial espionage. These many types of diffusion, often referred to as "spillovers," would suggest that technology gaps between countries should have eroded or even been eliminated. Some commentators even suggest that opportunities for innovation are increasingly similar everywhere.[20]

Table 1.5. Hourly compensation costs, in US dollars, for production workers in manufacturing covering thirty countries or areas and selected economic groups

Country or area	Hourly compensation ($)
Americas	
US	23.17
Brazil	3.03
Canada	21.42
Mexico	2.50
Asia and Oceania	
Australia	23.09
Hong Kong	5.51
Israel	12.18
Japan	21.90
Korea	11.52
New Zealand	12.89
Singapore	7.45
Taiwan	5.97
Europe	
Austria	28.29
Belgium	29.98
Czech Rep.	5.43
Denmark	33.75
Finland	30.67
France	23.89
Germany	32.53
Hungary	5.72
Ireland	21.94
Italy	20.48
Luxembourg	26.57
Netherlands	30.76
Norway	34.64
Portugal	7.02
Spain	17.10
Sweden	28.42
Switzerland	30.26
UK	24.71

Source: Data from the US Department of Labor, Bureau of Labor Statistics, November 2005, for the year 2004.

Table 1.6. McDonald's cashier or crew wages, "Big Mac" prices, and productivity

Country	Hourly wage rate ($)	"Big Mac" price ($)	Productivity estimate (wage rate/price)
India	0.29	1.26	0.23
Columbia	0.55	2.43	0.23
China	0.42	1.18	0.36
Indonesia	0.63	1.74	0.36
Venezuela	1.30	3.19	0.41
Thailand	0.57	1.34	0.43
Philippines	0.56	1.23	0.46
Russia	0.51	1.07	0.47
Brazil	0.89	1.65	0.54
Argentina	1.50	2.50	0.60
Malaysia	0.79	1.13	0.70
Korea	1.88	2.69	0.70
Turkey	1.75	2.32	0.75
Czech Rep.	1.16	1.42	0.82
Poland	1.15	1.33	0.86
Taiwan	2.20	2.33	0.94
Singapore	2.31	1.85	1.25
Hong Kong	1.86	1.31	1.42
Italy (2001)	6.00	2.94	2.04
UK	6.35	3.02	2.11
Germany	5.33	2.36	2.25
Canada	4.51	1.87	2.40
US	6.50	2.51	2.59
Sweden	7.07	2.72	2.60
Belgium	6.90	2.61	2.65
France	7.12	2.62	2.72
Japan	7.73	2.55	3.04

Source: Data from Ashenfelter and Jurajda (2001).[21]

Thomas L. Friedman argues that: "The scale of the global community that is soon going to be able to participate in all sorts of discovery and innovation is something the world has simply never seen before."[22] Yet, when it comes to "sheer economic horsepower and cutting-edge innovation," counters Richard Florida, "our world is amazingly 'spiky.'" Florida points to the high growth rates of cities as the world's demographic "mountain ranges." Innovation tends to occur most in particular countries, and in particular locations in those countries that attract the most creative people.[23]

Globalization does indeed reduce economic distances. The Internet and other advances in communication permit scientific collaboration across borders and increase the diffusion of innovative activity across the world. The trend is clear – but it is in its infancy. The rise of new centers of invention in China, India, and elsewhere may be the wave of the future. However, the support systems of advanced educational institutions, intellectual property rights, human capital, and industry R&D still matter. These support systems continue to be highly country-specific.

Innovation and knowledge differences continue to form part of the global mosaic. R&D and scientific and technological knowledge are centered in the industrial countries. Table 1.7 shows how inventive activity, based on US patents, follows the knowledge base, as indicated by the total of past patents. Table 1.8 shows the Technology balance of payments for selected developed economies, again showing a concentration of technology exporters. Many other countries are technology importers. Global managers must be aware of the technology gaps between countries: the uneven diffusion of invention and knowledge is likely to have a major impact on the location decisions of a firm and its competitors. The information and knowledge mosaic has a fundamental effect on the direction and composition of international trade.

The arbitrage principle

Cross-border arbitrage is the engine of international business. The simple prescription is to buy low in one country and sell high in another. As long as a product's prices differ across countries the arbitrage prescription works – the international business makes a lot of money. But if the roadblocks are substantial and trade costs too high, arbitrage is impossible and the price differences do not offer business opportunities.

Even in a frictionless world, economic differences between countries would remain. Endowments of resources differ across countries – consider the abundance of oil in regions such as the Persian Gulf or Central Asia. Brazil's Amazon rain forest offers unrivaled biodiversity. The geographic landscape plays an important part, from mountainous Nepal to Mongolia's endless grassy steppes, to South America's fertile pampas, to North Africa's Sahara desert. Economic differences reflect cultural values, social organization, work ethics, and educational institutions.

As globalization reduces trade frictions, some economic differences erode. The key economic differences are prices and wages. Why are price differences

Table 1.7. Number of US patents granted, by country of origin, in 2004, for top twenty-five countries

Country of origin	No. of patents in 2004	Total no. of patents for all years
US	94,129	1,725,546
Foreign Origin total	**87,193**	**1,376,170**
Japan	37,034	574,865
Germany	11,367	221,120
France	3,686	84,902
UK	3,905	83,991
Canada	3,781	63,944
Taiwan	7,207	57,606
Italy	1,946	36,883
Switzerland	1,405	36,802
South Korea	4,671	35,673
Sweden	1,388	29,696
Netherlands	1,537	28,256
Australia	1,093	15,876
Israel	1,092	12,348
Belgium	678	12,135
Austria	575	10,819
Finland	954	10,802
Denmark	530	8,649
China, Hong Kong SAR	641	6,449
Spain	312	4,821
Norway	255	4,253
USSR	0	3,902
South Africa	115	2,981
Singapore	485	2,719
China P. Rep.	192	2,361

Source: Data from the US Patent and Trademark Office, http://www.uspto.gov/.

evidence of untapped opportunities? The reason is that arbitrage eventually erases its own motivation: as businesses arbitrage across countries, price differences start to narrow.

Buying goods and services in the low-cost country uses scarce supplies and employs productive capacity. This creates upward pressures on prices. Moreover, as more and more companies are drawn to buy in the low-cost country, they bid against each other for scarce supplies and productive capacity, thus raising prices.

Suppliers in the low-cost country may respond by developing more supplies and investing in new productive capacity. Even so, the suppliers in the low-cost country start bidding against each other for scarce labor, land for

Table 1.8. The Technology balance of payments.

	Receipts (USD million)	Payments (USD million)	Receipts/payments ratio (%)
Canada[a]	2,033.6	1,050.4	194
Mexico	54.0	608.1	9
US	48,227.0	20,049.0	241
Australia[a]	103.0	224.9	46
Japan	13,043.6	4,862.8	268
Korea	816.4	3,237.3	25
New Zealand[c]	7.9	3.7	214
Austria	2,548.5	2,712.2	94
Belgium	5,872.5	4,757.3	123
Czech Rep.	187.9	548.8	34
Denmark[c]	1,657.4	1,055.3	157
Finland[c]	1,728.0	1,476.3	117
France	5,188.5	3,233.6	160
Germany	21,958.2	23,095.9	95
Hungary[c]	216.1	503.7	43
Ireland	205.4	16,115.1	1
Italy	3,108.4	3,794.6	82
Luxembourg	117.4	105.0	112
Norway	1,501.3	1,297.3	116
Poland[d]	136.0	813.4	17
Portugal	454.9	737.0	62
Slovak Rep.[a]	30.4	64.9	47
Spain[b]	190.4	1,025.6	19
Switzerland	4,553.1	4,792.1	95
UK	22,513.1	9,567.0	235
EU[e]	74,701.4	79,228.5	94
OECD total[e,f]	145,930.0	115,489.5	126

Notes:
Data are for 2003 unless otherwise indicated.
[a] 2001 instead of 2003.
[b] 1998 instead of 2003.
[c] 1999 instead of 2003.
[d] 2000 instead of 2003.
[e] Including intra-zone flows. Excluding the Czech Rep., Denmark, Hungary, Poland, and the Slovak Rep. Data partially estimated.
[f] Excluding Iceland and Turkey.
Source: Data from the Organization for Economic Cooperation and Development (OECD), Technology Balance of Payments database. OECD Science, Technology and Industry Scoreboard 2005.

production, and other local resources. In the end, costs rise, wages increase, land rents go up, and other local resources become more expensive. Increased exports drive up input costs in the exporting country.

Arbitrage effects cut both ways. As international businesses sell goods and services to the high-cost country, there is downward pressure on prices. As foods, clothing, toys, auto parts, furniture, appliances, electronics, and other goods come into the high-cost country, the prices of these goods start to fall. Retailers begin to cut prices to take advantage of their lower costs of buying these manufactured goods. Prices fall for all goods within the category that faces competitive pressures from imports.

Domestic producers in the high-cost country face a great challenge. They must improve their products to remain competitive, or they must find ways to cut costs. They must offer new product designs, launch marketing campaigns, and increase their sales efforts. They must invest in more efficient capital equipment to reduce operating costs. These efforts and the forces of competition put downward pressure on wages and salaries, not to mention reducing some employee benefits such as health care and pensions.

In a frictionless world, prices of goods and services in the high-cost country and the low-cost country quickly trend toward each other. Prices of inputs such as wages, rents on land, and resource costs also equalize. This competitive scenario sounds pretty frightening to workers and managers alike but, rest assured, we do not live in a frictionless world. Trade costs slow the pace of change. The international business manager knows that frictions exist and tries to adjust for their effects.

The global business manager examines cross-border arbitrage opportunities. Cross-border arbitrage may be feasible if the price spread between the supplier country and the customer country is greater than the costs of trade. Conversely, cross-border arbitrage is not feasible if the price spread between the supplier country and the customer country is less than or equal to the costs of trade.

The international business serves its customers by obtaining goods abroad that are not otherwise available. The international business provides goods with different features or that are produced with different methods. Customers benefit from imported goods with higher quality or lower costs than domestic offerings. They value the variety that comes with global brands. Customers enjoy products with innovative foreign designs.

The differences in relative abilities across countries are an important source of gains from trade. The different mix of merchandise and services across the world's regions provides an indication of the country differences, as shown in

Table 1.9. Exports and imports of merchandise and services, in billion dollars, for 2004

Areas	Exports		Imports	
	Merchandise	Services	Merchandise	Services
North America	1,324	379	2,013	335
South & Central America	276	56	237	58
Europe	4,031	1,126	4,140	1,025
Commonwealth of Independent States	266	33	172	50
Africa	232	48	212	55
Middle East	390	36	252	61
Asia	2,388	450	2,224	512
World	8,907	2,125	9,250	2,095

Source: Based on data from the WTO, *International Trade Statistics*, 2005, www.wto.org.

table 1.9. Underlying these trades is an incredible variety of goods and services: foods with national flavors; arts and entertainment from different cultural traditions; consulting, scientific expertise, and engineering from different technical backgrounds; and manufactured goods from labor forces with unique skills and capabilities.

Overview

The countries of the world form a great mosaic. The economic differences between countries create arbitrage opportunities. The international business plans its procurement based on offerings from different countries. The international business also adjusts its product offerings to handle the different needs of customers better than its competitors. Global business strategies make connections that benefit from the world mosaic.

The greater the economic distance, the lower is the incentive to trade, all other things equal. Economic distance is due to four trade costs, "the four Ts": Transaction costs; Tariff and non-tariff costs; Transportation costs; and Time costs. These costs are coming down and economic distances are shrinking – but it's still a big world, and distances between countries are still substantial.

The costs of trade make borders "sticky," thus helping to preserve economic differences across countries and within regions. Information about these economic variations provides the raw data of strategic analysis, see table 1.10. The manager feeds country and regional data into the "Star Analysis," which is

Table 1.10. Useful sources of data for the hands-on manager

International Monetary Fund (IMF)   www.imf.org
Organization for Economic Cooperation and Development (OECD)
www.oecd.org/home/
World Bank   www.worldbank.org/
United Nations (UN)   www.unstats.un.org/unsd/default.htm
World Trade Organization (WTO)   www.wto.org/english/res_e/statis_e/statis_e.htm

presented in chapter 2. This provides the basis for making the company's global competitive strategy.

Participating in the global economy does not guarantee success for a country's economy. That depends on a country's creativity, capabilities, and resources. A country's ability to add value depends on many underlying geographic differences between countries. These key differences include climate, availability of agricultural land, endowments of exhaustible natural resources – such as petroleum, natural gas, and metals – and access to renewable resources such as forests and fisheries. Differences in the human capital of a country's labor force play an important role, although work force skills can be improved through education and training.

A global business can build on its home country's geographic advantages and overcome its disadvantages through the creative use of international trade. This is why a global competitive strategy demands more of companies than a traditional domestic strategy. The world is not a flat featureless field: the manager must take into account the economic and geographic differences between countries.

The manager must be constantly aware of the historical, cultural, and social differences that distinguish nation-states. The global manager needs to understand how geographic differences affect the global market place. Transactions must adjust for differences in incomes, prices, and products across countries. The manager should structure transactions to take account of the costs of crossing borders. By playing to the strengths of countries, and by satisfying their different economic needs, businesses benefit from the global mosaic.

2 Global strategic analysis

Global business is where strategy meets geography. Five major geographic factors drive the international business. First, the features of the home-country influence its competitive performance. Second, the features of the countries where it engages in production and transactions with suppliers shape the company's competitive potential. Third, the features of the countries where it serves customers determine demand for the company's products. Fourth, the features of the countries where the company has partners that provide complementary goods and services affect the company's productive efficiency and appeal to customers. Finally, competitors' home countries, supplier countries, customer countries, and partner countries impact the competitive advantage of the international business.

Managers face significant challenges in designing global competitive strategy. To obtain the necessary information, the global business manager performs a "Star Analysis." The manager examines five major international geographic factors: the features of the company's home country, supplier countries, customer countries, partner countries, and the features of competitor countries. These five drivers are represented in figure 2.1.

These five major factors provide the *country context* of global business strategy. The manager should understand when the features of its home country enhance and constrain its strategic choices and when the company transcends its home country. The manager must determine how the features of supplier countries affect where the firm procures goods and services and carries out manufacturing. The manager should also be fully aware of how the features of target countries affect the firm's relationships with its customers. The manager needs to understand how the features of the countries where it forms partnerships can help extend its manufacturing and distribution capabilities. Finally, competitive strategy requires that the manager know the country context of its competitors.

The "Star Analysis" provides a general framework for gathering and processing data about global markets. The "Strategy Star" helps managers examine

1 Home-country features

- Company globalization
- Company history and culture
- Managers' background
- Brand nationality
- Corporate governance
- Home market – demand and supply
- Political, legal, and regulatory climate

3 Customer-country features

- Customer preferences
- Elasticity of demand
- Elasticity of substitution
- Income per capita
- Customer knowledge
- Society and culture
- Political, legal, and regulatory climate

2 Supplier-country features

- Worker wages and productivity
- Technology
- Finance capital
- Factor supplies
- Suppliers
- Political, legal, and regulatory climate
- Operating costs/risks

5 Competitor-country features

- Competitors' home, supplier customer, and partner countries
- Customer and supplier bypass
- Political, legal, and regulatory climate

4 Partner-country features

- Complementary products
- Complementary technology
- Complementary capabilities
- Market knowledge
- Political, legal, and regulatory climate

Fig. 2.1   The global business strategy "Star Analysis" for global competitive advantage

international economic features and develop information used for designing competitive strategy. Five important strategic prescriptions emerge from the "Star Analysis":

- Use the strengths of your company's home country but transcend its demand and supply limitations through international transactions
- Choose supplier countries to find the inputs best suited for your firm's strategy
- Target customer countries to maximize net gains from trade
- Choose partner countries to find the best demand-side and supply-side complements

- Expect competitors to make the best configuration of their home, supplier, customer, and partner country locations.

The "Star Analysis" is necessarily *dynamic* because national economies are in a constant state of flux. Not only are changes in the company's home country important, the manager must monitor changes in its supplier markets and customer markets. The "Star Analysis" provides a way for managers to bring some coherence to this ever-changing information.

Opportunities for transactions that connect countries are constantly changing as well. These opportunities appear as trade costs fall with globalization. Changes in technology, transportation, and trade regulations continually alter the returns to inter-country business. The manager observes new opportunities by monitoring changes in relative prices and wages between country pairs. The categories in the "Star Analysis" correspond to the needs of the manager who must formulate a global strategy and design a global business organization. The manager can identify critical changes in the business environment and decide what types of responses are required.

The international market place is vast in comparison with national economies. The total flows of international trade dwarf the retail sectors of any country, with world trade in goods and services three times the size of the US retail sector. International capital movements are a growing share of total investment. International trade comprises the full range of products, including basic metals and energy resources; agricultural goods; manufactured products such as cars, computers, and aircraft; luxury goods such as jewelry and high-fashion clothing; services such as software design, consulting, and customer call centers; transfers of technology and intellectual property; and entertainment – from music to movies.

The global business must operate simultaneously in multiple country environments and it must have the ability to create innovative cross-border transactions. These capabilities distinguish an international business strategy from a traditional competitive strategy. By crossing borders, the company captures some of the gains from trade between countries. However, to cross those borders the company will incur many costs of trade. A coherent strategy to address these difficult challenges is essential to gaining and sustaining international competitive advantage.

The "Star Analysis" works for companies based in emerging markets, such as Brazil, China, India, or Russia, as much as for international companies based in developed economies. The "Star Analysis" applies to companies that are contemplating international expansion and also to companies that already are established in global markets but are refining their international strategy. The

"Star Analysis" is not just for major international corporations but applies to entrepreneurial startups that must transact across international borders, as well as to small and medium-sized companies with international transactions. The "Star Analysis" is not intended for government policy makers promoting national competitiveness;[1] it is intended to guide international strategic planning by a company's senior management team and by managers of startups and growing businesses.

The "Star Analysis" is not confined to the country level. Sometimes there is substantial geographic diversity within countries, in local regions or cities. National averages can be misleading, so that detailed analysis of locations is a critical step in determining where to place a manufacturing facility or distribution center. The manager can adapt the "Star Analysis" to specific areas within countries – differentiating, for example, between China's coastal cities and its interior provinces, or between states in India. The main points of the "Star Analysis" combine geography with strategic analysis, but the manager can make the data and locations as specific as needed. The "Star Analysis" can be adapted to demographic differences as well – for example, the firm may identify the locations within a country that are best suited to serve specific groups of customers such as middle-class customers or home owners.

Home country: recognize benefits and transcend limitations

Does aircraft maker Embraer derive competitive advantages from its home country of Brazil in comparison with its Canadian rival Bombardier? The home country of the international business can exert a significant influence on the company's success. Some home-country effects fundamentally determine the firm's competitive advantages – they can greatly help or hinder the company in international competition. Other home-country effects have less influence because they can be enhanced, tempered, or overcome entirely through the company's international activities.

A company's *home country* refers to the country where the business has its headquarters. A company may benefit from a home-field advantage in meeting foreign competitors that enter its home market to compete for customers. A company can also benefit from home-country *strengths* by using the home country as a launching pad for international expansion.

At the same time, a global company need not be limited by its home country. The global company serves more than home-country demand – it finds customers in target countries abroad. The global company counts on more than home-country industries – it finds suppliers and partners abroad. The global company overcomes the shortcomings of its home economy by skillfully combining international transactions.

The home country gives only a partial picture of competition for the global company. Home-grown competitors are likely to have similar products, technologies, and employees. International firms entering the home market may pose a significant threat when they differentiate products with innovations from other countries. International entrants can pose a threat to the home market when they offer lower prices through world-class scale economies and low-cost production abroad. The greatest competitive threat to the global company is often not focused on the home market alone. The greatest threat comes from other international firms that the global company meets again and again in many customer countries.

How important is the home country to a particular international business? A quick snapshot of the company that can help to answer this question is to compare the percentage of the company's revenues, costs, and profits that come from inside the home country with those percentages from outside the home country. A company with a small percentage of domestic revenues, costs, and profits is more global and less dependent on the home country.

To obtain a dynamic measure of the globalization of the company, one can also consider the rate of growth of the company's revenues, costs, and profits inside the home country as compared to these rates of growth outside it. Many global companies, such as General Electric (GE), earn about half of their revenues abroad. In addition, GE anticipates higher growth rates outside the home country. GE finds new customers abroad for its family of products, and also benefits from the high growth rates of emerging markets such as China and India.

Since most companies do not change their home country, the home country is generally where the company was founded and where its managers and employees come from. The company's history reflects the home-country environment since that is where its first customers, suppliers, and investors were located. The features of the home country are thus often a good guide to the company's business practices, corporate culture, and core competencies.

The home country mainly affects the nationality, training, and characteristics of upper management. The company depends on the knowledge and abilities of the top managers, who generally are from the home country. The business education and business practices of the home country are likely to impact the corporate office. The company's management strategy often tends to reflect its home base.

The company's home country is thus a critical aspect of its identity. We often speak of companies in terms of their country of origin. We typically refer to Haier as a Chinese company, Tata Group as an Indian company, and Embraer as a Brazilian company. The company's identity plays a role in its ongoing relations with employees, suppliers, customers, partners, and competitors.

Brands have a nationality, as well. A company's brands are often closely tied to the company's home country, with Levis, Coca-Cola or Ford perceived as American brands and Sony, Kirin Beer, or Toyota perceived as Japanese brands. The nationality of the brand can help or hurt sales, depending on how customers feel about the brand's home country. The effects of a brand's nationality are likely to vary in different countries, providing competitive advantages in some locations but not in others. Some international businesses acquire and manage brands that are identified with countries other than their home country, such as Nestlé's acquisition of the Italian San Pelegrino water and of the American Dreyer's ice cream brand.

The home country is often in the same the place where the business is incorporated. The country of incorporation contains the legal jurisdiction in which the company is created and organized.[2] The designation "Inc." identifies a company as an American company. Related designations are Aktiengesellschaft (AG) in Germany, public limited company (PLC) in the UK, and Société Anonyme (SA) in France, Belgium, Ivory Coast, and elsewhere. Some companies have their legal home in a different country from their headquarters for regulatory and tax purposes. For example, the major conglomerate Tyco International is a Bermuda corporation, although its headquarters are in Princeton, New Jersey, US.

The legal jurisdiction that governs the company's headquarters exerts a significant effect on its corporate governance. Countries impose very different rules on their corporations. These affect accounting practices, how the company issues securities, and the membership and structure of the corporate board. Depending on their country of incorporation, the company's managers may place different emphases on maximizing shareholder value, providing customer benefits, and consulting with the company's employees.[3]

There are many features of the home country whose effect on competitive advantage varies considerably, depending on the context. For example, an important feature of the home country can be the size of the company's home market. A business can benefit from a large home market in which to launch, test, and develop its products. Yet, an international business need not be constrained by the size of its home market. Although Switzerland is a small country with a correspondingly small domestic market, the Swiss company Nestlé is the world's biggest food company, serving millions of customers around the globe.

The political, legal, and regulatory climate of the home country exerts an influence on the company. Its products, manufacturing processes, environmental policies, and working conditions in its domestic operations are subject to public policy actions there. A country that has an efficient legal and regulatory climate contributes to the competitive advantage of the companies that are based there. Restrictive regulations, high taxes, or government corruption can limit competitive advantage for an international business. Some countries treat their large corporations as "national champions" and provide tax breaks, subsidies, and trade protections. These protections can provide temporary advantages, but often limit the company's ability to develop competitive strengths.

The international business manager draws upon the strengths of the home country in establishing the company's headquarters, organization, and management team. The company takes advantage of the knowledge and resources of the home country. When the home country has a relatively open economy, the international business further benefits from the ability to import critical technology, skills, resources, parts and equipment, and capital finance.

The global business increasingly turns to international markets for such activities as production, procurement, R&D, and design. It seeks new markets for its products around the world. In an open economy, the international business turns to global markets to achieve growth, innovation, and diversification far beyond the opportunities offered by its home country. The higher are the trade barriers in the home country, the more firms based in that country must play defense against international entrants. The lower are the barriers to trade of the home country, the better are the global prospects of firms based there.

The business in a relatively flexible and open economy has the best chances of competing internationally. Going global means using the home country to best advantage, and using world markets in the most effective way. The home country benefits from opening markets by launching effective global competitors. To achieve global competitive advantage, the business must understand how best to balance its domestic operations and its international transactions.

Supplier countries: build global supply chains

Does the diversified candy maker Arcor gain a competitive advantage by concentrating production in its home country of Argentina in comparison with competing confectioners? Arcor, a family business, is the world leader in hard-candy production. The company primarily produces in Argentina, with additional facilities in Brazil and Peru. Arcor is vertically integrated into production of sweeteners, packaging, machinery, and dairy products.[4] Its competitors, Mars, Nestlé, Cadbury Schweppes, and others, are not so vertically integrated and they disperse production to many supplier countries? *Supplier countries* refer to those countries in which the international business transacts with its input suppliers and countries in which the international business manufactures its products. An international business may rely on a large number of supplier countries. The home country of the global business can, of course, be one of its supplier countries, but the company will choose the best options from the world market place.

Supplier countries are the foundation of the international business. The international business manager carefully studies the features of potential supplier countries, providing an essential context to the procurement and production activities of the international business. A key question for the international business manager is how to choose supplier countries: international business managers should evaluate the context of the countries in which they procure inputs and manufacture products.

Global managers have the luxury of searching the world for the best combination of prices, quality, and convenience. The international business can often put together a network of suppliers that transcends what is available to the purely domestic business. The challenge for the international manager is in finding the right suppliers, coordinating the company's sourcing activities, and harmonizing its procurement and production activities around the globe.

The international business can rely on arm's-length relationships with foreign suppliers, procuring goods and inputs across borders. Alternatively, the international business can become a multinational corporation (MNC) by establishing its own production (or distribution) facilities in multiple countries. Business can benefit from a large and skilled labor force in its home country to manufacture its products for both domestic and global markets.

The business need not be constrained by its home-country work force, however. It can manufacture around the world, either in its own factories abroad or through contracts and relationships with suppliers abroad.

Singapore is a relatively small country in terms of the size of its labor force. Flextronics, headquartered in Singapore, is a global leader in supply-chain management for industrial, automotive, and electronics companies with manufacturing and design facilities in over thirty countries on five continents. The international business has a potentially global work force.

In evaluating the work force in a supplier country, the international business manager closely examines both the productivity of labor and the wages paid to labor, as both affect the firm's cost of production. The manager is likely to encounter a trade-off, with some countries offering higher productivity at the cost of higher wages and others offering lower productivity at lower wages. The manager evaluates the ratio of wages to labor productivity so as to determine the cost of labor per unit of output in a given activity in the supplier country.

The manager considers the relative costs of labor in different sectors of a prospective source country. The manager is interested not just in average productivity but in specific productivity levels in manufacturing, agriculture, or distribution as a direct or indirect guide to how workers will perform in carrying out the company's projects. The manager evaluates additional factors such as the education and skill levels of the labor force, management–labor relations and unionization, labor laws, health care and social services, and the country's employment rate.

The technology of the supplier country is also of special interest to the international business manager. The international business can draw from technological advances and knowledge in its home country. However, the international business can overcome technological limitations in the home country by reaching out to inventors and technology suppliers in other countries. For example, Finland was not considered a world leader in computers and communications equipment; however, Nokia obtained customized microchips from Texas Instruments for its cell phones, helping the company to become the world leader in mobile communications. The international business can draw upon the cutting edge of global technology.

The international business may wish to purchase products that embody particular technologies, such as machine tools from the US, memory chips from Korea, or robots from Japan. The international business may purchase technology directly in the form of licenses for patents or blueprints. International businesses often obtain technology by establishing research laboratories in other countries, such as IBM's research labs in Beijing, Haifa, New Delhi, Tokyo, and Zurich. In addition, MNCs transfer technologies internally between their divisions operating in different countries, thus benefiting from learning in different production environments.

Finance capital is the critical ingredient for corporate growth. An international business is likely to be highly dependent on investors and capital markets in its home country to fund its projects at home and abroad. However, with the great mobility of funds in international capital markets, an international business can grow with financing from abroad. International businesses can obtain loans from abroad or offer shares on foreign exchanges. Mexico's Cemex has become one of the largest building materials companies in the world. The company raises investment capital in the US and elsewhere, with its American Depositary Receipts (ADRs) listed on the NYSE. The international business is not necessarily constrained by its home country's capital market since it can obtain financing on global capital markets.

The international business manager also considers the relative abundance of productive factors within the potential supplier country. The manager considers the relative abundance of labor, capital equipment, and natural resources. Beyond simply evaluating the size of the labor force or levels of investment in production facilities, the manager examines the extent to which manufacturing in the country tends to be labor-intensive or capital-intensive. Production methods reflect the underlying availability of productive inputs in the country. The country may have a high population density, reflecting a high ratio of labor to land. Depending on capital abundance, such population density might be reflected in labor-intensive agricultural production. The manager also considers the country's natural resources, including land, forests, and mineral and crude oil reserves.

The international business manager further evaluates supplier countries in terms of the prices and availability of products and services. The international business is generally not limited by supplies of goods and services in the home country because of the relatively high mobility of products that can be shipped to wherever they are needed for production or resale. International companies transcend the resource limitations of their home country as well: the energy giant BP, for example, explores and develops energy resources wherever they can be discovered around the globe.

A company depends on critical suppliers for necessary products and services. The international business is not limited to home-country suppliers because it can draw upon the best and the brightest around the world. Manufacturing companies are interested in obtaining local supplies of various parts and components. The manager considers the industry structure of potential suppliers and evaluates their productive capacity, technology, and performance.

The international business is likely to encounter trade-offs in terms of the purchase prices of products and the costs of doing business in the country.

The manager examines the costs of doing business and the adequacy of communications and transportation infrastructure. Thus, a supplier country may offer inexpensive parts but high costs of transportation while an alternative supplier country may offer more expensive parts with lower transportation costs. The costs of doing business also depend on characteristics of the companies offering those supplies. The manager will take into account the business practices and track record of suppliers, as well as their capabilities and product quality.

The manager of the international business is particularly interested in the political, legal, and regulatory climate of the supplier country. These government factors affect the business risk encountered by the international firm and the reliability of its supplies of goods and services. Thus, an energy company will evaluate the reliability of crude oil supplies that may be purchased in different countries. International businesses that enter into contracts with foreign suppliers can face a magnified contract risk because the contracts are often governed by the legal jurisdiction of the host country.

The political, legal, and regulatory climate of the host country is highly important for the MNC because it faces risk in recovering the costs of its irreversible investment in production and distribution facilities as well as a return on that investment. *FDI* refers to the expenditures made by MNCs in establishing oversees facilities or in acquiring a controlling interest in companies abroad. MNCs often use FDI as a quid pro quo to secure the political cooperation of the host country, as well as favorable tax and regulatory treatment. Through its FDI, a MNC becomes a domestic producer or distributor, employing local workers and contributing taxes and technology to the local economy.

The features of the supplier country affect a very important strategic decision, the extent to which the international business vertically integrates its activities at home and abroad. If the company relies primarily on spot purchases and procurement contracts, the company is not vertically integrated and does not own production facilities in the supplier country. If the company establishes or acquires production facilities in the supplier country, the company is vertically integrated in the supplier country. One way that the company can become an MNC is through its ownership of facilities in the supplier country.

Firms have many reasons for vertical integration. Ronald H. Coase was the first to identify transaction costs in the market place as a reason for internalizing transactions within the firm.[5] Vertical integration across international borders entails many additional benefits and costs. There are substantial costs of trade associated with transacting across international borders, as will be emphasized below. Firms derive benefits from vertical integration by internalizing international transactions and avoiding the market costs of trade. Vertical integration also entails costs, including the organizational costs of managing operating units in multiple countries. MNCs vertically integrating abroad face trade-related costs necessary to make investments in other countries and operate manufacturing and facilities there. The trade-off between the trade costs of arm's-length transactions and the organization and trade costs of vertical integration determine many of the activities of the international business firm.

The choice of the international business between arm's-length transactions (spot purchases and sales, technology licensing, contract purchases) and vertical integration (through growth or merger) is sometimes referred to as the firm's *mode of entry* into a foreign country. Another advantage of vertical integration is that the international business has greater control over its foreign affiliates, assuring a more rapid response to market events and compliance with company strategies and policies. The cost of vertical integration is that FDI entails, as we have seen, risks associated with the recovery of the costs of investment and a return on investment. Franklin R. Root suggests that companies with less knowledge about a foreign market will rely more on market transactions, but that they will turn to greater vertical integration as their knowledge of the foreign market increases.[6]

Companies around the world increasingly are turning to *outsourcing* of company activities, focusing on their core competencies. Outsourcing refers to reliance on outside suppliers for inputs of various goods and services rather than sourcing within the company's organization. By outsourcing activities, companies reduce the extent of their vertical integration. Managers can concentrate on those activities that are most critical to the company, such as product design or marketing. The company devotes greater attention to those activities at which it is relatively best, turning to suppliers for their special skills.

At the same time as the outsourcing trend, companies are turning to international sourcing, which is referred to as *offshoring*. The offshoring decision refers to either procurement or production abroad. The company produces offshore to take advantage of less costly or more efficient production opportunities, or to be closer to foreign customers. Alternatively, the company purchases from independent suppliers abroad, thus bringing together the outsourcing and the offshoring trends.

The combination of these two trends is changing the organization structure of the international business and the nature of international markets.

For example, US and European companies are hiring Indian firms such as Infosys Technologies, Tata Consultancy Services, and Satyam Computer Services for a wide range of IT and customer services. Many companies, such as Gap and Nike, outsource manufacturing through contracts with foreign producers. This has led to the vertical disintegration of the entire supply chain, with tasks along the value chain being allocated across many countries. Reductions in vertical integration among international businesses has increased the role of third-party logistics providers and supply-chain management firms. Standardized parts and components are sourced in many supplier countries, resulting in products that combine manufacturing and technology from around the world.

The supply side of the international business has been termed the "global factory." The global company's value chains cross multiple international borders, so that it is no longer bound by suppliers and manufacturing conditions in its home country. The global business coordinates a variety of procurement, production, assembly, and design activities in many supplier countries. These many sources of supply improve the firm's productivity, technology, and cost structure.

The global business manager selects from supplier countries to achieve the firm's objectives. The manager carefully compares the costs of trade incurred in accessing suppliers and developing manufacturing abroad. Using the global factory is a strategic imperative, since competitors are scrambling to obtain access to supplier countries. Global competitive advantage requires that the firm creates the best mix of supply sources from the global market place.

Customer countries: create global markets and adapt to local market segments

Targeting customer countries is crucial to the expansion of the international business. The international business manager considers features of customer countries so as to understand the nature and context of market demand. This information helps the manager to identify those countries where the company should serve customers, what types of products the company should provide, and what competitive strategies will be required.

The global business views the international market for its products as a single market. This is why the international business is increasingly organized by global strategic business units (SBUs), with each unit providing a set of related products to the global market place.

The most difficult task for the global manager is to define the company's target markets. For many types of goods, it is natural to identify particular countries as segments of the global market. Thus, within the SBU, the manager identifies regional or country-specific territories, but these report to the global product managers.

In other situations, the company's market segments are not country-specific. For example, companies that manage luxury brands view their customers as those with a sufficiently high income, wherever they are located around the world. This market definition necessarily crosses international borders. In fact, jet-set customers are highly mobile and the company wishes to serve them not only where they live, but wherever they travel.

Moët Hennessy–Louis Vuitton Group (LVMH) tends to view its market segments as crossing national borders. The company sees its mission as representing "the most refined qualities of Western 'Art de Vivre' around the world" (lvmh.com). It targets a group of consumers for its luxury wines and spirits, fashion and leather goods, watches and jewelry, perfumes, and cosmetics. Its handbag maker, Louis Vuitton, has "exclusive shops" in over fifty countries. Even for this company, however, location plays an important part in the demand for its products. LVMH Group's wine and spirits division earns about a third of its revenues in the US and a bit more than a third in Europe. In contrast, its perfumes and cosmetics unit earns less than 10 percent of its revenues in the US and almost 60 percent in Europe. The company's fashion and leather goods unit earns almost half of its revenues in Japan and the rest of Asia.

The firm's target markets can extend across country boundaries when it serves other global businesses. For example, a supplier to Wal-Mart must cater to the chain's international needs rather than identifying target customer countries. Wal-Mart, for its part, has a global procurement unit that operates in over seventy countries.

In serving target countries, the global manager seeks information about customer preferences. The international business earns incremental revenues from international growth by providing products to satisfy customer needs in its target countries. By understanding consumer preferences, the international manager can improve the combination of features of company products and adjust the variety of products that are offered to its various markets. Globalization no longer means that products must have standardized features and brand images across the globe. Often, products and messages must be tailored to local tastes.

To determine the firm's best pricing strategies, the international manager must understand how consumer's willingness to pay for the firm's goods and services can vary across countries. This key piece of information identifies the maximum amount the customer is willing to pay for the firm's product and reflects the benefits received relative to the best alternatives. The *price elasticity of demand* is a valuable concept that informs the manager how sensitive the market is to changes in prices.[7] When the elasticity of demand is less than one, demand is said to be "inelastic" and a price increase increases revenues while a price reduction lowers them. When the elasticity of demand is greater than one, demand is said to be "elastic" and a price increase reduces revenues while a price reduction raises them. Managers need to understand that customer sensitivity to price changes is likely to vary greatly across the countries that the company serves. They should have some estimates of customer demand elasticity in the customer countries the firm currently serves, and also in potential target markets.

International firms typically price to market, which means that they adjust their prices in each country, or even in different areas of each country, to reflect customer willingness to pay. The company uses the elasticity of demand to calculate the company's marginal revenue associated with a change in the company's output sold.[8] Pricing to market means choosing a price in each country that equates marginal revenue to marginal cost in that country.[9] Even within the Euro zone, prices tend to vary significantly across countries when comparing the cost of basic commodities, as well as branded goods such as automobiles, cameras, computers, and clothing.

The profit advantages or pricing to market must be weighed against the costs of keeping track of different pricing across countries, the costs of multiple price tags, and customer dissatisfaction if they become aware of price differences. For convenience, the fashion firm Zara showed its different country clothing prices on the same price tag but later discontinued the practice in favor of country-specific price tags.

The international business manager needs to have extensive marketing information, and that generally requires experience on the ground in the target country. The manager should have detailed information about customer requirements and lifestyle. The target country's society and culture is likely to affect customer preferences and consumption patterns. It is useful to understand the customer's knowledge and experience with products similar to those of the company – for example, a computer manufacturer should understand Internet usage and consumer familiarity with computers. The manager can observe past sales of similar goods, the size of the installed base, levels of education and training, and public institutions such as libraries and government offices that provide access to the technology.

The value that consumers place on product variety is an important aspect of demand for the international business. Consumer demand for a product will be affected by the availability and prices of substitute goods. Demand for wireless communications, for example, will be affected by the availability of traditional phone services. The elasticity of substitution in demand between products reflects consumer benefits from product variety. The elasticity of substitution measures how market demand for one product responds to changes in the price of another that is a substitute in demand. This has strategic importance, since the manager must know how prices of competing products affect the demand for the firm's own products, and how the firm's prices affect the demand for the products of its competitors. Different target markets served by the firm have different substitutes available to customers, which will create different local impacts on the demand for the products of the global business.

The global business creates value by bringing new differentiated products into national markets. Many believe that the main benefit of international trade is lower prices. A greater benefit of globalization is product variety. From the earliest times, people sought out other cultures for their unique and exotic goods. The ancient silk road that linked Europe with Asia brought gem stones, precious metals, ivory, and animals to Asia, while returning caravans took not just silk but also medicinal plants, furs, ceramics, jade, bronze objects, lacquer, and iron.[10]

People continue to enjoy the benefits of variety brought by international trade in such goods as food, clothing, jewelry, furniture, entertainment, and the arts. Global businesses earn returns by increasing the variety of products available in their target customer countries. Consumers buy imported European luxury cars because they value the different product features. Seeking variety, they consume French wines, Russian vodka, Colombian coffee, Darjeeling tea, Swiss watches, Brazilian music, and Hollywood movies.

Beyond customer preferences, a critical aspect of customer willingness to pay is the customer's income. The international business manager is highly aware of difference in income across countries, and income distribution within countries. A good first approximation is national income *per capita*. The manager should always take into account annual *per capita* income in evaluating customer countries.

The international manager will consider other critical factors underlying consumer demand. Consumer demand will also be affected by the availability and prices of complementary goods. For example, demand for automobiles will depend on the price of gasoline and the quality of roads. Consumer demand for complementary services such as product maintenance and other customer services are an important feature of the customer country. The international business manager should evaluate the availability of transportation, retail distribution, and package delivery in evaluating methods of distributing their products.

The political, legal, and regulatory climate is an important feature of the customer country. As in the case of supply options, the international business compares modes of entry into the target country. The international manager examines the relative benefits and costs of spot sales, contracts for selling through local wholesalers and retailers, and opportunities to establish or acquire wholesale and retail distribution facilities. Many countries regulate foreign ownership of companies. There are also regulations affecting retail and wholesale distribution. Finally, most countries have complex regulations in the form of product standards. International trade agreements continually create new challenges and opportunities that affect the choice of target customer markets for the international business.

The global business manager takes the information generated by target country analysis as a basis for competitive strategy. The global business serves world markets. The manager determines whether the appropriate market segments are regions within countries, entire countries, or groups of countries. The manager considers whether market segments are based on factors that cross national boundaries. The global business manager faces the critical challenge of determining what aspects of its product offerings should be standardized internationally and what aspects should be tailored to geographic market segments.

Partner countries: assemble a global team

Ken Kutaragi, the brash visionary who created Sony's PlayStation videogame franchise, was charged with revitalizing the company's electronics business. His strategy featured an unlikely global partnership between the Japanese company and one of its major competitors, Korea's Samsung. Sony would bring its expertise in consumer products design and marketing while Samsung would provide its flat-panel display technology.[11] Choosing the right partner was an essential part of Sony's competitive strategy: the partnership would combine the companies' complementary capabilities to achieve global competitive advantage.

Kutaragi knew Samsung's executive, Chang Won Kie, well; Kutaragi had dealt with him when Sony purchased the memory chips that it needed to launch the

PlayStation. That decision had helped drive PlayStation's explosive growth, with sales passing over 100 million consoles. Now, Kutaragi again turned to Samsung, this time for its ability to make liquid crystal displays (LCDs).

Without the alliance with Samsung, Sony would lack a critical technology for the large flat-panel TVs that were in high demand. Samsung's LCD knowledge was the result of its computer chip expertise and its huge investments in LCD R&D and manufacturing. Samsung's skills were complementary to Sony's since they were tuned to computer displays while Sony brought TV display knowledge. The two companies formed a 50/50 JV with Chang Won Kie at its head.[12]

The Sony–Samsung JV set up a massive manufacturing facility in Tangjung, South Korea. Kutaragi observed that the LCD panels from the JV would be "at the core of our flat-panel TV strategy."[13] The JV resulted in significant cost savings in R&D and manufacturing, and helped the companies gain substantial economies of scale in manufacturing. Sharing ideas stimulated product innovation, allowing Sony to boost its global sales of flat-panel TVs. Bravia, Sony's hit LCD TV brand, took a substantial share of the global market. Samsung also offered TVs with the same LCD technology.

Sony and Samsung decided to increase their cooperation through a broader alliance. They agreed to share patents for a variety of technologies – 13,000 patents from Sony and 11,000 patents from Samsung. The companies would hold back on sharing "differentiation" technologies, particularly Sony's PlayStation and Samsung's LCD displays. Samsung announced that the patent-sharing deal would help the companies keep up with advances in digital technologies that were driving innovations in the global market.[14]

The global partnership between Sony and Samsung showed that even major players needed to work together in the global market. Sony was the second-largest consumer electronics firm. Samsung was second only to Intel in the global market for computer chips.[15]

Sony also established a research JV with global partners IBM and Toshiba. Together, they developed the Cell chip that powered the Sony PlayStation 3. The companies split the high development costs and employed engineers around the world. The three partners then established a five-year research JV to develop chip manufacturing processes for the next generation of chips – chips with 32 nanometer circuits. Kenshi Manabe, president of Sony's semiconductor unit, stated that one JV would help the companies "accelerate the cycle from fundamental research to commercialization."[16]

The global market is so vast, and global competition is so challenging, that few companies can do it all. They must employ alliances, JVs, and other types of partnerships to achieve the necessary capabilities and innovations. JVs provide many benefits. Most importantly, the companies share the costs and risks of the common venture. This can yield significant cost savings for manufacturing or distribution JVs, particularly those resulting from economies of scale.

The global business manager must evaluate the features of the countries in which the partner is based and the countries where the partners will operate together. These are the "partner countries." An understanding of the features of partner countries is helpful to the global manager in evaluating the partnership's chances of success. Partner-country features are highly useful in determining the potential contributions that the business and its partner will bring to their joint activities.

A business has two basic types of partners, those on the demand side of the market and those on the supply side of the market. Global business needs both types of partners to succeed in the vast world market place.

On the demand side, partners provide goods that are complements in consumption. Computers and software are an example of demand-side complementary goods. The consumer must buy the two types of products to obtain the full consumption benefits. Without a computer, the software cannot operate. Some computer features enhance the value of the software, such as microprocessor speed. Some software is essential for the computer to operate, other types of software enhance the computer's value to the consumer.

Intel's Andrew Grove stresses the need for businesses to work with demand-side partners: "Complementors are other businesses from whom customers buy complementary products." Grove points out that complementors are businesses that "travel the same road" as your business, although demand shifts and technological changes can cause those paths to diverge.[17]

Producers of complements are potential partners because there are benefits from coordinated action. Because consumers obtain additional benefits from combining complementary goods, joint promotions can increase sales for two companies offering complements. Companies producing complements can capture these benefits by coordinating pricing and product introductions. For example, a company offering a videogame player and a partner offering games benefit from joint marketing.

Complementary products can be bundled together, offering advantages over competitors selling separate products. Bundling products allows partners to set a price for the bundle that generates greater revenues than separate sales. Customers may benefit from the convenience of one-stop shopping for product bundles. Prearranged bundles reduce the costs to customers of searching for complementary goods and matching compatible products. Product bundles help to inform customers about what complementary products work best together.

Demand-side partnerships are fundamental for global competitive advantage. It is unlikely that a business can supply all of the complementary goods that customers require, and the business can turn to the best providers of complementary goods in the world. Thus, the manufacturer of a videogame player can gain a competitive advantage by partnering with the best videogame designers in the world. The best partnerships will win in the global market.

Demand-side partnerships provide a way to customize for target customer markets. For example, a computer maker can partner with software providers that design for specific local-market applications, languages, and customer needs. The global business provides the common technology platform. The local and regional business partners customize for local preferences. With geographically targeted partnerships, the global business offers products with the best local complementary products.

Supply-side partnerships create production efficiencies. These inputs to the production process, referred to as complements in production, include components, capital equipment, capabilities, and technologies. Complements in production improve the quality of the goods that are produced. Complements in production also enhance the productivity of the manufacturing process and lower manufacturing costs. Samsung's LCD knowledge and Sony's television display expertise were complements in the production of flat-panel screens. Sony and Sweden's Ericsson created an international partnership in mobile communications, drawing upon their complementary skills in mobile phones.

JVs provide a way to outsource an activity that is not the core competency of the partners. The activity may be too important to hand off to an independent contractor but not so central as to keep within the central focus of the company. The partners farm out the manufacturing, distribution, or R&D to a special-purpose JV, keeping close control while not directly interfering with the central missions of the partner companies.

JVs have played a significant role in international business for a long time. Establishing a JV with a local partner is a way for an international business to customize its international operations to suit each country in which it operates. The global–local JV benefits from the brands, technology, scale, and knowledge of the global partner as well as the expertise, management, local knowledge, and investment of the local partner. Having a local JV partner puts a "local face" on company operations, greatly improving the treatment of the venture by government regulators and helping it gain customer acceptance and attract employees.

The global–local JV is also often necessary to meet host-country regulations that limit foreign ownership. The global–local partnership is in addition a way for global companies to test the waters, learning about a customer country or a supplier country before making a substantial commitment through full ownership. The global–local partnership confers substantial flexibility: the global company can choose to continue the JV, to opt out of the agreement, or to increase equity stakes in the venture. The global–local partnership increases the financial leverage of the global company because it is able to participate in larger local operations without having to shoulder the full investment costs.

Unilever used buyouts as a means of international expansion. The company partnered with companies offering popular domestic brands in many countries. Often, these partnerships turned into buyouts, with Unilever supplying the capital needed to grow the business. When it acquired Bestfoods, Unilever got its JVs with CPC/Aji, maker of Knorr Soups and Hellmann's Mayonnaise. By buying out the JV from Japan's Ajinomoto, Unilever gained full control over subsidiaries in Hong Kong, Malaysia, Philippines, Singapore, Taiwan, and Thailand.

Companies with complementary capabilities, such as production and engineering, can benefit from a JV without the cost of acquiring the other competency, particularly when the JV partners are different types of firms – say, a parts manufacturer and an original equipment manufacturer (OEM). Partners can contribute complementary inputs such as manufacturing facilities and engineering personnel. The global JV can speed up market entry if the partners already possess the necessary personnel, investment, and facilities. The partners share the risks of making capital commitments associated with entering a new supplier country or a new customer country.

Partnerships provide a way of mitigating competition. A global firm can rely on local partners for distribution rather than entering a country and competing with established distributors. A global firm can form manufacturing partnerships with local producers instead of entering a country and competing with existing ones. Distribution partnerships are ways for the global business to obtain local knowledge about customers. Manufacturing partnerships provide local knowledge about the labor force, real estate, and resource providers.

Global–local JVs allow companies to formalize their relationship with a local partner. Joint ownership of the venture allows international companies to comply with domestic content regulations, while providing the local company with access to international capital investment and technology. The international manufacturing JV, Cablecom International, was formed to produce connector cable assemblies for computer and mobile communications manufacturers. Based in Hong Kong, with production facilities in Shenzhen, China, Cablecom International was a partnership between the US Company ITT Industries, whose Cannon division provided the technology for connector manufacturing and design, and EDA, Inc. of Taiwan, which provided knowledge of low-cost supply channels and its experience operating in China.

Because they benefit from the market knowledge and relationships of local partners, global partnerships provide access to new suppliers and customers and to technological information. They reduce transaction costs relative to those incurred in going it alone. A partnership often is easier to form and maintain than a full merger: the partners maintain their corporate identity, management, and ownership structure intact, but take advantage of production efficiencies. Companies can rapidly expand their scope without the costs and commitment needed for an acquisition, merger, or internal growth. Partnerships can be dissolved or refocused as market conditions change, and partners can be added to expand into new markets.

R&D JVs allow companies to share the costs and benefits of research without duplicating their efforts. Companies can avoid a race to develop similar technologies. The inherent uncertainties of R&D heighten the need for cost sharing. R&D JVs are mechanisms for companies to cooperate in setting standards for new products, while sharing the costs of product development. Companies in an R&D JV benefit from pooling their ideas as well as their capital. Global R&D JVs take advantage of the different types of scientific and technical expertise that exist in different countries. They are also useful in establishing intellectual property (IP) protections for companies working across international borders.

Global JVs can reduce international transaction costs for the partners because the enterprise formed by the JV serves as an intermediary between the two partners. The JV employs specialized personnel and facilities that help to coordinate interaction between the parent companies. If the partners to a JV form a durable relationship, transaction costs are reduced by the specification of roles of the parent company and greater flexibility than might be achieved by contracts made directly between the parent companies. The JV can also improve communication between the partnering companies.

Understanding the features of the host country in which the partnership will operate is essential. JVs can create problems for the partners. When they involve complex business processes, the transaction costs of forming the JV can exceed the costs of more basic contracts between the partners. JVs create difficulties for the partners if free riding occurs, with one partner providing a greater share of resources or deriving a disproportionate share of the benefits.

As markets change, the partners' business objectives will evolve: it will become necessary to modify the partnership agreement or to dissolve the partnership. Changes in the agreement can be governed by the legal jurisdiction of the host country, so the global business manager needs to understand the legal and regulatory environment in which the partnership will operate.

Assignment of intellectual property rights from the JV can pose some difficulties. With unsuccessful JVs, one partner may use the JV to gain information about the partner's business plans. Such a problem can arise if the partner is acquired by another company. Managers establishing a JV should form an exit strategy, formally specifying how the JV will be dissolved if there are changes in market conditions or in the objectives of the partners. Managers should always understand the inherent risks of partnerships.

Michael Yoshino and Srinivasa Rangan argue that managers involved in global strategic alliances must carefully consider four objectives: "maintaining flexibility, protecting core competencies, enhancing learning, and maximizing value."[18] Managers face trade-offs in pursuing global partnerships; Yoshino and Rangan present a road map for forging strategic alliances that requires rethinking the business, crafting an alliance strategy, structuring the alliance, and evaluating its performance. They caution that: "Interfirm collaborations are plagued by ambiguities in relationships" and that there are "tensions associated with the need to balance cooperation and competition."[19] They stress the critical need for the involvement of top managers in continually supervising the ongoing relationship.[20]

Global partnerships, whether through JVs or other types of alliances, offer ways to extend the creativity and reach of global firms. They provide ways to bridge international borders and gain faster access to supplier and customer countries. The effectiveness of the global partnership strategy, of course, depends on how it is applied. Choosing the right partners, evaluating the geographic context of the target markets, and managing the relationship between the companies are critical to achieving success. The global partnership strategy provides a way of capturing and combining some of the abilities of diverse companies. The right mix of partners and their complementary capabilities can yield global competitive advantage.

Competitor countries: evaluate global and local competitive threats

Top managers at Boeing were intensely aware of the new strategy at Airbus, their main competitor in the global market for commercial aircraft. Airbus entered the super-jumbo aircraft category, spending over $12 billion to develop its massive A380 model.[21] The A380 would be the world's largest passenger jet, a double-decker plane projected to carry between 480 and 840 passengers in five passenger configurations for use on long-range routes, with a standard configuration of about 555 passengers.[22] Parts of the plane were built throughout Europe, transported by air, land, and sea, and assembled at Airbus headquarters in Toulouse, France.[23]

In understanding the strategy pursued by Airbus, Boeing's management needed to take into account the location of Airbus' headquarters and the ownership structure of the company. Airbus was majority-owned by the European Aeronautic Defense and Space Company (EADS), which was a Dutch company with EU headquarters.[24]

The European defense and aerospace industry had restructured in response to changing market demand conditions and the need to improve efficiency, a restructuring that took place against a backdrop of conflicting government objectives. The French government continued to maintain a large ownership share in the industry and to emphasize the need for government regulation and control, although it contemplated some privatization. The German government preferred private ownership but emphasized control by German investors. The British government favored private ownership and market-directed company strategies.[25] In the European defense and aerospace industry, according to Neil Fligstein: "Managers who face difficult economic conditions must make sense not just of what their competitors are doing but also of what their governments are prepared to accept."[26]

The involvement of European governments and their interest in Airbus was apparent to Boeing's top managers. In fact, many European leaders attended the unveiling of the super-jumbo, including Prime Minister Tony Blair of the UK, President Jacques Chirac of France, Prime Minister José Luis Rodríguez Zapatero of Spain, Chancellor Gerhard Schröder of Germany, and European Commission President José Manuel Barroso. Airbus received billions of Euros in subsidies from European governments in the form of low-cost loans called "launch aid." The diplomatic relationships of the European countries that parented the A380 super-jumbo would be helpful in its sales to national air carriers. Jacques Chirac of France signed aircraft deals in visits with Chinese leaders. Moreover, Airbus struck deals with state-owned aircraft manufacturers for a major assembly plant in China.[27]

The home countries of the companies that owned Airbus were also its supplier countries. Bringing the plane's parts together required extraordinary measures:

employees at an Airbus facility in northern Wales use 750,000 bolts, rivets, and other fasteners to attach pieces of the wings. The fuel system and landing gear arrive on trucks from another Airbus facility in Bristol, 115 miles away. Once the components are joined, workers transport the completed structures to a port on the Irish Sea and load them onto specially designed freight carriers for a five-day journey to Bordeaux.

At Bordeaux the wings take another water voyage – 12 hours on the Garonne River aboard barges equipped with a variable ballast system that enables the wings to pass beneath an 18th-century bridge . . . At the end of the river cruise, the wings are hoisted aboard specially designed trucks for a three-day drive to Toulouse.[28]

Airbus' home countries clearly played a significant role in the company's competitive strategy making. EU regulations also affected the company's labor relations and its corporate governance. The outlook of the company's managers had been influenced by government ownership of the company's parent organization. Executive hiring at Airbus was subject to political pressures, as reflected by the dual chairmen of the board at EADS. There also were dual CEO positions at Airbus that were held by a French executive and a German executive, leading to political conflicts.[29]

The home countries of Airbus and Boeing influenced their strategy making. Boeing was based in the US, with headquarters in Chicago, Illinois, and assembly plants located primarily in Seattle, Washington. It was a publicly traded company subject to shareholder oversight and the market for corporate control. In contrast to Airbus' strategy of developing a completely new design, Boeing initially planned to produce a revamped stretch version of its older 747 aircraft for a development cost of about $4 billion.[30] The Boeing 747 dated back to 1970; it was the original jumbo-jet, with incremental improvements spread over fifteen different model variations.

Boeing's strategy for product innovation was to be incremental change rather than following Airbus' strategy of offering an entirely new design.[31] Boeing's reasoning was that the market for 747-and-larger airplanes over the next two decades was small, little more than 1,000 planes, of which only about a third would be super-jumbos carrying over 500 passengers. Boeing expected demand for super-jumbos to be driven by growth of traffic on intercontinental routes and the need to deal with airport capacity constraints by carrying more passengers per flight.[32] Boeing initially attempted to pursue cost leadership as a response to its main competitor's product innovation.

Boeing's strategic reasoning was based on the expected size of the market and the anticipated needs of the airlines. However, customer reactions soon led Boeing to reverse its course. The company had received few, if any, orders for the stretched 747 while Airbus already had begun to receive orders for its super-jumbo. Accordingly, Boeing discontinued the project.[33] Boeing continued to offer the large 747 in other forms and introduced the smaller twin-engine 777, which was "the first jetliner to be 100 percent digitally designed using three-dimensional computer graphics."[34]

In this change of strategy, Boeing leapfrogged Airbus with a totally new design that would compete not on size but rather on energy efficiency. Responding to the operating needs of airlines, the Boeing 787 "Dreamliner" was launched. The 787, built with composite materials and offering new efficient engines, was cheaper to operate because of its greater fuel efficiency. Originally seating about 300 passengers, Boeing added a larger version of the Dreamliner for fifty more passengers under pressure from the airlines. Using ideas from its Dreamliner project, Boeing then introduced the enhanced 747 super-jumbo that would compete head-to-head with the Airbus 380.

The strategic change proved successful for Boeing. In the first six years, the Airbus super-jumbo attracted 160 orders, Boeing's Dreamliner in the same period obtained over 700 orders and another 500 orders for its larger planes including the 777.[35] Complicating matters further, Airbus ran into design problems and production delays with the 380 super-jumbo. Recognizing the competitive challenge, Airbus responded directly to the Dreamliner with the announcement of a newly designed plane, the Airbus 350, at a design cost of over $10 billion.

The competitive strategies in the aerial dogfight between the two global aircraft makers depended on the countries in which they operated. In responding to Airbus, Boeing needed to be aware of its competitor's location. Airbus' multiple home countries affected its strategy, as did Boeing's home country. In the case of Airbus, its European background indicated considerable government involvement in the oversight of certain management decisions. The super-jumbo project reflected national objectives as much as strategic considerations. Airbus' performance and competitive advantage also were fundamentally affected by its configuration of customer countries, supplier countries, and partner countries.

Boeing's challenge to Airbus demonstrates how a global business must understand the countries in which its competitors operate. The business manager completes the "Star Analysis" of the global business environment by examining the geographic context of its competitors. The manager considers the competitors' home country, supplier countries, customer countries, and partner countries. Effectively, the top manager attempts to understand what would be the competitor's own "Star Analysis."

The reason for analyzing the competitor's "Star Analysis" is to determine whether there are any critical differences between the geographic profile of the competitor and that of one's own company. Differences between companies are the source of potential competitive advantages. The manager considers the extent to which an advantage can result from differences with the competitor's home country, supplier countries, customer countries, or partner countries.

The manager begins by examining the extent to which a competitor's home country influences its strategy. The manager examines how the location of a competitor's headquarters affects the competitor's history, mission, and business practices. The manager considers whether the competitor's managers are affected by the company's location and how this might be reflected in their decisions. Is the competitor highly focused on the home market, reducing its effectiveness in other country markets? The competitor's home market affects the company's corporate governance, determining how the company raises capital for investment and the membership of its corporate board. The company's corporate governance affects its process of hiring of managers, the extent to which the corporation's shareholders scrutinize management decisions, and the strategic decisions of management.

How does the competitor's home country influence the competitor's business performance? Political, regulatory, and legal issues associated with the home country are often highly important in international trade. The manager examines whether the competitor is constrained by government regulations concerning such things as labor relations, health care and pension rules, the environment, product quality and safety, and corporate governance. The manager considers whether the competitor benefits from government subsidies or home-country trade agreements. For example, in the global competition between Boeing and Airbus, both countries accused each other of benefiting from government largesse. Airbus saw Boeing's defense business as subsidizing its commercial aircraft sales, and Boeing pointed out that Europe's low-cost loans provided subsidies to Airbus.

The manager determines what advantages and disadvantages the competitor may derive from its headquarters location. This can involve preferred access to resources, technology, investment capital, or management skills. The manager determines whether or not the competitor is particularly effective in providing service to customers in its home country. The manager examines how the nationality of the competitors' brands are perceived relative to the company's own brand nationality in the competitor's customer countries.

In examining a competitor, the global business manager considers the extent to which it is a global or local player. Does the competitor serve customers in many countries, work with suppliers in many countries, and partner with other companies in many countries? In contrast, is the competitor confined to a single country in its customers, suppliers, or partners? The global company Procter & Gamble (P&G) competed in many product categories and in many countries against other multinationals such as Unilever and Johnson & Johnson.

At the same time, P&G competed against many local companies. In China, for example, it faced intense competition from market leader Beijing Sanlu Factory. A state-owned company, Beijing Sanlu Factory offered its popular Dabao brand of herbal cosmetics including skin care, hair care, beauty care, perfume, and clinical products. The company recommended its consumers: "To make your skin brighter, . . . use Dabao day and night." P&G adjusted its pricing and marketing to counter the lower-cost and local appeal of Beijing Sanlu Factory. The Jiangsu Longliqi Group was a large-scale chemical company with 95 percent of its sales within China. Jiangsu Longliqi provided competing products such as skin care, cosmetics, toothpaste, soap, shampoo, and bath lotion.[36] Another major competitor was the C-BONS Group based in Hong Kong, with production in Guangdong and Hubei Provinces and a sales network throughout China. C-BONS offered cosmetics, personal hygiene products, hairdressing products, and pharmaceutical products.[37] These competitors required that P&G adjust its strategy in China to take into account both local and global competitors.

Competitors who serve larger customer country markets or many customer countries benefit from economies of scale in production. The number of customer countries served by the competitor also affects the competitor's return to R&D, since innovations can be spread over a wider market. The location of customer countries served by the competitor are likely to reflect the competitor's market knowledge, which may be extensive or confined to specific regions or particular of types of economies. The manager examines whether the competitor spreads its operations across many markets or whether it focuses its energies on defending a specific set of markets.

The manager should consider how the competitor's customer market footprint differs from the company's own footprint. For example, the manager looks at whether the competitor primarily serves countries in a geographic region. The manager also examines whether the competitor serves countries in developed economies or in emerging markets. The pattern of countries served by the competitor may reveal regions that are not fully served, or it may indicate areas of head-to-head competition. This is critical in evaluating a company's prospects for achieving global competitive advantage.

The manager considers the supplier countries of its competitors. The cost structure of a competitor will be affected if the firm produces in low-cost or high-cost countries. If the competitor manufactures in multiple countries, it is also useful to determine whether or not the competitor coordinates its international operations. There is evidence that many MNC's operate independent country-specific affiliates without the cost efficiencies that come from international coordination of their activities.[38] In contrast, the global cement company Cemex gains a competitive edge by close integration of its manufacturing operations across many countries (see chapter 8).

The manager should examine whether his or her company relies on the same or different supplier countries in comparison with competitors. Different sources of supply create opportunities for competitive advantage. It can matter a great deal if a competitor is sourcing parts and services from a lower-cost emerging market or a higher-cost developed economy. A competitor's cost advantage may be mitigated by turning to similar suppliers – say, for example, providers of standard computer components produced in China. Companies can have similar costs of call centers by outsourcing to comparable service providers in India. Alternatively, different supplier countries can provide a competitive advantage. The technological capabilities of suppliers, particularly when suppliers rely on the technology of their home country, can affect their product offerings. A company might obtain an edge by turning to more technically advanced suppliers from different countries than those working with competitors.

Supplier countries also affect the costs of trade. For example, the manager considers whether a competitor has suppliers or production facilities that are located closer to or farther from customer countries than the manager's company. The company may gain a competitive advantage over competitors by turning to suppliers that are situated more conveniently for serving customer countries. Do competitors have the same profile, sourcing in the same supplier countries and serving the same customer countries, or do they have substantially different global network configurations?

The manager should carefully observe competitors' partner countries. Chen *et al.* point out that, in many industries: "the large number of participants in the Asia market and the vast differences in cost structure between global players, regional players and small local players mean that competition will be much more intense than in other parts of the world."[39] Rather than engaging in large-scale entry through vertical integration, global companies can benefit from this intense competition in Asia through partnerships with local players. In this context, local partnerships can yield a substantial competitive advantage, The manager should evaluate whether its global competitors gain government connections and other advantages through their local partnerships.

With growth in outsourcing and increased international trade in services, global businesses increasingly use partnerships to reduce their costs and improve distribution. Partnerships allow the business to extend its geographic coverage. Local partnerships increase the effectiveness of entry into local markets. As a result, the locations of competitor partnerships increasingly impact competitive advantage for global business. The manager should examine whether competitors benefit from supply-side partnerships that provide essential components, technology, or capabilities. These can be an important source of competitive advantage. The manager should also consider competitors' demand-side partnerships to determine whether complementary goods are a source of competitive advantage. The manager should also look at the distribution partnerships of competitors.

If a competitor benefits from effective local partnerships, on the supply side or the demand side, this can require a company to seek similar partnerships. Such local partnerships will help the company to carry out entry into supplier or customer markets. The manager should also consider whether it can use global partnerships to differentiate its production processes or products from those of its competitors. The company's local and global partnerships can be essential to meeting the needs of a large-scale global market while addressing the needs of local target markets.

Overview

The "Star Analysis" is intended for all types of cross-border business activities. As a result, the "Star Analysis" works for companies that do business internationally whether or not they are MNCs that operate facilities abroad. The framework applies to international trading companies, financial firms, consulting firms, e-commerce firms, and business services. In addition, the framework applies to companies with substantial capital investment abroad, including manufacturing companies, transportation and logistics companies, communications companies, and retail and wholesale distribution companies.

A global management strategy integrates both economic and geographic forces. As globalization continues its rapid pace, business managers must have the tools and expertise to discover new ways to obtain gains from trade and new ways to reduce the costs of trade. The international business manager must bring original approaches, capabilities, and strategies to succeed in world markets. Developing international knowledge is the foremost management challenge in the emerging global market place. The "Star Analysis" provides a method for applying this knowledge to obtain international competitive advantage.

Based on the results of the analysis, the manager is prepared to formulate the company's global business strategy. By understanding the opportunities and constraints offered by the company's home country, the manager is poised to devise an international expansion strategy. Managers should no longer count on trade barriers for the luxury of a protected national market. The forces of globalization mean that most businesses are likely to face challenges in their home market. Most businesses will also need to engage in their own international expansion to obtain the necessary size to meet the international competition. Most businesses already source abroad to obtain the products, components, services, technology, and expertise to stay competitive.

By applying the "Star Analysis," the manager prepares to select locations for manufacturing operations and customer sales. Based on supplier-country features, the manager determines the extent of the company's vertical integration, choosing between spot purchases, contracts, and vertical expansion through FDI. Based on the features of customer countries, the manager chooses the extent of vertical expansion into distribution, choosing between spot sales, contracts, and ownership of distribution. By understanding partner-country features, the manager develops more effective international alliances and JVs.

The "Star Analysis" provides a method for analyzing the global business environment. It systematically integrates country-level data with competitor analysis. The different country profiles of the company and its competitors provide avenues for creating global competitive advantage.

3 Global competitive advantage

The global business locates its activities around the world for competitive advantage. The company draws on the strengths of its home country, supplier countries, and partner countries. It targets a desired group of customer countries. The global business then *coordinates* its global purchasing, manufacturing, alliances, distribution, and sales to generate value. The global business uses its transactions and activities to connect markets across country borders. I refer to this as the company's *global value connection.*

The global value connection does *not* mean choosing the lowest-cost supplier countries or the highest-income customer countries. The global business chooses the *best match* between its home country, supplier countries, partner countries, and customer countries. Toyota produces cars in the US, with relatively high labor costs, to build customer relationships and respond quickly to changes in market demand.

In choosing country locations, the global business also must take account of its own market knowledge, technical skills, and organizational capabilities. Nokia assembles phones in relatively high-cost Finland to control its technology, component sourcing, and worldwide product distribution. In addition, the company operates manufacturing facilities in Brazil, China, Germany, Great Britain, Hungary, India, Mexico, and South Korea.[1] The company handles 100 billion parts per year, achieving both global scale and local-market customization for the phone operators that it serves.[2]

A global business gains a *competitive advantage* when it is able to create greater value than its competitors. The global company creates value by harnessing the power of international trade. The value generated by the global business equals the *gains from trade across countries net of the costs of trade.* The global business succeeds by creating and capturing the greatest net gains from trade.

The global value connection

The global business creates value by connecting markets in its home country, supplier countries, partner countries, and customer countries. The company's global value connection constitutes its set of international market transactions and organizational activities. This is illustrated in figure 3.1.

There are many alternative ways to establish a global value connection. Some involve bricks-and-mortar manufacturing and distribution and others rely on transactions and relationships. International oil companies establish their global value connection through a system of multiple-country facilities in exploration, oil field operations, crude oil transportation, refining and petrochemical manufacturing, wholesale distribution, and retail service stations.

The global value connection also can be achieved through transactions that cross national borders. Companies that are global electronics supply-chain managers set up their global value connection through a network of contracts with product designers, component makers, assemblers, and customers.

Hong Kong's Li & Fung Group served the needs of major retail chains in the US, Europe, and in Asia, including The Limited, Gymboree, and Abercrombie and Fitch. Li & Fung managed a worldwide supply chain primarily for clothing manufacturing, as well as footwear, toys, fashion accessories, furnishings, gifts, handicrafts, home products, stationery, sporting goods, and travel goods.[3] The company's trading unit did not own manufacturing plants, but instead operated a virtual global factory. Its sourcing networks were spread throughout Asia and expanded to the Mediterranean, Eastern Europe, and Central and South America. Its sourcing network was enhanced by its long-term relationships with suppliers. The company's global value connection brought together its extensive supply network with its group of retail chain customers.

The global value connection involves the best match between a company's abilities and its global market opportunities. The global business manager applies information generated by the "Star Analysis" to design the company's global competitive strategy. By understanding the gains from trade and the costs of trade, the manager can choose those cross-border transactions and activities that yield the greatest global competitive advantage.

The international manager takes account of the strengths and limitations of the company's home country. The manager coordinates location choices for its purchasing, manufacturing, partnering, distribution, and sales. The choice

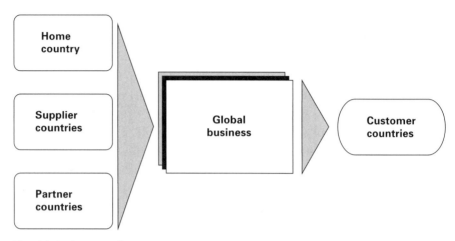

Fig. 3.1   The global value connection

of a country location for purchasing is thus related to the choice of the location for manufacturing and assembly operations. Choosing the location of manufacturing and assembly also depends on the choice of target customer countries.

The company creates value through its cross-border business transactions and operations. The international business combines procurement or production in its supplier countries with sales in its customer countries. *Gains from trade* equal benefits to customers in the firm's target countries net of the firm's costs and those of its suppliers in other countries. The main sources of gains from trade are spelled out in the next section of this chapter.

Managing the firm's value creating activities and transactions is difficult because they cross international borders. The international business manager must considers the impact of the *costs of trade*. Recall the four main costs of trade considered in chapter 1: transaction costs, tariff and non-tariff costs, transportation costs, and time costs. The costs of trade are the costs of coordinating and connecting transactions between supplier and customer countries.

The costs of trade offset the potential gains from trade. The costs of trade are sufficiently important that they can change the firm's choices concerning what countries should be sources of supply and what countries should be target markets. The international business manager then structures the company's international activities and transactions to maximize the net gains from trade.

The international business also considers the costs of completing the international transactions. Therefore, the *value created* by the firm equals the benefits obtained by the firm's customers minus the total costs of inputs

Fig. 3.2   Creating global value: choose country connections to maximize net gains from trade

provided by the firm and its suppliers, and minus the costs of trade.[4] The calculation of the net gains from trade is illustrated in figure 3.2.

It is important not to make these choices separately. A global strategy requires coordinating import and export activities. The global business manager chooses where to carry out procurement, where to make partnerships, and where to serve customers to maximize the net gains from trade. Decisions about the origin and destination of business transactions are necessarily interdependent.

For example, the manager may choose a transaction between two countries that has relatively low gains from trade but also low costs of trade. This can occur if a competing alternative with higher gains from trade is simply not worthwhile because of its costs of trade. To illustrate this possibility, suppose that the firm wishes to provide a product to a customer in Country A. The question is whether to purchase the product from a supplier in Country B or Country C. The customer may have a higher willingness to pay for the product from Country B than the product from Country C. Country B might also have lower manufacturing costs than Country C. This implies that gains from trade are greater if the product is purchased in Country B (and sold to the customer in Country A).

The manager should choose country pairs to maximize the gains from trade net of the costs of trade. In this example, suppose that Country A imposes higher tariffs on imports from Country B than it does on imports from Country C. These import duties may be sufficiently high as to offset the difference in gains from trade. Then, with Country A as the customer country, the firm should choose Country C as the supplier country. The manager chooses the customer country and the supplier country together to obtain the greatest net gains from trade.

The international business creates value by making connections between many markets in different countries. For any given configuration of countries, the manager maximizes value created. To increase the value that it creates, the company increases the benefits to its customers, lowers the costs of its suppliers, uses its resources more effectively, or combines suppliers and customers in new ways. The firm's ability to create and capture value depends on the firm's capabilities and its strength in comparison to competitors.

Competition with local and global rivals requires the firm to share the value that it creates with its customers and suppliers. To attract customers away from competitors, the company must provide sufficient customer value as compared to rival firms. To attract key suppliers away from competitors, the company must offer sufficient supplier value. To attract investment capital in competition with other market investment opportunities, the company must increase the value of the firm for its investors.

To obtain a competitive advantage, the company must create greater total value than its competitors. The firm can capture the added value that it brings to the market. The competitive advantage of the firm equals the difference between the overall value that is created by the industry when the firm is in the market and the overall value that would be created by the industry when the firm is not in the market.[5] *Global competitive advantage* is the extra value created by the firm in comparison to its competitors in the global market place.

Capturing the firm's added value is the source of the company's profits. The international firm provides products to customers in many countries through its international innovation, purchasing, manufacturing, assembly, and distribution activities. The value created by the company is based on the difference between the benefits received by the company's customers and the cost to the company's input suppliers, including the cost of the company's self-supplied inputs.

Value creation stems from the benefits received by the final customers, as determined by the customer's willingness to pay. The costs of supplying customers depend on the market value of goods and services provided by the firm and the inputs obtained from its suppliers. The costs incurred by the firm and its suppliers are the purchase costs of all inputs, including labor, natural resources, manufactured parts and components, technology, and capital equipment. Supplier costs further include the costs of all services obtained by the firm, including the costs associated with completing transactions, such as legal, accounting, marketing, and sales costs. The costs of the supplier also include the cost of capital, whether that capital is obtained through debt or the sale of equity.

When Michael Dell started his company, he observed that IBM sold a personal computer for $3,000 even though it contained $600 worth of parts.[6] He knew that the difference was too high, which suggested that IBM's other costs were too high and that IBM's markups were too high through lack of competition. Michael Dell realized that the costs of assembly and delivery could be lowered considerably, thus increasing the value created. Later, by operating online, Dell Computer dramatically lowered its transaction costs still further. By lowering its markups, Dell Computer was able to share the increased value with its consumers and suppliers. For a $2,000 computer, Dell Computer's cost of goods sold was approximately $1,600 and its overhead (selling, general, and administrative costs) was about $220, so that the markup was about $180.[7]

With increasing globalization, there has been an important change in the computer market. A computer company must establish a global value connection. Supply chains cross international borders more than ever before. Makers of monitors, screens, memory chips, microprocessors, batteries, and other components are located in different countries. Assembly is carried out in multiple countries chosen to lower costs. Distribution systems often involve multiple countries in systems of logistics, transportation, and warehousing. The firm's internal value chain often is global as well, as the MNC's activities are located in many countries. The global factory operates in many industries, including petroleum products, cell phones, automobiles, and clothing.[8]

The concept of the global value connection provides an important linkage between the steps of the strategy process. The manager's "Star Analysis" yields information about the company's customers and their willingness to pay for the company's products. The "Star Analysis" gives the manager information about the company's suppliers and their costs. The "Star Analysis" further informs managers about how partners can enhance the company's cost efficiency and its appeal to customers. This information enters directly into the manager's consideration of how to structure the value connection across countries.

The manager's "Star Analysis" also provides information about the company's competitors: their costs, their prices, and their products. This information is very useful in determining whether the company's transactions with its customers and suppliers create value in competition with other firms in the industry. Do the company's customers derive greater or lesser benefits from purchasing the products of competitors? Do the company's suppliers incur greater or lesser costs in serving competitors? These considerations will be important to the manager in evaluating what value the company adds to the market.[9]

The manager looks most carefully at the competitor's global value connection. The comparison between the company's global value connection and that of its competitors should help to reveal potential sources of competitive advantage. For example, ExxonMobil and Royal Dutch–Shell have different geographic configurations of exploration, production, refining, and retail distribution. These yield different global value connections in terms of the value of crude oil reserves, the cost of crude oil extraction, the cost of refining and distribution, and customer demand for the final product. The result will impact the relative economic performance of the two companies.

The five gains from trade

There are five major sources of gains from trade in international business:
1 Preference for variety and economies of scale
2 Comparative advantage
3 Comparative availability of factors of production
4 Differences in preferences and endowments
5 Innovation and technology transfer.
Each of these sources of gains from trade explains why countries specialize in particular activities.

To profit from gains from trade, the international business manager must understand the underlying international economics. In addition, the manager must develop transactions and activities designed to capture these gains.

Managers should determine what types of goods and services are the best candidates for international trade. They should understand why there are market opportunities to provide goods and services that originate in a given country to customers in other countries. Understanding the sources of gains from trade helps managers anticipate the *direction of trade* – that is, what should be exported from and imported to a particular country.

The manager uses the direction of trade as a guide to determine the best countries in which to find suppliers, partners, and customers. The international business obtains a competitive advantage if it is better than its competitors at anticipating opportunities generated by gains from trade.

It should be emphasized that gains from trade are a *dynamic* phenomenon. Significant shifts in opportunities for cross-border trade arise as a result of technological change, natural resource discoveries, and demographic trends. Changes in a target country's income and customer preferences alter demand patterns and open opportunities for new forms of international trade.

Gains from trade: 1 – preference for variety and economies of scale

A major source of gains from trade comes from the combination of consumer preferences for increased variety and the advantages manufacturers derive from economies of scale. The international business creates value by taking advantage of the love of variety and cost efficiencies from greater scale.

International trade brings a greater variety of goods to a country, providing benefits to its consumers. From 1972 to 2001, the number of goods imported to the US increased from 7,731 to 16,390. The number of product variations for these goods increased from 74,667 to a staggering 259,215. The result was a substantial increase in consumer benefits in the US, with even greater benefits in many other countries that experienced similar increases in variety.[10]

Companies expand their production through sales abroad, lowering their unit costs as a result of economies of scale. The international business creates value by seizing upon both sides of this process. Auto makers are increasingly trying to consolidate production of multiple varieties to obtain economies of scale. At the same time, they are exporting and importing multiple types of automobiles to provide consumers with greater variety.

The pursuit of scale and variety drives the globalization of the automobile industry as auto makers consolidate multiple national automobile companies to provide a global web of both production and sales. Thus, in addition to their traditional US brands, General Motors (GM) owns Saab, Vauxhall, Opel, and Holden, while Ford owns Volvo, Mazda, Land Rover, and Aston Martin.

Renault and Nissan's Alliance was formed to obtain the benefits from product variety and scale economies. The alliance provided economies of scale in production that was situated in many countries, and also provided variety not only by bringing their products into new country markets but also by offering multiple brands with a range of car models.

To achieve the benefits of scale and variety, auto makers are expanding the use of platforms to share parts, components, and technology across models. This creates economies of scope that reduce the costs of providing variety. Globalization of automobile markets makes each automobile a complex collection of many international elements.

Globalization continues to drive industry to consolidate its activities. As the economies of countries are increasingly integrated, the size of the market place is the sum of the markets of the countries. Economies of scale are measured not relative to national needs but relative to the needs of the many countries that obtain the product on international markets.

Manufacturing companies in such industries as steel must pursue the greatest plant-level economies. This means closing inefficient small-scale plants and building more efficient large-scale plants. Manufacturing companies also must pursue multi-plant economies, building the best network of manufacturing plants to operate efficiently.

At the same time, globalization increases variety. Increased scale economies in the global market place lower unit costs, and thus reduce prices. This results in increased demand. Through international trade in the same types of goods, each country can have many kinds of cars, computers, appliances, cell phones, foods, entertainment, and clothing. Increased variety is achieved by involving more countries without the need to scale down production. International business is not just a matter of lower costs, it also involves improved customer benefits from a greater choice of products.

The growing importance of scale economies in the global economy does not suggest that one country can capture the market for all kinds of goods. On the contrary, producing too many goods in a given country will mean sacrificing economics of scale. Economies of scale require that every country specialize. Companies should build and operate large-scale facilities in countries that offer the best combination of costs and access to customer markets.

The need to provide customers with product variety drives specialization within countries. Even if a country's industry has not reached the technological limits of scale economies that does not imply that additional production should take place just to get the benefits of lower unit costs. The market limits further growth in a product's demand since customers are willing to pay for variety. Competition between companies providing different varieties results in a mix of scale and variety.

Gains from trade: 2 – comparative advantage

In *An Inquiry into the Nature and Causes of the Wealth of Nations*, Adam Smith (1776) observed that the division of labor was limited by the extent of the market. In the familiar illustration of the pin factory, employees improved their productivity by specialization, limited only by the scale of the factory. Smith pointed out that these benefits of specialization extended to the nation, because countries that did not trade were limited in their ability to specialize. Nations benefited from trade by focusing on those sectors where they were relatively more productive. Smith pointed out that great civilizations developed where water transportation permitted international trade.[11]

The theory of *comparative advantage*, the foundation of international trade economics, is generally associated with David Ricardo (1817), who pointed out that by trading wine for wool, Portugal "would obtain more cloth from England, than she could produce by diverting a portion of her capital from the cultivation of vines to the manufacture of cloth."[12] Comparative advantage continues to have major implications for international business.

Country differences persist, and they are major. Countries vary significantly in terms of productivities, capabilities, and competencies. The gains from specialization have begun to be tapped through over $10 trillion in international trade, but the world has only scratched the surface. With the opening of China, India, Russia, and South-east Asia to international trade as never before, and the potential development of Africa, new horizons are appearing for companies. The economic development of these new traders does not suggest that they will take over the world, as some pundits predict, but rather that all countries can increase their investment in those activities in which they have a comparative advantage.

No country can produce everything, as many fear. Every country gains from specialization. Thus, China or India have large and still underutilized labor forces. However, it is in the best interest of companies operating there to specialize in activities where they have a comparative advantage. Attempting too many activities means that the country's work force, management, investment, and other resources are not put to their best uses. A country always gains by specialization and reliance on others.

The international business can create value by developing new import and export activities and by participating in the expansion of activities within country borders. Companies such as GE are riding the boom with sales to businesses in developing countries, and companies such as Wal-Mart are doing the same with sales to consumers in those countries.

For the international manager, comparative advantage provides a practical rule of thumb. Recall the discussion in chapter 2 of supplier countries in which the ratio of the wage to labor productivity determined the cost of labor per unit of output in a given activity. In evaluating two countries, the country with the lower unit cost of labor will tend to export to the country with the higher unit cost of labor.[13] All other things equal, the manager will obtain products from the country with lower unit costs of labor and provide products to the country with higher unit costs of labor.

The competitive actions of firms that pursue these strategies at the level of individual products determine national comparative advantage. Countries end up specializing in those products where they have relatively lower unit labor costs as compared to other countries. These choices are not made by countries themselves, of course. It is the actions of firms operating in the global market place that determine what goods will be imported and exported by countries. The strategic actions of firms reflect the underlying comparative advantages of countries.

Gains from trade: 3 – comparative availability of factors of production

The comparative availability of factors of production – labor, resources, and capital – provides another source of specialization and gains from trade.[14] In trade between two countries, one country will specialize in the production of goods that take advantage of that country's relatively more intensive factor as compared to the other country. If one country has a higher capital–labor ratio than the other country, it will tend to export more capital-intensive goods and import less capital-intensive goods. Each country moves along its production possibilities frontier and exchanges the additional production of the goods undergoing expansion with those goods of other countries undergoing expansion.[15]

For example, China increases its production of household appliances, such as air conditioners and washing machines, while the US increases its production of machine tools. Customers in both countries are made better off by the exchange of goods for which each country has a comparative advantage. Managers of companies engaged in international business take advantage of these potential gains through their manufacturing and sales decisions.

Gains from trade: 4 – differences in preferences and endowments

Countries may simply obtain gains from trade from international exchange of final goods and services or natural resources. The overall trade flows between the countries effectively add up to barter of final goods and services.[16] These gains can occur, for example, when countries have different endowments but similar consumer preferences, or different preferences but similar endowments. A landlocked country with extensive forests and a coastal country with an arid climate are likely to benefit by trading lumber products for seafood. Middle Eastern countries export crude oil and import agricultural goods. The growth of trade in natural resources and finished goods continues to illustrate these most traditional gains from trade.

International business plays an important role as an intermediary that carries out international transactions. The international business need not be a manufacturer. Managers of the international business find important sources of value by enhancing the efficiency of international markets and by connecting new buyers with new sellers. The international business creates value by bringing buyers and sellers together across borders.

Gains from trade: 5 – innovation and technology transfer

A rapidly developing source of gains from trade stems from differences in technologies across countries.[17] Since the same technology can be applied repeatedly in production in many different countries, it can be sold again and again. This creates gains from international trade in the technology itself.

The international market is expanding in licenses, blueprints and industrial processes, and knowledge transfers within MNCs. Other market transfers of technology take the form of business services such as consulting, training, and software development. Many types of specialized technology embodied in parts, components, and capital equipment are traded internationally.

Companies also benefit from combining diverse research efforts internationally to improve their chances of success. Gains from trade result from knowledge transfers, cooperative R&D, and competition between inventors in the global market place of ideas. International business is taking advantage of these developments by participating in the import and export of IP and the new application of innovations traded internationally. MNCs are establishing international divisions for internal transfers of knowledge to take advantage of gains from trade in ideas.

Maximizing global added value

The international business creates value through cross-border activities and transactions. The value created equals the benefits received by the firm's customers minus the costs incurred by the firm's suppliers, and minus the costs of using the firm's own assets. The international business earns returns by capturing some of the value that it creates.

The problem faced by a manager is how to make this system operational, and he or she has specific guide posts to aid in the task. The most important guide posts are the prices of goods and services. Additional guide posts are provided by descriptions of country differences obtained from the "Star Analysis."

To illustrate how price guide posts work, consider the most basic application: cross-country arbitrage. Take a hypothetical example in which an international business wishes to procure crude oil from a producing country and provide it to a refinery in a consuming country. The crude oil costs about $5 per barrel to the producer to extract from the ground. The refinery obtains value of about $50 per barrel from the crude oil. Gains from trade are the difference between the value to the customer and the cost to the supplier. Thus, gains from trade equal $45 in this example; if the costs of trade associated with this transaction equal $2, then the net gains from trade equal $43.

It may be difficult for a purchaser to observe the producer's costs. One indicator can be the freight-on-board (fob) price – at, say, $40 per barrel – that is charged by the producer. This is considerably above costs and reflects the scarcity of the resource and the higher costs of alternative sources. On the buyer side, the purchase price for the refinery is $43. The price difference of $3 indicates to the manager that there are some gains from trade, at least equal to $3, that can be created by the transaction.

The company seeking to engage in arbitrage incurs the $2 costs of trade. Since this is less than the gains from trade of $3, the transaction creates net gains from trade of at least $1. If the company can transact at these prices by buying from the producer and selling to the refinery, it makes a profit of $1 per barrel, thus capturing some net gains from trade.

Clearly, goods and services flow from the low-price country to the higher-price country. The price spread indicates that there are gains from trade and shows the direction of trade. The general rule for the manager is as follows: there are available net gains from trade if the spread between the ask price in the importing country and the bid price in the exporting country exceeds the costs of trade.

The international business has many instruments for making a global value connection, including the nine listed below:
- Export–import arbitrage
- Export–import brokerage
- International technology licensing
- International logistics services
- Cross-border supply-chain management
- Cross-border distribution-chain management
- Distribution abroad with international procurement from manufacturers
- International procurement of components and assembly
- Multi-country manufacturing for export.

A global business may perform one or more of these activities, and may combine multiple activities in their international operations.

Table 3.1. Global manufacturing of toys: "My First Tea Party Barbie"

Mattel captures value of approximately $1 per doll

	($)
Retail price (US)	10.00
Shipping, ground transportation, marketing, wholesale margin, retail margin	7.00
Overhead and management (Hong Kong)	1.00
Materials (China, Japan, Saudi Arabia, Taiwan, US)	0.65
Labor (Asia)	0.35
Mattel earnings per doll	**1.00**

Key locations for production of Barbie Doll:
El Segundo, CA: Mattel, Inc.
US: Cardboard packaging, paint pigments, molds
China: Factory space, labor, electricity
Saudi Arabia: Petroleum
Hong Kong: Management, shipping
Taiwan: Refines petroleum into ethylene for plastic pellets for Barbie's body
Japan: Nylon hair

Source: Data from US Commerce Department; Chinese Ministry of Foreign Trade and Economic Cooperation; Mattel, Inc.; Hong Kong Toy Council. This example is presented in Rone Tempest, "Barbie and the World Economy," *Los Angeles Times*, Part A, p. 1, September 22, 1996, Sunday, Home Edition.

The global business obtains gains from trade by a complicated mix of home-country activities, multiple supplier countries, partner countries, and customer countries. The global value connection is enhanced by brand recognition, productive efficiency, and efficient global operations and transactions. The global value proposition is illustrated by the example of Mattel, Inc. toy production in table 3.1.

To achieve global competitive advantage, a company must design international transactions that address potential gains from trade. The international business must make the best mix of customers, suppliers, and partners. It must also make the best match between its organizational skills and market opportunities.

Few, if any, competitive advantages can be sustained indefinitely, so the company is continually seeking opportunities to create the most value. Managers monitor global markets, comparing industry capacity to market demand. They closely examine their company in comparison with competitors to distinguish those features that are critical to success. To outbid competitors for customers, suppliers, and shareholders, the firm must create total value at least as great as that of its competitors.

Companies tend to differ in terms of production methods, product features, brand names, technology, and capabilities. They differ in terms of home-country features and the configuration of their customer, supplier, and partner countries.

The critical differences between companies are the sources of competitive advantage. The company can obtain no more than the additional value it creates over and above that of its competitors. The earnings realized by the firm depend on the share of additional value that the firm is able to capture. Competitive strategy therefore requires both value creation relative to competitors and the capture of a portion of that value through relationships with suppliers and customers.

Competitive advantage equals the difference between the value created by the company and the potential value created by its competitors. There are three main components of value: customer value, supplier value, and the value of the firm. Customer value is the customer's benefit net of the expenditure to purchase the product. Supplier value is the supplier's revenue net of cost. The value of the firm is the share of value created that is captured by the firm.[18]

To attract customers, the firm must create customer value that is at least as great as that offered by its competitors. A competitor's product or service may provide the customer with a different combination of price and product features. To bid away the customer from competitors, the firm must offer a better deal. The customer derives net benefits known as customer value or consumers' surplus from purchasing the good. Both price and benefits are elements of customer value,[19] which is equal to customer benefits minus the price the customer pays for the good.[20]

The firm attempts to capture a greater share of value by raising prices to customers or by lowering payments to suppliers, or by using its assets more efficiently. Capturing a larger piece of the "value pie" depends on the strength of competition for customers and suppliers, and the company's abilities.

The firm also tries to create greater value by increasing the size of the "pie." Creating greater value is accomplished in three ways:

1 Operating more efficiently by providing customer benefits at a lower cost or by lowering supplier costs
2 Providing greater benefits to customers by improving products and services
3 Developing innovative transactions that offer new value to the market.

The three strategies for creating greater value correspond to three types of competitive advantage: cost advantage, differentiation advantage, and transaction advantage.

The *value of the firm* equals the net present value (NPV) of expected cash flows. The value of the firm determines what is the value of the firm's debt and the value of the owner's equity. Investors have many alternative opportunities for capital investment, so the company's owners and lenders must be compensated for the cost of capital. To attract investment capital, the firm must provide sufficient value to investors so that they earn a rate of return at least as great as the comparable investment alternatives.[21]

The traditional strategic alternatives of product differentiation and cost leadership are disrupted by global competition. Product differences are significant, involving world-class product designs and global brands. Manufacturing cost differences are substantial because of variations in wages and worker skills across countries and innovations in global supply chains. Market segments tend to differ substantially, with the need for local tailoring of many product features, marketing messages, sales methods, and customer services.

Growth and value creation

The international company's ability to create value depends critically on world industry conditions. The potential for value creation depends on how the growth of global market demand compares with the growth of global industry capacity. Although these tend to balance out in the long run, through price adjustment and investment in new capacity, there are likely to be many short-run imbalances. Capacity imbalances are familiar events in markets for agricultural goods, energy resources, and manufactured goods.

As globalization proceeds, and country markets are increasingly linked by international business; capacity shortages in some countries balance out capacity surpluses in others. However, world markets are in a constant state of flux and imbalances inevitably result. In addition, business cycles and political conflicts have regional and world impacts. International business creates value by responding to demand and supply changes.

There are two main scenarios. If market demand outruns industry capacity, practically all companies can operate profitably and add value by providing scarce products to the market. If, on the other hand, industry capacity outruns market demand, some companies may not be profitable, and companies will need to have a competitive advantage to survive.

Industry capacity refers to the total capacity of the companies operating in an industry. To compare market demand with industry capacity, it is necessary to determine the price at which market demand equals industry capacity. That price is a critical determinant of the state of the industry. If the price at which market demand equals industry capacity is greater than the unit cost of the highest-cost company in the industry, then market demand is said to outrun industry capacity. If the price at which market demand equals industry capacity is less than the unit cost of the highest-cost company in the industry, then industry capacity is said to outrun market demand.

Demand outruns industry capacity

As President John F. Kennedy remarked: "A rising tide lifts all boats." During a period of rapidly rising demand there are significant opportunities for value creation. When total market demand outruns industry capacity, it means that individual firms have encountered short-run capacity constraints and cannot serve the entire market. In consequence, industry capacity is scarce relative to market demand, so that many companies in the industry can be profitable. This has the important strategic implication that individual firms can create value even without a competitive advantage.

Global businesses adjust their strategies to address imbalances between market demand and industry capacity. With demand outrunning capacity, competition exerts less downward pressure on prices. The lowest-cost firms cannot use prices to expand market share beyond the limits of their productive capacity. Because capacity is scarce, even the highest-cost firms are able to operate. This means that the capacity offered by even the highest-cost firms adds value to the market.

Because companies with different cost levels can operate profitably, there is room for firms with a cost disadvantage. Firms can be profitable with differing levels of productive efficiency and different types of productive technology. Companies with obsolete plants may operate side-by-side with companies with modern facilities. The market can be served by many different types of firms, including larger established companies with scale economies and new entrants with the high costs that startups often encounter.

When demand outruns capacity, firms with products of differing quality can serve the market, so that even firms with lower-quality products are profitable. Multiple firms with similar or generic products can also compete effectively. Moreover, firms that offer different prices for similar products can serve the market simultaneously. The firms offering price discounts cannot capture the market as long as they face capacity limitations.

Demand can outrun capacity for many reasons. The industry can experience relative high demand growth because of worldwide economic growth. Demand spikes can result from economic expansion in large emerging markets, such as Brazil, China, and India. Increased demand in emerging markets for energy, metals, and other commodities lift prices for these goods on world markets.

Reducing barriers to international trade can induce a demand boom, as companies take advantage of import and export opportunities and discover new markets for their products abroad. Lowering of trade barriers often stimulates demand for imports of foreign music, movies, food, clothing, and electronics. Changes in government regulation also lead to demand booms, as happened when deregulation of telecommunications led to an explosion in the demand for mobile phones, fax machines, and other communication devices.

As more developing economies open to world trade, world demand for some goods increases, just as productive capacity also increases. Higher consumer income, greater employment, regulatory reform, and tax cuts stimulate country economies and lead to growth of demand in many industries. Industry demand growth can also occur due to shifts in population – an increased demand for housing followed the migration from rural to urban areas in China, particularly in coastal areas, for example.

Many types of factors stimulate demand growth in specific industries. Business cycles can drive demand growth in specific countries. Shifts in customer tastes can favor a particular type of product. For example, changing lifestyles of working families in industrializing nations lead to increased demand for restaurant meals and preprepared foods. The success of complementary products creates demand shifts. The increased use of personal computers (PCs), for instance, stimulated demand for software applications such as spreadsheets and word processing programs. The growth of the automobile industry in emerging markets, including China and India, has spawned a wide range of other industries, including petroleum refining, automobile repair and service stations, motels, and companies producing parts such as tires and batteries.

The introduction of new technologies has often led to demand booms as customers discover new products. Consider the opportunities created by the introduction of new modes of transportation, from the railroad to the automobile to the jet aircraft. New methods of communication including the telegraph, the telephone, the Internet, and the wireless phone have led to significant demand booms as customers adopt the new product. New technologies such as advances in information and communication can stimulate demand by changing the organizational structure of companies and the organization of markets. With less vertical integration and increased outsourcing, companies have an increased demand for information processing and communications equipment.

Technology effects often are associated closely with new product introductions, and help to explain the growth phase at the start of a product life cycle. Typically, the product life cycle is said to involve four stages: introduction, growth, maturity, and decline. Sales and profit rise during the introduction and growth stages and fall during the latter part of the maturity stage and the decline stage. The product life cycle has limited predictive powers because the time at which turning points occur is difficult, if not impossible, to observe or to predict. However, the product cycles that do occur reflect underlying patterns of customer demand changes and firms' capacity investments.[22]

Firms still have incentives to be efficient during a demand boom. Companies still earn greater profits by lowering their costs. Moreover, companies can stimulate sales through greater product quality. However, because competitive pressures are substantially reduced or eliminated during booms, it may be useful for companies to delay investments that have little short-run benefit, focusing their efforts on taking advantage of current sales growth. Managers may use the boom to prepare for future investment to reduce operating costs or enhance product features.

Scarcity of supply relative to demand can take many forms. Companies that supply natural resources, such as metals or energy resources, experience booms during periods of economic growth. Real estate demand booms result in the sale or rental of all available space, rising prices, and new construction. Manufacturing industry booms lead to shortages of production capacity for manufactured inputs, components, and final goods. The manufacture of computer notebooks has been hindered at various times by shortages in LCD screens. Companies may benefit from industry-level scarcity of distribution capacity or shortages of sales personnel. Finally, there may be limits on all kinds of competencies, from technological knowledge to management skills.

Demand growth attracts inputs to the growing industry, as demand for final products leads companies to expand production. Thus, demand booms attract funds from venture capitalists, banks, and securities investors. Entrepreneurs are drawn to the opportunities provided by a booming industry. Booms lead to higher wages and increased hiring, which in turn attract managers and employees to the industry. Suppliers of parts, components, and services are motivated by the opportunity to serve companies who are in a booming market.

Why does demand outrun capacity? Part of the problem for companies responding to a demand boom results from lags in establishing capacity. The demand boom may come as a surprise, so it takes the industry time to respond. When energy prices rise, it takes time to increase exploration and drilling for new petroleum and natural gas resources. When there is increased demand for computers, it can take several years to build a new plant to manufacture semiconductors. When there is an increased need for particular skills, such as surgeons or computer programmers, long training times lead to delays in obtaining qualified personnel.

Because capacity is costly to establish, companies cannot adjust capacity perfectly in tune with demand fluctuations, so that the market naturally experiences periods of capacity shortfall. Moreover, established companies experience adjustment costs – that is, the increased costs associated with installing new capacity and integrating that capacity with existing operations. Competitive advantage is not essential to profitability when there are delays in new entry or expansion of firm capacity. The shortage of capacity creates incentives for established companies to expand their capacity and for companies to enter the market with new capacity, and competition intensifies.

Industry capacity outruns demand

When global industry capacity outruns market demand, the strategic situation changes considerably. The industry must shed its excess capacity because it is usually very costly for companies to carry it. As a result individual companies need to reduce their productive capacity or exit the market altogether. Some companies may merge as a means of lowering costs as well as retiring duplicated parts of their capacity. The main strategic implication is that companies need a competitive advantage to be profitable and survive. Therefore, it is often the case that when industry capacity outruns market demand companies need to have a competitive advantage to create value in the market.

Industry capacity can outrun market demand for many reasons. Economic forces, as discussed previously, such as changes in income, employment, or other business cycle effects can result in a slowdown in the growth of demand or a decline in the demand for a given industry.[23] Excessive capacity in the global automobile industry at the start of the twenty-first century led to mergers and consolidation, such as the acquisition of Chrysler by DaimlerBenz.

Even if industry demand continues to grow, an unexpected slowdown in demand combined with continued growth in industry capacity can cause companies' building capacity to overshoot. Industry-specific effects, such as changes in customer tastes, can also reduce industry demand below industry capacity. Industries that produce outmoded products experience declining demand. An industry in a specific country can experience declining demand as it competes with lower-cost or higher-quality imports.

Even with substantial demand growth, capacity can outrun demand as a result of discovering economies of scale and scope. If technological change allows individual companies to expand their capacity while realizing economies of scale, then market demand can be served by a smaller number of companies. As companies expand their potential scale, competition will drive them out of the market. Companies with a smaller inefficient scale will be driven out by more efficient companies with greater scale economies. Companies that realize scale economies will compete on cost efficiencies.

In some industries, economies of scale are so significant that there is room in the market for only a small number of companies. For example, in large jets, the global market can apparently support only two companies, Boeing and Airbus. Their scale economies result from the complexity of designing, manufacturing, and assembling large aircraft. In computer operating systems, the high fixed costs of writing software and the minimal costs of producing an additional copy of the software give Microsoft the scale economies to easily supply software to run 90 percent of personal computers. In retailing, large companies such as Wal-Mart and Target take advantage of scale economies in distribution networks, but the retail sector also includes many small specialized stores that offer convenience and service.

In some markets, including computer operating systems, the benefits customers derive from standardization create winner-take-all industries. However, in other markets, the benefits of variety create opportunities for many companies. Although there are benefits from standard formats for computer games, such as those offered by Nintendo and Sony, the need for many diverse games has created opportunities for a host of game designers.

In newly established industries, there is a tendency for capacity to outrun demand. The celebrated economist Joseph A. Schumpeter observed "the appearance of entrepreneurs in clusters" – that is, innovative startup companies tend to enter the market at around the same time.[24] Schumpeter attributes this "clustering" in part to the elimination of obstacles to entry by pioneers who show the way. Pioneers may inspire entrepreneurs to enter into a specific industry; sometimes, pioneers in one industry can encourage entrepreneurs to enter into many other industries if they demonstrate how to overcome general types of obstacles.

Entrepreneurs often enter an industry simultaneously in search of the potential rewards of establishing a successful business. Entrepreneurs tend to be rational profit maximizers, taking a calculated risk even if they enjoy creating a new business. They are not likely to be irrationally exuberant gamblers who overestimate the chance of success. The end result is the same: when excess capacity enters a market, some businesses will succeed and others will fail and exit. The growth of market demand and the entry decisions of firms determine whether the rewards of the winners outweigh the costs to the losers. Bringing innovation to market requires taking risks.

Capacity is also likely to outrun demand in new industries because of technological uncertainty. If production technologies are not well understood, each entrant will try out a different production process. More capacity enters the market than is needed to satisfy demand because each entrant believes that their variant of the production technology has a chance of being the best. As production begins, companies discover the costs and efficiencies of their technology, and competition weeds out the inefficient processes.

Similarly, when new types of products are introduced, each entrant will test a different type of product. Excess capacity enters the market because each entrant believes that their product has a chance of proving to be superior to those of its competitors. As customers try the products, companies discover how various product features are viewed by customers, and competition weeds out inferior products.

When capacity outruns demand, a shakeout results. Firms experience a reduction in their market share and some firms exit the market. The pattern of growth, rapid decline, and leveling off has been observed in many new industries. Shakeouts have characterized the early history of a wide range of industries: hundreds of car companies entered the market at the beginning of the twentieth century, but a combination of cost differences and product differentiation weeded out most of them.

As total industry capacity outruns demand, the least efficient firms, or the firms with the least attractive products, generally are forced to exit the market. However, there is still room for a diverse set of firms to operate. The capacity limits of firms that are operating in the market continue to allow less efficient firms, or firms with less attractive products, to operate profitably. This explains in part the great diversity of firms within any given industry. Limits on individual firm capacity imply that supplying products to the market creates value.

When industry capacity outruns customer demand there often is a shakeout of industry capacity. Some firms will exit the industry by closing capacity; other firms will merge to consolidate their capacity and close down inefficient plants. The second-largest disk-drive manufacturer, Maxtor, bought Quantum, and Hitachi bought IBM's disk drive manufacturing business. Companies need to have a competitive advantage to continue operating in the industry and survive the shakeout Those companies with a competitive advantage sometimes are able to grow their capacity at the same time that the industry is shedding its less efficient capacity. Having a competitive advantage also enables the company to pursue its strategy through the ups and downs of the business cycle.

Overview

Global competitive advantage requires that the firm create greater net gains from trade than its competitors. The five gains from trade are:
• Preference for variety and economies of scale
• Comparative advantage
• Comparative availability of factors of production
• Differences in preferences and endowments
• Innovation and technology transfer.
The four costs of trade are: transaction costs, tariff and non-tariff costs, transportation costs, and time costs.

A global business chooses country locations and links markets through its activities and transactions. The source of global competitive advantage is the firm's global value connection. Making these value connections is difficult and complex, as supply chains, distribution chains, and company operations cross national borders.

Reductions in the costs of trade drive the process of globalization. By making more cross-border transactions economically feasible, more gains from trade become available and the international business is able to create a more effective global value connection. The global business seeks competitive advantage by discovering new sources of gains from trade, by developing new transaction methods to reduce the costs of trade, and by linking new combinations of markets across countries. In this setting, competitive advantage can involve both cost advantages and differentiated products. By building global value connections through innovative transactions, the global business stands to gain a competitive advantage.

4　Global competitive strategy

Global competitive strategies must address the two sides of the global challenge: a company must be able to cope with the sheer size of the global market place while addressing the great diversity of local markets. To resolve this dilemma, the global business must turn to its advantage both the vast dimensions and local variations of global markets. This chapter and chapter 5 present five key global competitive strategies, which comprise the "G5 strategies" for achieving global competitive advantage.

Of course, all such advantage is necessarily temporary. Highly variable consumer tastes, production methods, information technologies, and public policies affect global trade. The global strategies presented here offer ways for a company to anticipate and adapt in a rapidly changing world. These strategies may be used in combination – they are not mutually exclusive. Also, the list of strategies does not exhaust the possibilities, but instead highlight the many opportunities that exist for global firms.

Global platform strategy: scale and variety

Carlos Ghosn was the "hottest car guy on earth," according to the *Wall Street Journal*.[1] He became the head of the Japanese auto maker Nissan Motor Co. in 1999, when it formed an alliance with the French auto maker Renault. Then, in 2005, six years after the Renault–Nissan Alliance was formed, Ghosn also was made the CEO of Renault. Uniting the Alliance partners under the same management, Ghosn had a 10,000-mile commute between Paris and Tokyo.[2] Under his leadership at Nissan, the Alliance became a pacesetter in the global auto industry.

Ghosn's international roots prepared him well for the challenge of integrating the two companies. A French citizen, he was born in Brazil to Lebanese parents and spoke fluent English, French, Arabic, and Portuguese. After obtaining his second degree in engineering, Ghosn joined the French tire company Michelin, rose to the position of CEO of Michelin North America, and then moved on to Renault.

Formed by cross-share holdings, the Alliance made rapid strides. Within five years, the Alliance was among the top four car companies in the world and it achieved a global market share of one-tenth of total sales. The Alliance trailed GM, Ford, and Toyota, but surpassed Volkswagen, DaimlerChrysler, and other car companies. Ghosn had turned Nissan around, changing the company to a dynamic and profitable operation with many new successful models including the Nissan 350Z, the Murano, and the Infinity G35.

Although the Alliance pioneered many important management innovations, its *global platform strategy* was crucial. The two companies stressed cooperation in all major areas of the business, which resulted in cost savings, product innovation, and marketing benefits. The platform strategy exemplified the international coordination between Renault and Nissan and such a global platform strategy was critical not just for partnerships but for many global firms.

At the time the Alliance was formed, Nissan had twenty-four vehicle platforms. Under Ghosn's direction, Nissan began reducing the number of these, a process known as *platform consolidation*. Nissan also began the corresponding process of creating more vehicles that would use the same platform, which is referred to as *platform extension*. Within five years, Nissan had reduced the number of its platforms to fifteen, and the top five platforms accounted for over 90 percent of its production.[3]

For cars, the *platform* is primarily its chassis (frame, suspension, steering, and wheels) and an associated family of engines and transmissions. Auto makers then create *variants* by putting different bodies on top of the same platform, allowing multiple car models to use it. A platform becomes truly global when it is sold in multiple countries, often with well over 1 million cars per year on one platform. A platform can not only support multiple car models simultaneously, it can extend across multiple model years. The auto maker can update the model in ways that customers will appreciate while keeping the same underlying platform.

The Renault–Nissan Alliance set an objective of jointly creating ten shared platforms by 2010. One of those shared platforms was called the Alliance B platform, and the Alliance used it to launch nine small cars. On the Nissan side, the cars on the B platform were March, Cube, Micra, Tiida, Tiida Latio, and Note. On the Renault side, the cars on the B platform were Modus, Clio III, and Logan. Another common platform, the Alliance C platform, supported the Nissan Lafesta minivan, the Nissan Serena van, and the Renault Mégane II automobile, which became the highest-selling car in Europe.[4]

The Alliance maintained the integrity and independent identity of its brands – Nissan, Infinity, Renault, Dacia, and Samsung. The two companies cooperated closely in product planning. In some cases, the same vehicle was sold under both badges, such as the Renault Kangoo and Nissan Kubistar Sport Utility Vehicles (SUVs). They worked closely to develop and share engines and transmissions. Cooperation extended to R&D, and navigation and communication systems. The companies consolidated their parts purchasing, manufacturing, information systems, quality control, sales financing, and all types of logistics.[5]

Common platforms were at the heart of the international competitive strategy of the Renault–Nissan Alliance. By creating global platforms, they achieved *economies of scope*, which refers to the cost savings that a firm achieves by jointly producing multiple products. For example, if the cost of developing a platform equals $4 billion, the cost per variant is $1 billion if there are four variants, $0.5 billion if there are eight variants, and so on. Producing multiple variants per platform thus yields economies of scope.

Developing a platform is likely to cost more than developing an individual product. As the number of variants increases, the platform approach becomes worthwhile. With enough variants, the platform is less costly than multiple unconnected products. The international business pursuing the global platform strategy must have the long-term perspective needed to invest in the platform; it must also have the global vision to create platforms that can support a variety suited for many countries.

The global platform strategy yields additional cost benefits in the form of *multi-product economies of scale.*[6] The company can spread the costs of IT, R&D, and management across multiple products and reap cost advantages from scale. Additional scale economies come from flexible manufacturing that allows more effective use of manufacturing capacity. There are cost advantages associated with increased production of each of the firm's products.

The other major benefit of global platforms is incremental revenues from product variety. By adding variants on a common platform, Renault and Nissan could offer each country they served a car model that most closely fitted consumer tastes and income. The ability to increase product variety improved their responses to competitors' offerings.

All of the major global auto makers use platforms to achieve economies of scope and to provide variety to the market. Simply having platforms does not confer a competitive advantage, however. Rather, it is the way that the global platform strategy is applied that has the potential to create competitive advantage.

DaimlerChrysler's experience illustrates that merely having a platform strategy is not enough. The company failed to implement the strategy effectively after the acquisition of Chrysler. The company's managers were so intent on preserving the separation of the Mercedes and Chrysler brands that they strongly resisted common platforms; moreover the managers, led by company chair and CEO Jürgen Schrempp, conceived of Mercedes as the luxury brand whose product identity in the premium car segment would be tarnished by an association with Chrysler. Schrempp's strategy was to merge with Mitsubishi and to implement global platform-sharing. Mercedes would lead the way with technological innovations that then would be shared with Chrysler and Mitsubishi after a lag of a few years. This strategy, while inherently flawed, was further damaged when DaimlerChrysler dissolved its association with Mitsubishi after failing to bail out the struggling Japanese auto maker.

After being acquired by DaimlerBenz, losses began to appear at Chrysler. Mercedes itself faced increasing consumer doubts about the quality of its cars relative to other brands in the luxury segment. Dieter Zetsche, who was appointed to head Chrysler, began the process of turning the company around. Having met with success in Detroit, Zetsche was named CEO of DaimerChrysler, replacing Schrempp. A critical change was the sharing of platforms. The Chrysler Crossfire sports car and the Dodge Magnum station wagon were the initial results of the common platforms. The announcement of the Chrysler Crossfire stated: "Dreamed in America. Crafted in Germany. Infused with passionate American design and precision German engineering."

GM and Ford encountered problems and losses as they struggled to compete with global firms entering the US market. In the mid-1990s Jack Smith, then CEO of GM, wanted the company to "Run Common, Run Lean and Fast, Grow, and Go Global." This meant that GM would emphasize global platforms and share components and engineering across its domestic and international operations. Some of GM's platform-sharing projects did not work – for example, GM abandoned an alliance with Italy's Fiat that would have involved common platforms. GM shared platforms with Saab, Daewoo, and Isuzu, but these drew mixed reviews.

Ford expected to increase platform-sharing in its Way Forward Plan. The company developed a common platform for cars made by Mazda, Volvo, and Ford Europe, but much consolidation still lay ahead. GM and Ford each announced multiple plant closings. Between GM, Ford, and the Chrysler division of DaimlerChrysler, actual and planned job cuts in a six-year period starting in 2000 totaled 140,000, about a third of their North American workforce.[7] The effects of global competition were very evident.

The global platform strategy can become a source of competitive advantage when it effectively achieves two tasks. First, the company must achieve sufficient economies of scale and scope by reducing the number of platforms and increasing the number of variants per platform. Second, the company must offer sufficient variety, by having enough platforms to cover the critical market segments in terms of car sizes and functions, and enough variants to serve different countries with the right car features. The global platform strategy thus yields competitive advantage if companies achieve the right mix between economies of scale and scope and provision of product variety.

The global platform allowed the Renault–Nissan Alliance to develop a world car for emerging markets – the Logan – that would sell for less than $6,000. Western Europeans wanted the car, too, so Renault–Nissan added some features and offered the car there for a little over $9,000. The car was built on the Alliance B platform. Kenneth Melville, the head of the car's design team said: "The Logan is the McDonald's of cars."[8] The Logan was designed for cost-effective production in emerging markets, including Romania, Russia, and India and potentially in China and Brazil. The low cost would make the car competitive for low-income consumers while its roominess and design features would extend Renault and Nissan brands to many new customers – the 80 percent of the world's population who live in emerging markets.

Whatever the industry, companies in the global market place face a difficult choice. They must have world-class cost economies to be price competitive, which requires *standardization*. They must address different customer requirements and competitor products in the many countries they serve, which requires *tailoring*. These objectives were viewed traditionally as mutually exclusive, but the global platform strategy is a way of harmonizing these dual objectives. The global platform helps firms to address the trade-off between costs and product diversity, and the strategy has begun to transform many industries – not only cars, but also computers, mobile phones, appliances, machine tools, and jet aircraft.

Any company can apply a global platform strategy. The company must decide what activities should be standardized across their worldwide operations, and what activities should be adapted to specific countries or regions. Managers of the international business should review their activities to determine what should be "global" and what should be "local". These activities include:

- Product R&D
- Technology and inputs
- Product features
- Manufacturing operations and methods
- Brands
- Marketing
- Sales and service.

The activities that are standardized across the globe are the company's *platforms* and the activities that are tailored locally are the company's *variants*.

For example, Wal-Mart offered global platforms through its four store formats: Supercenters, Discount Stores, Neighborhood Markets, and Sam's Club warehouses. Wal-Mart's local country variants were achieved by tailoring its product offerings to local tastes and incomes. In China, for example, Wal-Mart discovered that customers often visited the store daily for fresh food. Chinese customers also preferred smaller package sizes (because of limited storage space) and detergent for hand-washing laundry. Wal-Mart made the necessary adjustments in its procurement, inventories, products, and prices.

Taiwan's Acer adapted its computers to different country markets, using what it called a global vision with a "local touch." Acer implemented what was essentially a global platform strategy using its "fast food model." Stan Shih, Acer's founder and chairman, created four centralized global functions: brand management, logistics, customer service, and IT. The company centrally produced the elements of the platform in its "central kitchens": motherboards, monitors, power supplies, and keyboards. The global product platforms included the company's global brand and common technology. Acer then tailored its product *variants* to the local markets it served by creating local production sites and assembly plants, and shipping the right mix of components that would be needed for local models. Most importantly, Acer express shipped those components such as microprocessors that would be "perishable" as local demands varied.[9] Acer's global platform was exemplified by a computer design that facilitated local tailoring. The company developed motherboards that could easily handle different types of central processing unit chips, a computer assembly process in which parts snapped together without fasteners, and a standardized assembly process that was used in all its local production locations.[10] By moving assembly close to the customer, Acer's products could develop variants that adjusted to local demand conditions.

Whirlpool pursued a global platform strategy in appliances, reaching a lead position in India, Latin America, and North America. The advantages of global platforms were faster product innovation, better transfer of technology and knowledge across international units of the company, and more focused parts procurement. Dave Whitman, Whirlpool's chairman and CEO, observed: "We recognize that consumers are different around the world. They have different tastes, cultures, and usage patterns with our products." Whitman emphasized the importance of customer loyalty: "the global platform strategy enables us to accomplish our goal."[11]

The global platform strategy, when executed effectively, creates customer loyalty by solving the central conundrum of international business. Platforms provide the economics of scope needed for global price competition, as well as the product variety needed for product differentiation in many customer country markets.

Global network strategy: coordinating comparative advantage

Victor Fung and his brother William headed up Li & Fung, Hong Kong's largest export trading company. Grandsons of the company's founder, who established the business in 1906, the billionaire brothers built Li & Fung into the world's leading supply-chain manager for clothing and toys. Central to the company's success was its *global network strategy*.

Li & Fung's supply-side sourcing network consisted of 7,500 suppliers in almost forty countries. Using its far-flung network, the company created customized supply chains for each of its customers, who were generally American and European retail companies. The company also operated three retail chains with over 750 stores in China, Indonesia, Malaysia, Singapore, South Korea, and Thailand. The retail chains were Circle K, Toys "R" Us, and Branded Lifestyle offering branded outlets such as Salvatore Ferragamo, Mango, Country Road, and Calvin Klein Jeans. In addition, the Group's distribution division offered "value-chain logistics," a collection of marketing, logistics, and manufacturing services.

Describing the company's trading business, Victor Fung colorfully illustrated the company's intermediation role:

I have a picture in my mind of the ideal trader for today's world. The trader is wearing a pith helmet and a safari jacket. But in one hand is a machete and in the other a very high-tech personal-computer and communications device. From one side, you're getting reports from suppliers in newly emerging countries, where the quality of the information may be poor. From the other side, you might have point-of-sale information from the United States that allows you to replenish automatically.[12]

Li & Fung coordinated its vast set of suppliers to create the best mix of activities for each item it produced. Only 2,500 of Li & Fung's 7,500 suppliers were active at any one time.[13] This allowed the company's suppliers to pursue other manufacturing projects and reduced excessive reliance on Li & Fung orders.

According to Victor Fung, the company's novel concept was "breaking up the value chain" through dispersed manufacturing. Li & Fung supplied the upstream functions of design, engineering, and production planning. It then organized and outsourced the middle stages of production, including raw material and component sourcing and managing of production by contractors in factories around the world. Finally, Li & Fung provided the downstream functions of quality control, testing, and logistics, as well as the marketing and sales interaction with its customers, the retail companies.[14] As Victor Fung stated: "We orchestrate this great big network, from yarn to fabric to garments, moving to shipping and warehousing."[15]

Through its global network strategy, Li & Fung assembled a vast work force in many countries, numbering perhaps a million people, who worked for their suppliers. Li & Fung's network was structured carefully to benefit from the *comparative advantages* of many countries. Each country had a different labor force, with varying wage structures and productive skills. Taking into account differences in wages and productivity, Li & Fung could match its supplier countries with particular types of clothing production or assembly work. By relying on independent suppliers, Li & Fung could respond flexibly to changing relative wages or the development of new labor capabilities.

Li & Fung structured its organization to maintain personal relationships in its dealings with its many suppliers, delegating considerable autonomy to the company's buyers. These relationships were critical to the company's competitive advantage. Li & Fung's knowledge of the competencies of each supplier was the product of considerable experience, and would be difficult for a competitor to duplicate. The mutual trust between Li & Fung and its suppliers also would pose a challenge to a new competitor seeking to enter the market by forming a comparable network.

Another key source of the company's competitive advantage stemmed from its efficiency in coordinating the large number of suppliers along its supply chain. The company's suppliers might produce only one component of the finished product – for example, the zipper or the shell of a parka. Li & Fung determined the best sources for the individual components and coordinated design, final assembly, and quality control. By choreographing the activities of its supplier network, the company obtained the best mix of goods and services needed to produce efficiently any particular garment or toy.

By relying on its network of outside suppliers, Li & Fung achieved a flexibility that might not be possible with vertical integration into manufacturing. Li & Fung could shift production to those countries where suppliers had excess capacity; this meant that the company's large supplier network was a market for productive capacity. Li & Fung could reduce its supplier usage in countries where capacity was scarce and increase supplier usage in countries where capacity was abundant. In this way, it could use its network of suppliers to become a market maker in productive capacity. Because its suppliers also offered specialized skills in garment and toy manufacturing, Li & Fung was also a market maker in productive skills. The network allowed rapid responses to changes in the availability of productive capacity and capabilities.

Although gains from trade were important, Li & Fung was not guided simply by the production costs and capabilities of its suppliers. It had to take account of the costs of trade. The company was acutely aware of the country context of its suppliers and the implications for "the four Ts": transaction costs, tariff and non-tariff barriers, transportation costs, and the costs of time.

Li & Fung used its global network strategy to minimize transaction costs. By establishing a network of trusted suppliers, Li & Fung could transact efficiently with them on a repeated basis to operate its supply chain for clothing and toys. Li & Fung's established supplier relationships, IT, and management systems provided a source of competitive advantage.

The transaction costs a competitor would incur in recreating such a network were substantial, but a knowledgeable firm could attempt the task. Where Li & Fung gained an edge was in comparison with potential bypass by its customers or suppliers. For a customer to assemble a supply chain would involve much higher costs because Li & Fung had the advantage of scale and scope: its supplier network was used for many projects carried out for many customers. A customer would face significantly greater transaction costs in duplicating a part of Li & Fung's supply-chain management. The same was true for Li & Fung's suppliers: an individual supplier could not replicate Li & Fung's entire supply chain. Also, an individual supplier might serve only a few retail chains and would lack access to Li & Fung's many retail-chain relationships.

Transportation costs were critical to Li & Fung's supply chain for clothing and toys. Materials had to be shipped in and finished goods shipped out.

Logistics played a critical role. Clothing and toys were seasonal items and highly dependent on fashion. Transportation infrastructure within a supplier country and the location of the supplier country in relation to customer markets affected the efficiency and speed of transportation. Li & Fung constructed its network and logistics to keep down shipping costs and drastically reduce time to market.

Tariff and non-tariff barriers were particularly significant for Li & Fung. With textile quotas imposed by customer countries, including the US and European nations, Li & Fung could use its global network to allocate production across supplier countries so as to come in under quotas that would limit exports. This provided a competitive advantage over producers with limited geographic reach who would be more constrained by country quotas.

The competitive landscape changed dramatically with the end of the international MFA and the gradual relaxation of textile quotas by the US and the EU. This potentially removed a source of Li & Fung's competitive advantage. The textile industries of Hong Kong and China had effectively become integrated, with their combined forces representing one of the most competitive garment exporting countries.[16] Li & Fung faced increased competition from companies in China and elsewhere that had their manufacturing operations and suppliers within a single country. By locally clustering manufacturing and sourcing, a clothing company could avoid much of the costly logistics and cross-border transactions that had been needed to comply with textile quotas. Li & Fung's global network would have to yield benefits that went beyond compliance with trade regulations.

Time is essential in the fashion business. The shorter the product cycle, the better a retailer can anticipate and respond to changes in demand. Errors in the product mix result either in unsold inventory or shortages of popular items. Li & Fung could take an order and have the product on shelves in the US within five weeks.[17] Retailers gained the ability to reduce the size of orders and limit end-of-season sales.[18] Companies that relied on Li & Fung for production could focus on marketing and product development knowing that its products would be available quickly.

Li & Fung served such clothing retailers as The Limited, Gymboree, Abercrombie & Fitch, and American Eagle Outfitters, while producing apparel for Reebok, giftware for Avon, home items for Bed, Bath & Beyond, and consumer goods for Warner Bros. shops.[19] Li & Fung faced competitive threats from a variety of sources. In addition to competition from other supply-chain managers, the company could be bypassed by major retailers who did their own sourcing. Gap International ended its connection to Li & Fung to do its own purchasing.[20]

Another major competitive challenge was the creation in China of textile and garment cities. Producers were located side-by-side, allowing for ease of coordination with less need for logistics. China Textile City, in Zhejiang Province, evolved from an informal market place, with products displayed in shacks, into Asia's largest distribution center for synthetic fabrics and a major center for a wide variety of textiles.[21] Ningbo, China's fashion city located next to Shanghai, offered thousands of small and large textile manufacturing businesses, serving many international clothing firms. Many other industries clustered in Ningbo, which in ancient China created the "silk and porcelain road in the sea."[22]

Li & Fung's global network strategy would need to address the competitive challenges of customer bypass and supplier clusters. The key would be its coordination of international supply chains and the realization of trade flows that reflected the comparative advantages of nations. The threat of supplier clusters could be addressed because Li & Fung's network was sufficiently flexible to incorporate them. This would allow Li & Fung to take advantage of the suppliers' geographic concentration to improve the performance of its own network.

The global network strategy uses the countries of the world as parts of a value chain for all kinds of purposes, including R&D, design, manufacturing, logistics, and distribution. Companies that operate global supply chains include Flextronics and Solectron in electronics, Acer in computers, and Honda in automobiles.

Solectron Corporation, one of the largest electronics manufacturing services companies, provided outsourcing solutions to leading electronics OEMs in such industries as computers, computer peripherals, networking, telecommunications, semiconductor equipment, industrial controls, medical electronics, avionics, and consumer electronics. Solectron's global network strategy promoted speed, efficiency and cost containment throughout the entire supply chain. Solectron maintained a vast global network of customers (OEMs) and suppliers (component manufacturers). Solectron reduced communication costs by applying electronic data interchange, centralizing data collection and analysis, and jointly monitoring manufacturing and fulfillment processes.[23] The centrally managed network allowed outsourcing transactions to be managed at far lower costs than if the OEMs and component suppliers were to transact directly with each other.

A company with a global network of suppliers presents a single face to its customers, who see only a seamlessly constructed final product of the global factory. The many countries that contribute to the product remain in the background. When the global network company provides the product, its customers do not know what functions have been performed in-house and what functions have been outsourced around the world.

The global network strategy applies to distribution as well. Franchising provides a good example of a network of distribution contracts. 7-Eleven is the world's largest operator, franchisor, and licensor of convenience stores, with 28,000 stores worldwide, of which about 22,600 are operated by licensees. Many of these franchise operations are outside the US; the company has over 10,800 stores in Japan.[24] Franchising offers a company such as 7-Eleven a way to extend its brand and earn revenues in many countries without incurring the cost of investment needed for market entry. The franchise firm can pursue a global network strategy by selling the right to use its brand and to apply its business model. Other leading international franchisers include McDonald's, KFC, Pizza Hut, Subway, Starbucks Coffee, and Häagen-Dazs.

The global network strategy can be extended through master franchising agreements. Under this arrangement the franchiser contracts with a company, who then operates outlets or finds franchisers in the host country. Cendant franchised Century 21 Real Estate this way in France and China. Cendant is the world's largest franchiser of real estate brokerages; the company's Century 21, ERA Real Estate, Coldwell Banker, Coldwell Banker Commercial, and Sotheby's International Realty have almost 15,000 independent real estate offices worldwide. The size of the company's global network gives it the "power to provide an unmatched worldwide referral network, international brand awareness, national marketing and advertising campaigns, and access to alliance partners."[25]

The franchise network provides a way for the parent company to reduce the total investment needed to build a worldwide network, and franchising offers a related type of benefit for the franchisee. A franchise operator is able to become part of a recognized established business with only the capital necessary to purchase a franchise. The limited initial investment required of franchisees makes this model highly attractive for emerging markets:[26] the franchise network can expand with the economic growth of the host country, allowing the franchise company to extend its worldwide network flexibly and efficiently.

The global network strategy can dramatically extend the reach of the international business. This includes both supply-side networks like Li & Fung and demand-side networks like Cendant, see figures 4.1 and 4.2. The company that successfully executes the global network strategy becomes an essential hub for international transactions, see figure 4.3. Suppliers gain access to

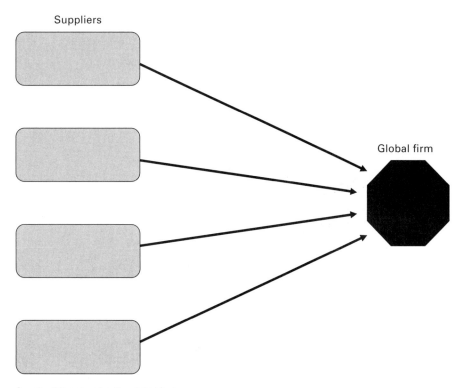

Suppliers

Global firm

Fig. 4.1   Supply-side networks: the global factory

many customers; customers gain access to many suppliers. The firm that organizes the network is an intermediary. The firm receives returns based on the value created by transactions that come through the hub of the network.

The firm's global network improves the efficiency of international transactions by vastly reducing the number of transactions compared to a point-to-point network. The centralized hub-and-spoke network needs only one relationship between the firm and each individual customer or individual supplier. In contrast, a complete point-to-point set of transactions would need links equal to the number of suppliers multiplied by the number of customers, as shown in figure 4.4.

The global network can be built on informal relationships or on formal contracts. The network helps the global business to coordinate its international activities. Increasing the size of the network enhances the firm's ability to generate value by widening the number of potential international connections between suppliers and customers. The firm offers value to its suppliers and customers in part from providing *access* to the global network. As Jeremy Rivkin observes in *The Age of Access*: "Access is becoming a potent

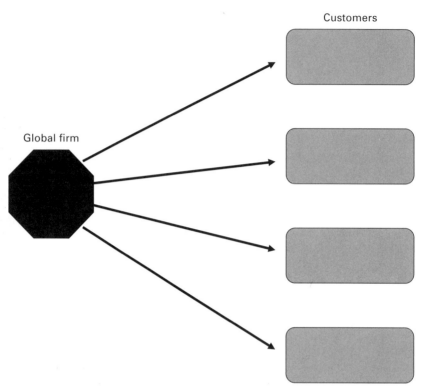

Fig. 4.2   Demand-side networks: the global store

conceptual tool for rethinking our world view as well as our economic view, making it the single most powerful metaphor of the coming age."[27]

The firm's global network can transmit not only physical products, but also information, technology, services, and entertainment. Indian programmers can provide services such as customized software design, medical diagnoses, legal services, call center operations, and engineering expertise over a firm's global network. The firm's global network provides a system of *trust*, allowing many buyers and many sellers to deal with the firm as a trusted partner. This works even though buyers and sellers may not know the identity of others in the network. This system of trust is particularly critical in an international setting because transactions cross international boundaries – buyers and sellers would have difficulty forming relationships outside the network. The cross-border relationships that the global business forms with its customers and suppliers are especially valuable because they make inter-country connections between the more strongly tied networks that exist within countries.

The global network strategy is a vital source of competitive advantage. The strategy extends the reach of the international business, allowing it to achieve

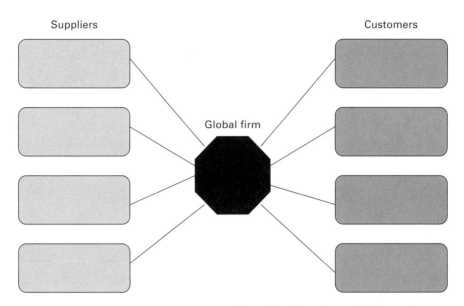

Fig. 4.3   Combining supply-side relationships and demand-side relationships to form a global transaction network

an almost unlimited extension of its activities. The strategy is costly to implement because it rests on building relationships, but it is correspondingly difficult to duplicate. The firm's global network increases in value per member as it grows because of opportunities to create new connections. The network creates economies of scale and scope because centralized management, logistics, and IT are shared across the network's branches. The network grows without requiring proportional increases in investment because the global firm relies on the investment and ownership of its suppliers and customers.

The firm obtains the greatest source of competitive advantage from a global network if it effectively coordinates transactions across the network. Compared with in-house transactions, a network is more likely to be locally tailored since the firm delegates some ownership and control to its suppliers and customers. The global network strategy creates a competitive advantage by increasing the value of the firm's market relationships.

Global intermediary strategy: matchmaking and market making

Pierre Omidyar drew upon his computer programming skills to set up a website for trading collectibles, after his fiancée expressed an interest in getting together with other collectors of Pez candy dispensers. The response

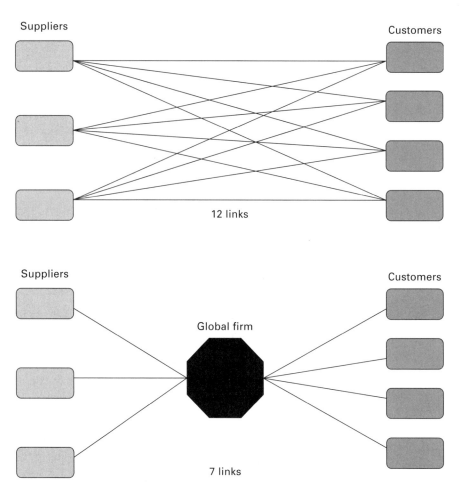

Fig. 4.4   Comparison of a point-to-point network with a transaction hub offered by a global firm

to the basic website was unexpected and overwhelming and soon led Omidyar to found eBay in 1995. Omidyar's company had created a universal auction mechanism for individuals to buy and sell almost any type of product, whether new or used. The company blossomed in the US, quickly becoming a leading online market place.

Omidyar's innovations did not end there. eBay applied a *global intermediary strategy* to gain a global competitive advantage. Billing itself as "The World's Online Marketplace," eBay attracted over 100 million registered members worldwide. The company's mission was "to provide a global trading platform where practically anyone can trade practically anything."[28]

From its initial US focus, eBay individually targeted auction websites to twenty-four countries throughout the Americas, Europe, and the Asia–Pacific region. The company also obtained a strong presence in Latin America through its stake in MercadoLibre.com. eBay offered buyers and sellers a "Global Trade resource center where you can search, buy, and sell across the global eBay marketplace." Traders could use eBay's online tools, including international payment services, worldwide shipping assistance, currency conversions, language translation, and a time zone calculator.

eBay acted as a global matchmaker, bringing together individual buyers with individual sellers through its transaction software. Buyers and sellers could find each other and transact easily even though they might be located in different countries. What distinguished eBay from the local flea market was not only its sheer scale; it was eBay's creation of a unique online community. The company brought buyers and sellers together to transact with each other and to share common interests. Visitors to chat rooms could converse with other collectors about their favorite area but were warned "No business please!" Chat rooms were devoted to such categories as antiques, Beanie Babies, coins, computers, dolls, Elvis, glass, jewelry, photo equipment, pottery, stamps, toys, and trading cards. Buyers and sellers were urged to communicate with their counterparts in other countries on an "international community discussion board." eBay's services added value to transactions, further enhancing the company's matchmaking.

eBay also acted as a global market maker, bringing many buyers together with many sellers through its online auctions. eBay served as an outlet not only for individual sellers but also many small and medium-sized businesses, which used eBay as their mode of access to international trade. eBay offered buyers a choice of auctions or fixed posted prices. eBay's auctions and price mechanisms made the company a global market maker. As well as then introducing individual buyers to individual sellers, the company aggregated buyers and aggregated sellers, helping to clear markets for many types of products by balancing supply and demand.

eBay focused on convenience. The system was designed to allow buyers and sellers to search easily across categories and to participate in auctions with as little friction as possible. Within any category, such as computer hardware, auctions in any subcategory could be identified easily, along with featured auctions and hot items. Online tutorials lead newbies through the basics of bidding. Users could customize the service, keeping track of bids made and offers received and their account status. Buyers and sellers were provided with access to payment intermediaries and could complete more efficient transactions.

Margaret Whitman, CEO of eBay, set up customer focus groups to evaluate the experience of buying and selling through the company. Once, the company proposed charging 10 cents for sellers to delay the start date of their auction but checked with users first. Such a small charge met with considerable resistance from users and was dropped. Whitman, who came to eBay from the FTD flower network, emphasized the returns to listening to customers: "It's far better for a car dealer to hear about eBay from another car dealer than from our sales force to call on them." She continued: "Buyers attract sellers, who in turn attract buyers, and so on. That's been the success formula in every category on eBay so far."[29] Whitman helped extend eBay's global reach, with nearly half of the company's revenues coming from outside its home country. She noted that Europe was one of eBay's fastest-growing markets: "Markets evolve at different rates, but there's no difference in people wanting to better their lives."[30]

The company, with a global intermediary strategy, creates and operates world markets. The international company gains a global competitive advantage through innovative cross-border transactions. As a *matchmaker*, the company earns returns by bringing together buyers and sellers located in different countries. As a *market maker*, the company achieves success by aggregating both the demand for and the supply of goods and services across countries, creating transaction efficiencies at a global level.

The costs of cross-border transactions can be substantial. In international markets customers are likely to encounter additional costs of searching and shopping, learning about product features, finding out prices, negotiating the terms of exchange, placing orders, keeping track of payments and receipts, and arranging for delivery. Moreover, suppliers in international markets often incur extraordinary costs of marketing, sales, purchasing, hiring, and financing. Sales personnel incur the costs of time spent searching for customers, informing customers about prices and products, and conducting the sales transaction. Transaction costs include the costs that companies incur in negotiating contracts, writing contracts, and monitoring the performance of contract partners. Transaction costs also include the cost of additional back-office processes within the organization, involving such activities as billing and invoicing.

The international business gains competitive advantage by innovative cross-border transactions. These lower the transaction costs for their customers and suppliers by automation of the exchange process, applying computer technology to complex transactions and employing enhanced communication methods. The application of IT to back-office processes further lowers transaction costs. Small changes in transactions have far-reaching effects on global competition, because transaction costs are a significant part of overall costs.

Communication of transaction information allows buyers and sellers to transact with the firm at remote locations and at different times. Thus, the buyers and sellers in an auction on eBay need not be in the same country and can participate in the auction at different times. This reduces transaction costs by avoiding the costs of travel and reduces the time costs of transacting. Technological change in information processing and communications results in innovations in the technology of producing international transactions.

The international matchmaker lowers transaction costs by providing customers and suppliers with accessible distribution channels, distinctive sourcing techniques, superior contract designs, and better information. The firm creates value through services that enhance the value of the match between sellers and buyers.

Matchmakers alleviate *search costs* for buyers and sellers by operating central places of exchange. Since the beginning of civilization, people have met in central market places to trade goods and services; towns provided a central market place in which farmers and buyers could meet conveniently on market day. Global matchmakers such as e-Bay are central places of exchange for world markets. Amazon.com's online bookstore has many country-specific websites and offers "Earth's Biggest Selection™ of products, including free electronic greeting cards, online auctions, and millions of books, CDs, videos, DVDs, toys and games, and electronics."

Companies that are *market makers* achieve an important type of transaction advantage by creating and managing their markets.[31] A market is a centralized exchange where buyers and sellers meet each other directly, or trade through dealers. Market makers provide these institutions of exchange by coordinating interaction between many buyers and many sellers. Market makers operate the market by adjusting prices and balancing purchases and sales. In contrast to intermediaries, who match up a particular buyer with a particular seller, market makers add up the demands of many consumers and add up the supplies of many producers and create a market by combining demand and supply. Market makers create markets by standardizing products, from basic commodities to manufactured parts.

Market making creates new opportunities for creating value across countries. Companies that bring buyers and sellers together raise the efficiency of markets by lowering transaction costs. Market makers generate benefits for customers and suppliers by improving transactions, and perform several major functions. First, they coordinate exchange between buyers and sellers by reducing the costs of search and bargaining. Second, they adjust prices to influence buyer demand and to give incentives to sellers, while providing information to the market. Third, they adjust purchases, sales, inventories, and production to balance supply and demand. Finally, they allocate sales and purchases of products across market segments, in response to differences in buyer valuations of the products and differences in the productive efficiency of suppliers.

In financial markets, where the term originates, market makers are dealers that stand ready to buy and sell a particular financial asset if there is not a buyer or seller available.[32] Market makers thus provide *liquidity* by keeping a stock of a particular asset for possible sale, as well as cash on hand to buy that financial asset. An investor knows that they can enter the market to buy or sell at any time, since they will always find someone to transact with. More investors are willing to invest in a bond or security knowing that it will be possible to sell the asset in the future. In turn, the more buyers and sellers that participate in a market for a financial asset, the more liquid the market becomes.

In a similar way, market makers reduce the risk for buyers and sellers in product markets by standing ready to purchase or sell. By selling when customers are ready to buy and buying when suppliers are ready to sell, firms provide an *immediacy* to product markets that is similar to liquidity in financial markets.[33] Retailers perform market making functions in product markets: a consumer is able to make shopping plans with confidence if they know that gasoline will be available at the service station or specific products will be on the shelf at the grocery store. Customers rely on retailers having a wide variety of goods in stock, including food, clothing, furniture, hardware, appliances, computers, or other general merchandise. Customers dealing with the retailer have convenient access to the products of many different suppliers without having to deal directly with them. Suppliers to the retailer have convenient access to the retailer's many different customers without having to deal directly with them.

Wholesalers also perform market making functions. A manufacturer is able to plan production with greater confidence if it knows that their supplier of chemicals, energy, or parts is standing ready to serve it. Holding inventory is costly, not only because of the costs of storage, but also because of the capital costs of holding the unsold goods. Manufacturers can lower inventories if they can expect JIT purchase and delivery. Wholesalers often aggregate the products of many manufacturers and aggregate the demands of many buyers.

Market makers include large-scale companies that create worldwide markets. Oil companies ExxonMobil, BP, and Royal Dutch–Shell manage major portions of the worldwide oil markets for crude oil, natural gas, petrochemicals, and refined gasoline. Companies such as Cargill and Archer Daniels Midland create worldwide markets for all types of grain and agricultural products. Dealers that act as market makers include major retailers and general merchandisers such as Wal-Mart, Carrefour, Target, Home Depot, and Best Buy. Major wholesalers such as Genuine Parts, W. W. Grainger, TruServ, Wesco International, Ace Hardware, and Ingram Micro aggregate demand and supplies for manufactured goods. Financial firms such as banks, insurance companies, and diversified financial companies create markets for financial assets and products.

Manufacturers also act as market makers, although their transaction activities are intertwined with their productive activities. Nokia manages a large portion of the worldwide market for mobile phones, creating generic platforms and adjusting components so that mobile phones have features that meet local needs. Auto-parts makers such as Delphi and Siemens create international markets for standardized parts and components. Purchasing productive inputs and selling outputs are critical activities for most companies. By understanding the relationship between these activities, managers can enhance the market making functions of the company. It is useful for managers to perceive the company's buying and selling activities as a *service* that coordinates the transactions of its customers and suppliers.

People often speak of the "world price" of a good. These prices are frequently the result of important market making activities carried out by leading international firms. While it is sometimes convenient to say that "the market sets the price," price setting is not carried out by an invisible auctioneer. Rather, pricing is often an integral part of competitive strategy. Moreover, pricing is an essential aspect of the firm's intermediation between its customers and its suppliers. Because pricing is at the heart of competition, the prices chosen by managers reflect strategic interaction between the company and its competitors. A global market making strategy can involve clearing world markets by balancing supply and demand. This creates economic efficiencies by avoiding local shortages or local excess supplies.

Retailers and wholesalers make innumerable adjustments in the quantity of inventories purchased to increase turnover. Firms order based on demand projections and daily monitoring of the pattern of sales. Items that sell quickly are reordered, while less is ordered of slower-selling items. Advances in computerized inventory management and bar coding of products has allowed retailers to monitor sales as they occur, permitting shorter reordering times and closer adjustment of inventories to demand patterns. This allows the retailer or wholesaler to keep fewer inventories at the store or the warehouse while reducing the likelihood of stockouts. Thus, the amount sold and the amount purchased by the retailer or wholesaler track each other more closely over time, bringing the quantities bought and sold in the market closer to being in balance.

Manufacturers play an important market making role by adjusting production to reflect changing demand information. Dell and other computer makers assemble computer systems to order, thereby adjusting instantly to demand patterns. Increasing automation of inventories allows manufacturers to reduce their inventories of parts and materials. The use of JIT inventory management often has been promoted as a cost-cutting activity. By reducing the time that inventories sit idle, manufacturers reduce the time cost of investment in inventories. However, JIT inventory management also should be seen as an important market making activity. The reduction of parts inventories by manufacturers means that the firm's demand for parts is more closely synchronized with the supply of parts. This helps balance demand and supply in the market for parts.

The flexible factory has helped to eliminate delays in both production and distribution. By producing multiple products on the same assembly line, the flexible factory allows a manufacturer to tailor its production more closely to local demand patterns without building substantial inventories or operating multiple production systems with excess capacity. The flexible factory allows a multi-product firm to achieve the benefits of economies of scope. Like JIT inventories, JIT production and the flexible factory also perform market-clearing roles by improving the adjustment of production to market demand information. Toyota changed its strategy from "sell the customer what we have" to "sell the customer what he wants."[34]

By adjusting inventories and production to international demand and supply patterns, firms provide critical services and help to bring world markets into balance. Improvements in computer and communications technology allow firms to track customer demand patterns. JIT inventories and flexible production techniques then allow rapid adjustment to customer requirements, while reducing costly inventories and production capacity. These developments are critical to the market making functions of firms. The market is closer to being in balance since demand and supply are continually brought closer together. Matching demand and supply more closely is not just a question of lowering inventory costs. Managers should use market demand and supply information in adjusting the quantity and variety of the company's products.

The international business provides a valuable market making service by allocating its products across different countries. It creates value by allocating products to markets with the highest-value users. Global companies respond to customer needs and supplier availability through sophisticated international distribution logistics and supply-chain management. The global business must make complex allocation decisions that coordinate its deliveries to different countries based on demand projections, production capacity, transport costs, trade regulations, and competitor reactions. Effectively implementing the global intermediary strategy through cross-border matchmaking and market making generates competitive advantage.

Global entrepreneur strategy: creating new combinations and businesses

Paul Otellini, CEO of Intel, took the stage in 2006 at the International Consumer Electronics Show in Las Vegas. He told the audience that in technology "rapid evolution and change are the new normal." The introduction of Intel's Centrino mobile technology had "created a new normal in computing"; within a few years, the Centrino chip had taken computer laptops by storm, while Wi-Fi hotspots had spread rapidly around the world.[35] Otellini observed that the results of Centrino had been "astounding." In only one year, computer makers had sold 30 million Centrino notebooks.[36]

Otellini continued: "To improve the entire mobile experience, we combined the microprocessor, the chipset, Wi-Fi, and software to form Centrino." The result was longer battery life, greater computing power, more portable notebooks, and easier wireless connections.[37] Intel's success came in part from application of the global platform strategy. The Centrino was a collection of technologies that allowed global standardization and local customization. The origins of the Centrino, and its later development, illustrate something else – a *global entrepreneur strategy* – creating new businesses by turning inventions from multiple countries into global innovations.

The story begins with Intel's design team in Haifa, Israel. The team was working on a low-cost variant of Intel's Pentium III to be used in budget desktop computers. The low-cost chip, known as Timna, although ready, was cancelled just weeks before its release. According to a contemporary account:

For Intel's Israel design team, the death of Timna was like the loss of a family member. A CPU [central processing unit] that they had worked feverishly on for quite some time was now never going to make it to fruition; and the most painful part of all, especially to an engineer, was that the Timna failure had absolutely nothing to do with the design of the chip, and everything to do with the outside factors that a design team cannot control. Things were so bad for the Israel design team that when they were immediately summoned to begin work on a dedicated mobile processor, they were almost in a state of depression. How would you feel if your blood, sweat and tears were poured into something that just ended up a lost memory? Luckily, for the sake of the Israel design center and Intel's mobile computing plans, the Timna team didn't spend too much time mourning their loss and quickly began work on designing Intel's first truly mobile processor.[38]

The focus would be on mobility rather than pure speed. The result was a chip that was significantly different from the Pentium family.

The project generated three compatible components: the Pentium-M CPU, associated chips sets, and wireless chips. Intel named the technology the Centrino. According to industry observer Anand Lal Shimpi, Intel's approach would be hard for competitors to duplicate: "It requires dedicating an entire design team to a project that will be taking significant risks and will be relying on perfect execution on the manufacturing side of things to meet product cycles."[39]

Intel's strategic shift had two sources. On the demand side, customers were interested in greater mobility as laptops became more popular. On the technology side, Intel's engineers hit a wall as their traditional quest for greater clock speed meant chips that ran hotter and used more power. The problem even meant that Intel had to disband one of its leading advanced design teams.[40] Centrino addressed the customer need for mobility by offering lower power usage, smaller size, and wireless connectivity.

Intel's strategic shift meant organizational changes. The company would need to overcome the attachment to speed and to motivate its engineers toward the goal of better mobility. Otellini, then Intel's president and chief operating officer (COO), put in place a planning process in which the company's business units cooperated in new ways. This meant that the chip platforms would be used jointly by the business units serving markets for home computers, business computers, mobile devices, and network infrastructure equipment.[41] The Centrino project meant transferring technology *internationally* within the company. The mobile platform group in Haifa worked closely with other Intel design teams in Israel and California.[42] As Otellini said: "We are not playing the same game we played for 15 years."[43]

Sharing knowledge across countries is a key aspect of the global entrepreneur strategy. Global companies are establishing R&D facilities in multiple countries to tap into diverse local talent. Companies such as Cisco Systems, GE, IBM, Intel, Motorola, and Texas Instruments have established R&D facilities in India and filed significant numbers of US patent applications.[44] GE, IBM, Intel, Microsoft, Motorola, and other companies also have research centers in China.[45] Just as production is carried out by the global factory, so

R&D is fragmenting into the global lab – with stages of research performed at the most effective location.[46]

Having established global R&D networks, these companies benefit by applying the technology developed in each center across their international operations. US pharmaceutical companies conduct R&D in multiple countries and transfer technology within their organizations, and also extensively license drugs from independent inventors in Europe and Japan.[47] There also is growing evidence of globalization of R&D. China, India, and other emerging market countries contributed 17 percent of world R&D expenditures although they provided a small share of inventions, with less than 1.5 percent of patent families.[48]

The global entrepreneur strategy involves bringing together buyers and sellers across borders in new ways. Adam Smith observed long ago that innovations are made by "men of speculation, whose trade is not to do anything but to observe everything; and who, upon that account, are often capable of combining together the powers of the most distant and dissimilar objects."[49] The global entrepreneur discovers new forms of business organization, new types of contracts, new sources of supply, new ways of serving customer needs, and new applications for R&D. Entrepreneurs then act as international intermediaries between suppliers of technology and those who derive benefits from employing the new technology, whether they are consumers or firms.

The global entrepreneur establishes new businesses that span borders. The international context presents some difficulties for the entrepreneur, particularly in developing countries. Obstacles to new businesses include restrictions on hiring and firing workers, registering property, protecting investors, enforcing contracts, and closing a business.[50] Most significantly, the time it takes to start up a business varies greatly across countries, mostly because of differences in government regulation. The countries with the fastest startup times are Australia (2 days), Canada (3 days), Denmark (4 days), the US (5 days), Puerto Rico (7 days), France and Singapore (8 days). The countries with the slowest startup times include Venezuela (116 days), Azerbaijan (123 days), Burkina Faso (135 days), Angola (146 days), Indonesia (151 days), Brazil (152 days), Mozambique (153 days), Democratic Republic of Congo (155 days), and Haiti (203 days).[51]

The World Bank found that procedural complexities, bureaucratic delays, the cost of official fees, and minimum capital requirements posed challenges for entrepreneurs in many countries.[52] The global entrepreneur strategy for an international business should be adjusted to recognize country differences. The international business manager may avoid creating subsidiaries in some countries with high transaction costs and high costs of starting a business. In some countries, however, the international business may recognize an opportunity to start up new businesses by using its expertise to speed up the process of establishment. The global business can use its access to international capital markets to provide the necessary startup capital. The global business can also apply its knowledge and investment to assist local entrepreneurs in establishing new business. This can provide new customers, suppliers, and partners for the international business in emerging markets.

Entrepreneurs create firms that offer new combinations of products, processes, and transactions. Established companies or entrants create entrepreneurial innovations by bringing together their suppliers and customers in novel ways. Companies developing and applying entrepreneurial innovations need not be the original creators of product, process, or transaction innovations. Rather, they bring one or more of those innovations to the market place. Entrepreneurial innovation creates competitors with original combinations of products and services, manufacturing technology, and transactions.

The noted economist Joseph A. Schumpeter describes an entrepreneur as someone who introduces technological change to the market place. He gives the now-classic example of an individual who first introduced the powerloom to some segments of the textile industry during the Industrial Revolution in Britain; prior to that time the textile industry had relied on manual labor. The entrepreneur does not need to be a manufacturer, either of the capital equipment or of the final product. The profit earned by the entrepreneur is not a return to ownership of capital equipment nor is it a return to ownership of the firm through the provision of finance. The entrepreneur's profit is not a return to the research that produced the innovation. Finally, the entrepreneur does not need to be the risk bearer, unless he chooses to self-finance.[53]

The entrepreneur earns a return from making the deals needed to introduce the innovation, and by founding new businesses. By introducing the powerloom to the textile industry the entrepreneur earns the initial returns due to the increased productivity in textile manufacturing. Generally, he earns the initial returns to the new combination, but after a time competitors imitate or surpass the innovation, eroding the returns.

Entrepreneurs discover arbitrage opportunities. Arbitrage, as we have seen, refers to profit making activities that connect suppliers and customers. The firm resells or transforms products and services obtained from suppliers to meet the needs of its customers. Arbitrage profits depend on rapid action since arbitrage opportunities can be eroded in the blink of an eye in the most competitive markets. Managers must have up-to-date knowledge of shifting supplier capabilities and changing customer requirements. Managers must develop the ability to recognize these opportunities and to execute rapidly the necessary transactions.

What makes entrepreneurial arbitrage possible is the existence of substantial *market frictions*; without these frictions, arbitrage opportunities would be negligible. Transaction costs are pervasive in international business, including the costs of gathering and comparing price and product information and the costs of searching for customers and suppliers. The ability to create better transactions is offset by the potentially high costs of negotiating, writing, and monitoring contracts. Moreover, managers have different perceptions and possess asymmetric information about technology, customer characteristics, and supplier capabilities. Natural limitations on the cognitive capacity of market participants constrain their ability to discern complex market opportunities, even with the aid of advanced data processing techniques.

Entrepreneurial innovations combine customers and suppliers in new ways, through new products and services, or by adding new customers and suppliers. To create entrepreneurial innovations requires managers to monitor markets continually for potential arbitrage opportunities. The tools of external analysis of customers, suppliers, competitors, and partners outlined previously are essential in discovering new combinations.

Managers should ask some or all of the following questions:
- Are there innovative products and services that have not been brought to target countries that would serve customer needs?
- Are there customers whose needs are not being addressed by competitors?
- Are there advances in transaction technology that permit the introduction of new goods and services?

For established companies, discerning transaction opportunities depends on the encouragement of creativity within the organization. The "Star Analysis" should support these activities.

An important source of entrepreneurial returns is to bring existing technology to new applications.[54] In addition, entrepreneurs bring new technologies to market by acquiring the technology from inventors and reselling it to companies that will apply it to produce goods and services. Identifying technology for acquisition requires monitoring innovative startup companies, university and government laboratories, and other technology sources.

Global managers need to determine the quality of the company's business processes and its ability to develop innovative transaction technologies:
- How sophisticated are its customer transactions, including sales and customer service?

- How effective are its supplier interfaces?
- How efficient are its back-office systems?
- How well integrated are its demand-side management systems and supply-chain management systems with the company's enterprise management systems?

The manager should determine how well the company's cross-border transaction systems perform in comparison with market alternatives. In addition, the manager should consider the organization's ability to carry out improvements in transaction technology, or whether it should rely on customers, suppliers, or partners for such enhancements.

To innovate as a global entrepreneur, the company must continually refine and improve its market monitoring capability. Managers need to determine the company's ability to identify new technologies and customer applications. It is commonly recognized that organizations can become less entrepreneurial over time: companies may become less willing to take risks or to embrace different approaches to the business. Managers should adjust internal rules and procedures to take advantage of market opportunities.

The global firm disperses its value added activities around the world. The interactions between the parent company and subsidiary managers are important drivers of company decisions.[55] Julian Birkinshaw, in his study of entrepreneurship in global firms, emphasizes the benefits of internally driven changes in strategy and organizational structure. Birkinshaw notes that local subsidiaries in international business should take the initiative because they are at the intersection of the local market, the company's internal market, and the global market. The manager of the local subsidiary can act as an entrepreneur by taking the initiative for change. Birkinshaw points out that even though MNCs have a strategic imperative to listen to the ideas and advice of subsidiary managers, "the evidence clearly shows that many MNCs disregard it."[56]

The global entrepreneur strategy yields a competitive advantage for the international business that continually creates innovative cross-border transactions. By drawing on inventions from its dispersed R&D units and transferring that technology around the world, the international business creates global market innovations. By considering carefully the ideas of local managers, products from subsidiaries, and business methods from local units, the international business gains a richer and diverse source of business innovations.

The international business employs the global entrepreneur strategy by establishing international markets through new connections between customers and suppliers in different countries. This transaction-based approach differs substantially from international expansion based on finding incremental revenues by selling a known product to additional target markets. The global entrepreneur strategy involves gathering and distributing knowledge within the organization as a basis for creating new markets.

Overview

This chapter has set out the first four of the "G5 strategies" for global competitive advantage. The manager applies the "Star Analysis" set out in the introduction to determine the opportunities and competitive challenges in the global market. Depending on the company's capabilities, the manager chooses the best match between the company skills and market opportunities. The manager then applies the best strategy or combination of strategies to gain competitive advantage.

Global strategies demonstrate the difficulty and complexity of strategy making in an international setting. There is much more room for maneuvering than choosing just low-cost or high-product quality. The global business manager has a full set of alternatives in selecting technology, product features, business methods, and transactions. These strategic alternatives are augmented by geographic considerations: the global business manager chooses supplier countries, customer countries, and partner countries so as to effectively implement the firm's strategy.

The "G5 strategies" address global challenges. The international business must achieve world-class levels of innovation and efficiency while still meeting the diverse requirements of many individual country target markets. These strategies provide a method of strategic reasoning for global markets: many more strategic alternatives are waiting to be discovered.

5 Global investment strategy: choosing the best mix of transactions and investment

Global business is far from virtual. International companies invest heavily in bricks and mortar around the world. Instead of relying on arm's-length transactions or contracts, they place value at risk by investing capital in many different host countries. Although companies such as Nike outsource abroad but own no factories, many global businesses such as Toyota own facilities throughout the globe. Maximizing the value of the international business requires an effective *global investment strategy*, the fifth of the "G5 strategies."

The global investment strategy provides another way to address the dual global challenge of meeting the need for global scale while catering to the diverse needs of local markets. Where necessary, the global firm turns to bricks and mortar, putting the necessary production or distribution capacity in the host country. These investments provide the capacity to serve global markets and meet local needs. Where political risk, high production costs, and the need for flexibility prevent this approach, the global firm responds with spot purchases and contracts with local suppliers and distributors. These transactions use the capacity of others to build scale and tailor offerings to local tastes. The middle ground between these approaches is to rely on global partners, applying alliances and JVs to share the costs and benefits of investment.

Investing internationally offers many attractive opportunities. Most notably, foreign production facilities benefit from proximity to natural resources, labor, and suppliers. Companies build global factories by establishing value chains that cross national borders. Many international firms gain from placing production, distribution, or R&D facilities close to their customers abroad. This chapter gives the manager a guide to global investment strategy.

A business that owns and operates production or distribution facilities in multiple countries is called a *multinational corporation* (MNC). The MNC establishes facilities abroad either through greenfield investments, investment in *joint ventures* (JVs) or through mergers and acquisitions (M&A).

Greenfield investment, JVs, or M&A across borders constitute *foreign direct investment* (FDI).

There are two main types of FDI: horizontal and vertical. A firm that engages in *horizontal FDI* invests in facilities abroad that are at the *same stage* of the value chain – for example, Mittal Steel builds steel plants in different countries. A firm that engages in *vertical FDI* invests in facilities abroad that are in *different stages* of the value chain – for example, BP invests in crude oil exploration and production in some countries, refining capacity in other countries, and retail service stations in yet others.

Investing internationally entails risk because of uncertainty regarding public policy or economic conditions in the host country. The global business must understand both the risks and rewards of its foreign investment strategy. Nations restrict global investment just as they restrict international trade. There are worries that "hot money" from global capital markets may create economic instability. Some assert that global capital markets pose a challenge to national sovereignty. Many people fear that foreign purchases of companies, real estate, or government bonds threaten national security and personal freedom. These anxieties, while often unfounded, nevertheless pose a serious challenge to companies investing abroad.

Government restrictions on investment also mean that major business opportunities continue to exist for those firms that can overcome the barriers. The world of capital investment is not flat, but is highly contoured (see figure I.1). This means that strategic FDI can yield big returns. FDI continues to be a key to understanding global competitive advantage.

Horizontal FDI

By the time Aditya Mittal was thirty years old, he had overseen $30 billion worth of international acquisitions. Mittal was the president and chief financial officer of Mittal Steel and likely to succeed his father Lakshmi as CEO. Lakshmi Mittal, who had started the company in Indonesia, was the third richest man in the world. Working with his father, Aditya Mittal built substantial experience in investment strategy by helping to complete over fifty global acquisitions. Aditya, who had visited steel plants almost as soon as he could walk, observed: "It's about doing something that will stand the test of time."[1]

Mittal Steel, the world's largest steel company, was also the most geographically diversified steel firm. The company had production facilities in 14 countries, sales and marketing offices in another 11 countries, and 5,000 customers in a total of 120 countries.[2] The company went on a global M&A spree, buying what turned out to be undervalued assets. Often, Mittal Steel bought privatized assets in emerging markets, such as bankrupt steel mills in Kazakhstan. Within a year, these mills were operating effectively and exporting steel to China.[3]

Mittal Steel's production, measured in millions of metric tons, was regionally diversified. It produced about 26 percent in China, 18 percent in the EU, 14 percent in the Russian Commonwealth of Independent States and other parts of Europe, 13 percent in North America, 11 percent in Japan, and 4.5 percent in Central and South America. It also produced a total of 14 percent of its output at various locations in India, South Africa, the Middle East, and other parts of Asia. The company used its production to support global market making, with sales of its steel crossing international borders and trading between continents. Mittal Steel employed 164,000 people, with 44 percent in Europe, 42 percent in Asia and Africa, and 14 percent in the Americas.[4]

The company's transactions varied geographically. Mittal Steel shipped its product primarily under spot sales or contracts of less than six months' duration in Asia and Africa, and used spot sales or contracts for 90 percent of shipments in Europe. In the Americas, more than half of its shipments were under fixed-price long-term contracts of more than six months' duration.[5]

Mittal Steel consistently pursued an FDI strategy, not only acquiring facilities around the world but upgrading them as well. According to the company: "[it] invested heavily in the plants it has acquired, modernising facilities, expanding capacity, and improving product mix. Mittal Steel has built a reputation for turning acquired companies into world-class operations through the implementation of this strategy."[6]

Mittal Steel argued that its success was based on "a consistent strategy that emphasizes size and scale, product diversity and quality, and a strong customer focus." The company sought the advantages of industry consolidation and stressed the need for a worldwide presence to serve customers who were themselves global. Mittal Steel also reaped the benefits of aggregate global purchasing, which allowed the company "to source raw materials at advantageous prices" and to access "new supplier bases."[7] The company thus attributed much of its competitive advantage to its global investment strategy.

Aditya Mittal readied himself for a difficult acquisition of the world's second largest steel maker, Acelor. The deal would diversify Mittal Steel still further by adding Acelor's facilities in Brazil and Western Europe. The company's bid faced political and cultural resistance: Acelor's CEO Guy Dollé referred to Acelor's steel as " 'perfume' compared with the 'eau de cologne' produced by Mittal."[8] The French finance minister, Thierry Breton, expressed doubts "that the cultures of the two groups could function and live together."[9] Former French president Valéry Giscard d'Estaing warned against the economic "laws of the jungle."[10]

The Mittal–Acelor merger tested Mittal's management skills and international diplomacy. The Mittals worked with European governments and trade unions to explain the potential benefits of the merger; they paid a substantial premium and ceded some of their corporate ownership to entice investors. The acquisition was ultimately successful and the company was well positioned as a global leader. With over 330,000 employees in over sixty countries, the combined company initially would produce over 130 million tons per year, about 10 percent of the world steel market, with further projected growth.[11] The company would have the necessary scale to serve global markets while producing the diverse steel products required by different industry applications, but it faced the difficult task of integrating its many operations around the world.

Mittal Steel's investment in M&A and capacity expansion illustrate the many benefits from horizontal FDI, as well as the problems that firms can encounter. Putting production or distribution facilities in a foreign country reduces the costs of trade incurred in serving customers in that country. The company avoids the transaction cost of shipping the product from facilities elsewhere. Transportation costs are lowered since facilities are closer to customers in the host country or other countries in the region. The firm becomes a domestic producer, thus avoiding tariff and non-tariff barriers designed to keep out imports. Moreover, the firm becomes a domestic employer, giving it political clout, while its capital investment may earn it a quid pro quo from public policy makers. Because the firm's production and distribution facilities are closer to suppliers or to customers, the time required to react to changes in market conditions is considerably shortened.

Horizontal FDI creates a global network of production and distribution facilities. The company can benefit from proximity to critical resources or close relationships with suppliers of parts, services, and technology. The location of production facilities close to low-cost or highly skilled labor forces boosts returns to capital investment. Horizontal FDI provides geographic diversification of production facilities. The company can use its geographic diversification to pool the risks of changes in operating costs; it also can adjust capacity utilization in response to changes in local cost conditions or demand fluctuations.

Geographic diversification helps the company become a global market maker since it can adjust to market shifts by shipping product from low-cost to high-cost locations. Horizontal FDI is important for distribution companies as well. Wal-Mart and Carrefour must build retail and warehouse facilities near its customers. Placing production facilities near customers benefits manufacturers, who can tailor their manufacturing mix to nearby local or regional markets.

Horizontal FDI offers many additional opportunities for competitive advantage through international M&A:

- Companies can use cross-border M&A to increase their size without adding capacity to the global market.
- M&A lets companies increase their market share and potentially *increases* their market power as well.
- Cross-border M&A is used to acquire critical technologies or brand names.
- M&A is a quick way to enter a country without building greenfield facilities.
- M&A allows growth in capacity commensurate with the size of world markets.
- M&A provides a way to expand global scale and scope while increasing market power with local and global suppliers.

Traditionally, FDI has focused on manufacturing. This emphasis has shifted dramatically over time, with services now accounting for almost two-thirds of FDI. Much of this is driven by M&A in financial services, as companies such as Citigroup (US), UBS (Switzerland), and Allianz (Germany) extend their international reach.

The effects on the global economy of FDI by MNCs are significant. The accumulated stock of FDI outflows approaches $10 trillion. The total assets of foreign affiliates of MNCs are estimated at $36 trillion. The total foreign assets of MNCs grow at a rate of about four times that of the inward stock of FDI, reflecting the growth of the foreign affiliates and the financial leverage employed by MNCs. The largest MNC in terms of foreign assets is GE, followed by the UK's Vodafone. Two major groups of leading MNCs in terms of foreign assets are automobile companies (GM, Ford, and Toyota) and oil companies (BP, ExxonMobil, Royal Dutch–Shell, and Total). The top five developing country MNCs ranked on foreign assets are Hutchison Whampoa (Hong Kong), Singtel (Singapore), Petronas (Malaysia), Samsung (Korea), and Cemex (Mexico).[12]

The activities of MNCs constitute a huge share of the global economy, contributing not just to international trade but providing a substantial share of the combined GDPs of countries around the world. There are about 70,000

MNCs in the global economy, and together these companies have about 690,000 foreign affiliates, whose total annual sales equal almost $19 trillion. Foreign affiliates of MNCs are estimated to employ over 57 million people, and the gross product of these foreign affiliates approaches one-tenth of global GDP.[13]

Global annual flows of FDI, after increasing steadily for years, hit a peak of nearly $1.5 trillion in 2000, after which they fell by about half. The main driver of global FDI is cross-border M&A. Two-thirds of FDI is through equity investment, in which the acquiring company has a controlling interest, with the remaining one-third of FDI taking the form of intra-company loans and reinvested earnings. Most FDI inflows and outflows are concentrated in developed economies, increasingly, however, FDI is heading toward developing countries. China is the leading FDI destination among developing countries, and India is joining many countries by adjusting its regulatory policies to attract FDI. Over 100 countries changed their policies toward FDI in 2004.[14]

The main drawback to FDI is the risk of not recovering the company's investment and not earning a return on that investment. This risk transcends normal business risk from competition, technological change, or varying demand. The problem concerns changes in public policy in the host country: the worst-case scenario is outright confiscation, referred to as nationalization. Often, host countries change their rules and regulations governing trade and foreign ownership. FDI places capital at risk in a host country whose business practices, social customs, and laws can differ greatly from those of the firm's home country.

Political resistance to FDI is a common occurrence. Sometimes governments express national security concerns – for example, the US blocked the acquisition of port management operations by DP World, owned by the government of Dubai in the United Arab Emirates (UAE). DP World had obtained the ports management operations as part of its larger acquisition of a venerable British company, Peninsular & Oriental Steam Navigation (P&O), which had managed US port operations for years without any public outcry.

In another incident, an agency of the US Congress raised national security concerns when the US State Department sought to buy Lenovo Computers, because the company was partly owned by the Chinese government. The objections posed a political risk to Lenovo's investment in purchasing IBM's personal computer unit, even though the US government's Committee on Foreign Investment had approved the IBM acquisition.

Political roadblocks to FDI are another form of trade protectionism. Just as some oppose imports of foreign goods and services, others express opposition to foreign capital based on "economic nationalism." These are closely connected. A country with a trade deficit in its current account buys more goods and services abroad than it sells. This deficit in the current account returns to a country in the form of investment, creating a corresponding surplus in the capital account. Looked at correctly, the current account and the capital account are just two sides of the same balance of payments: the two accounts reflect the relative attractiveness of markets for goods and services and the relative attractiveness of investment opportunities.

As emerging markets increase their exports and also attract investment, they have money to spend abroad. Some of that money is used to import consumer goods and services and to purchase manufacturing equipment and technology. Some of that money is used to invest abroad, either in financial markets or in the form of FDI. The population of industrialized countries may express surprise and even reluctance when faced with unfamiliar investors from an emerging nation such as China or an oil-rich Middle Eastern country.

Many people express concerns that foreign investors will acquire companies only to lay off workers. For example, the government of Luxembourg opposed Mittal Steel's offer to buy Acelor because it was worried about a decline in employment of steel workers. Luxembourg also feared that Mittal Steel would close Acelor's headquarters, a palatial structure in the style of Versailles.

The international business must adjust its global investment strategy for political risk, and must be sensitive to public perceptions of FDI. Managers should determine whether there are national security problems and foreign relations issues associated with the investment. Managers should examine whether layoffs and restructuring are likely to raise greater concerns when carried out by a foreign owner. Managers should also consider how foreign ownership will affect interaction with the customers, suppliers, and partners of the business. A global investment strategy can generate great political support if it is seen as providing jobs, technology, capital for growth, and access to world markets. Global managers should understand these opportunities and problems when planning FDI.

The manager can adapt standard tools of NPV analysis to prepare a global investment strategy, using NPV analysis to compare different supplier countries or customer countries as investment targets. Investments should go to the country offering the highest NPV projects. Global business should not target countries unless they offer a positive NPV of returns. Clearly, domestic operations should not subsidize foreign operations, nor should foreign operations subsidize domestic ones: each of the company's countries should make positive contributions to its NPV.

NPV analysis also gives managers a useful method of incorporating political risk calculations. It is critical for managers to adjust the discount rate for political, legal, and other business risks that the firm will encounter in each host country. This means that the firm should appropriately discount returns for country-specific risk. The firm may prefer lower earnings in a lower-risk country since this will generate greater NPV. In some cases, the firm may enter a high-risk country if its market research suggests that the returns are sufficient to justify the risk. Mittal Steel made successful investments in countries that others considered too risky because its research revealed hidden opportunities. The firm's NPV analysis showed that certain emerging and underdeveloped countries offered sufficient returns to overcome any difficulties in establishing and managing their operations.

Vertical FDI

In 1901, an Englishman named William Knox D'Arcy obtained a concession from the Shah of Persia to explore for oil and develop deposits of the resource. The enterprise in its initial years was plagued by "severe weather, difficult terrain, the absence of a developed infrastructure, the shortage of skilled local labor" and political conflicts.[15] Within seven years, after struggling with these and other difficulties, D'Arcy's engineer George Reynolds made the "first commercial oil discovery in the Middle East." To develop D'Arcy's concession and the resulting oil discovery, the Anglo-Persian Oil Company was formed two years later. Some critical funding came from the British government shortly before the First World War, reflecting Winston Churchill's desire to secure fuel oil for Royal Navy ships.[16]

The Anglo-Persian Oil Company was later to become British Petroleum (BP).[17] The company was one of the largest global businesses, with facilities located around the world. BP was present at all stages of the energy value chain: exploration, development, transportation, refining, chemicals, wholesaling, and retail service stations, and the company's global profile exemplified vertical FDI.

BP actively explored for oil and gas in twenty-six countries. It produced oil and gas in twenty-three countries with proven reserves second only to ExxonMobil. For example, BP explored for and developed oil and gas in the deep water off the shore of Angola. BP owned in whole or in part twenty-one refineries, of which five were in the US, with a combined capacity of over 3.2 million barrels of crude oil per day. The company also had shares of chemical plant capacity equal to 35 million tons per year. Finally, BP had 28,500 retail service stations. Most of these assets were the result of BP's vertical FDI.

Much of BP's FDI took the form of greenfield development of oil and gas resources, refinery capacity, chemical plants, and service stations. In addition, the company engaged in significant vertical M&A. BP gained substantial assets in many countries at each stage of the value chain, acquiring Standard Oil of Ohio (1978), Amoco (1998), ARCO (1999), Burmah Castrol (2000), and Veba Oel AG and Aral AG (2002).

BP's then-CEO, Lord John Browne, observed that the company's strategy rested on four key elements:

1 Economies of scale
2 Geographic scope
3 Integrated know how combining technical, commercial, and diplomatic skills
4 Corporate capacity to manage a large portfolio of different projects.[18]

The company's vertical structure was summarized by its mission statement: "Our business is about finding, producing and marketing the natural energy resources on which the modern world depends."[19]

The vertically integrated structure of a global business such as BP requires it to operate a complex chain of coordinated businesses that must connect across national borders. The vertical FDI decision requires that managers answer two key questions:

• Should we *outsource* this activity or perform the task *in-house*?
• Should we take this activity *offshore* or perform the task in the *home country*?

Vertical FDI requires a decision to perform a task in-house, but also a decision to take that activity offshore. Four possibilities are shown in table 5.1:

• What are the strategic motivations for these choices?
• What is the strategic interplay between two key decisions: assignment of activities and location of activities?

If the firm's managers choose to outsource some activities, then FDI is not necessary. The firm can turn to suppliers either at home or abroad. If the firm contracts with suppliers abroad, it is "offshoring" those activities.

If the firm's managers choose to perform production or distribution activities in-house, and they choose to keep the activities in the home country, there is again no need for FDI. The firm is vertically integrated, which requires investment in the facilities necessary for these tasks. However, investments stay within the home country.

Vertical FDI becomes necessary only when two conditions hold. First, the managers want to keep certain activities in-house. Second, the managers

Table 5.1. Four strategic options for vertical integration and location of activities

Assignment of activity Location of activity	Outsource	In-house
Offshore	Contracts abroad	Vertical FDI
Home country	Contracts at home	Vertical integration without FDI

want to split up the value chain across national borders. Keeping activities in-house may be caused by the need to preserve expertise or to develop competencies in key tasks, or it may be caused by the need to keep control over vital IP. The firm's managers may find that coordination and control are better achieved in-house. On the other hand, the managers may move in-house activities offshore to take advantage of the skills or low wages of foreign workers, or proximity of production to customers, among other factors. This combination of in-house production and offshoring of the activities requires vertical FDI. For example, the firm might manufacture components in one country to reduce labor costs or to work with parts suppliers, and it might then assemble the final product in another country where its customers are located.

To outsource or to stay in-house?

The manager first determines whether or not an activity should be delegated to others – suppliers, customers, or partners. If the activity is left to others, particularly suppliers or partners, it is *outsourced*. If an activity is performed in-house, the firm is *vertically integrated*.

Vertical integration means that the firm carries out two or more activities along the value chain. Those activities that managers choose to perform in-house must still be performed well; they must be judged as highly effective even when compared to market benchmarks. That is why activities performed in-house often are identified by the manager as the firm's *core competencies*.

When facing global competition, performing tasks in-house means that the organization must judge its performance against global benchmarks: the organization must execute tasks with sufficient efficiency to beat feasible alternatives almost anywhere. Otherwise, global competitors can capitalize on any inefficiencies. This requires a tougher standard for best-in-class performance. The firm should perform only tasks for which it has *global core competencies* – at least in those areas where it faces competitive challenges.

Managers even outsource some activities that are *not* best performed by others. The reason is that the managers and employees of the firm must make the best use of their time. This is closely related to the idea of *comparative advantage* discussed in chapter 1. Performing some routine tasks in-house is a distraction for managers and employees who need to focus their efforts on critical strategic challenges. If performing a task to world-class standards takes attention away from other activities that have higher value to the firm, it is time to outsource.

Managers face the difficult task of coordinating many disparate activities. Purchasing, production, and distribution must match demand to avoid the costs of holding unsold inventories or missed sales from insufficient inventories. Parts and components must meet specifications for products to be manufactured. Product designs must match customer needs to compete effectively.

These types of coordination may be costly to achieve through arm's-length transactions with suppliers. If the information systems of a company and those of its potential suppliers cannot be linked electronically, there may be coordination advantages from in-house production. Improvements in IT, particularly in software that allows companies to coordinate their production requirements, potentially reduces the advantages of vertical integration.

If the firm operates in a market with high variability of customer demand, it may be easier for managers to adjust internal production levels by work orders rather than for purchasing managers to adjust orders from outside suppliers through contractual arrangements. Long-term relationships with suppliers mitigate the transaction costs of changing orders. Suppliers who are accustomed to order variability may offer flexibility and lower costs. A company that relies on internal production capacity to deal with variable demand will inevitably carry costly excess capacity; an outside supplier can avoid some of these costs by pooling orders from many sources. The decision to use the company's own capacity to deal with highly variable demand thus depends on the costs of holding excess capacity as compared to the costs of adjusting outside orders. Cemex handles this problem by manufacturing about half of its cement requirements and relying on external suppliers for the other half.

Under some conditions, managers favor vertical integration for strategic reasons. Some suppliers are concerned that they may not sell all of their output unless they own the distribution channel, while some distributors are concerned that they may not have adequate product availability if they do not own manufacturing facilities. Such concerns may not justify the costs of operating a vertically integrated company. If supplies are generic, there is little advantage to distributors from owning supply capacity. If supplies are differentiated, distributing the company's own products will not yield a competitive advantage unless those products yield greater benefits for consumers than those of competitors. The competitive advantage comes from the superior products, not from the vertical integration of production and distribution. Accordingly, there may also not be an advantage to distributors of owning supply capacity if products are differentiated. Conversely, suppliers gain little advantage in owning distribution: if specific distribution channels have a competitive advantage over others, that advantage is not likely to be enhanced by vertical integration into supply.

Major oil companies such as BP, ExxonMobil, and Royal Dutch–Shell have traditionally been fully vertically integrated from the oil field to the final customer. They engage in exploration, production, transportation, refining, chemicals manufacturing, wholesale distribution, and retail distribution of refined petroleum products. Each of these activities and other functional services within the major oil companies could operate as a large-scale stand alone business. The major oil companies operate internationally, exploring for crude oil and natural gas in fields around the world and serving final customers in many countries. The vertical integration structure of these companies suggests that the market transaction costs of international coordination have been greater than the costs of operating vertically integrated companies. However, as the transaction costs of international business fall and as trade agreements lower tariff and non-tariff barriers to trade, the major oil companies likely will contemplate restructuring their organizations.

Competition has spurred many companies to recombine and restructure their extensive vertically integrated organizations to accomplish strategies targeted to market segments. Companies require *flexibility* – that is, a rapid response to changes in production technology, in supplier performance, or in customer preferences. In some cases, vertical integration into manufacturing or distribution may improve *short-run* flexibility if companies can achieve internal coordination at lower costs than coordination with their suppliers. However, outsourcing increases *long-run* flexibility in a number of ways. By relying on outside suppliers for parts, components, and resources, managers can concentrate on customer service. Specialized suppliers can shorten product cycles, allowing the company to adapt to changes in customer preferences. For example, supply-chain manager Li & Fung offers faster product cycles to major retail-chain stores, allowing the stores to respond quickly to fashion trends and to adjust inventories more accurately.

Moreover, by dealing with outside suppliers, the company achieves long-run flexibility because it has the option to switch to new suppliers who offer more up-to-date equipment, parts, or product designs. In the computer industry, companies such as IBM were originally vertically integrated, producing their own software, processors, memory, and other computer components. As the industry developed, companies such as Dell relied on outside suppliers to obtain the best software and computer components.

Often, a higher degree of vertical integration creates a company bureaucracy that slows down the company's response to market conditions and hinders even short-term flexibility. Managers are busy supervising a larger vertically integrated company and their concern with activities within the organization may take time away from external analysis.

Many CEOs have struggled to keep pace with organizations that have rapidly expanded through M&A. Referring to the large organizations operated by new behemoths such as DaimlerChrysler and Citigroup, the *Wall Street Journal* asked: "Can anyone run these monsters?" Extensive overseas operations, armies of employees, and a deluge of market data put strains on management decision making at companies such as GM and P&G. A. G. Lafley, CEO of P&G, with well over 100,000 employees, acting on concerns about the speed of decision making, shed vertical layers in the company and urged managers to focus on the company's core businesses.[20]

Many vertically integrated companies undertake extensive capital investment to establish manufacturing facilities for parts and components, assembly plants, and distribution facilities. Vertically integrated petroleum companies, for example, invest in equipment for oil exploration and production, tankers and port facilities, refining plants, and retail outlets. Vertical integration does not in itself increase capital investment in an industry but concentrates that investment within large firms who must raise substantial amounts of capital and allocate it within the organization. Managers should evaluate the advantages and disadvantages of combining investment in multiple stages of production within a single firm.

If a company can allocate capital within its organization at a lower cost than capital markets, then there are returns to vertical integration. For this to occur it is necessary both that managers of the company are better informed than investors about the performance of its business units, and that managers allocate capital more effectively than would capital markets. This may be the case for startup companies if managers are effective venture capitalists. Problems arise, however, if internal capital allocation hides the performance of the company's activities, allowing the good performance of some units to cover up the poor performance of others. This suggests that internal allocation of capital is not a sufficient reason for vertical integration. Accordingly, if the business units of a company do not belong together for strategic reasons, internal capital allocation cannot justify vertical integration.

Transaction costs are a critical element in the manager's design of the firm's vertical organizational structure. Although transaction costs are sometimes difficult to identify, managers ignore them at their peril. Generally, transaction costs are the *indirect* costs of the company's market transactions, including management and employee time, legal services, back-office operations, and information systems. Transaction costs affect management choices regarding modes of market entry and the firm's asset ownership.

In designing the organization, the manager must be concerned with total cost. The manager should choose a higher-cost supplier if the cost premium is justified by transaction costs savings. For example, the company might obtain office supplies at a purchase price of $100, but it might spend an additional $20 in transaction costs to research the market and contact the providers of those supplies.

Consideration of transaction costs has a fundamental impact on strategic decisions. Dealing with multiple suppliers may lower costs through competition, but may raise total costs because of the need to manage multiple relationships. Dealing with suppliers on a spot basis rather than through contracts may confer flexibility and lower short-term purchase costs, but may entail higher transaction costs through the need for repeated negotiation. A domestic supplier may charge more than an overseas supplier, but the total costs of dealing with the domestic supplier may be lower because of the costs associated with arranging the overseas purchase, including the costs of communicating with the supplier, scheduling transportation, obtaining import documentation, and converting currencies.

Transaction costs include many types of management and employee labor costs associated with obtaining financing, acquiring technology, hiring personnel, and finding and negotiating with suppliers of inputs and services. In addition, transaction costs are encountered in dealing with customers, including many types of marketing and sales costs and all manner of back-office process costs associated with sales and purchasing, such as billing and invoicing. Transaction costs often represent a major share of the company's communications and IT expenditures. Transaction costs also entail costs associated with negotiating, writing, and monitoring contracts with suppliers and customers. They also include the costs of accounting that are needed to gather and provide information in the company's dealings with governments, capital markets, and business partners.

Advances in telecommunications technology have drastically lowered the costs of communication and information exchange between the firm and its suppliers and partners. This also has helped to lower the costs of coordination within the firm's organization. The increasing reliance on outsourcing suggests that technology and market changes have lowered the transaction costs of market contracting more than they have lowered the costs of managing production within a large vertically integrated organization.

Companies lower transaction costs by exchanging data on demand and inventories with their suppliers, allowing for production and deliveries to respond rapidly to demand shifts. Companies can have JIT deliveries rather than holding large inventories. Companies can link electronically with their suppliers, bringing down the costs of ordering, billing, and monitoring deliveries. By connecting internal computer systems to external buying and selling decisions, companies can update their inventory records and production decisions, achieving coordination in business-to-business transactions that previously were limited to production within the organization.[21]

Managers must coordinate and supervise market transactions just as they must devote effort to coordinating and monitoring organizational activities. In-house manufacturing of parts and supplies brings advantages of greater coordination, but comes at the cost of a large organization with a potentially unwieldy bureaucracy. Outsourcing provides benefits by reducing the size of the organization and increasing management effectiveness.

In the global market place, transaction costs are even greater than within countries. Independent suppliers or distributors located in other countries can be difficult to deal with because they have different languages, cultures, customs, business practices, and operating procedures. This has tended to make the global business very vertically integrated – perhaps more so than many companies with a single-country or regional focus.

In-house interaction lets the vertically integrated business communicate across countries without having to go through complex international transactions and negotiations; the company can use its standard organizational communication systems and IT. Commands from headquarters require less translation and interpretation than would requests made to arm's-length distributors, suppliers, and service providers.

The vertically integrated firm avoids the costly interruptions in distribution or manufacturing that can result from dealing with a foreign partner. Yet, the rapid rise of international trade in parts and components, and JIT production by global businesses, show that many companies have solved key logistics and coordination problems. As firms switch from vertical integration to out-sourcing, the search for the best suppliers and partners soon expands from the home country to encompass the global market place.

Modes of entry

Few firms are sufficiently large and diverse that they can serve global markets singlehandedly. There are some notable exceptions. Giant retailers Wal-Mart and Carrefour have their own networks of stores and distribution centers that span the globe. Auto maker Toyota covers the world with its pro-duction and design facilities, although it relies on networks of parts suppliers and retail dealers. Major oil companies such as ExxonMobil or BP circle the globe with vertically integrated supply chains going from far-flung oil fields to refineries to their own gas stations. These firms choose FDI and full owner-ship of facilities as their mode of entry. Other firms rely on spot transactions and contracts as their mode of entry into supplier markets and customer markets.

The *mode of entry* refers to the extent to which an international business vertically integrates into production and distribution. At one end of the spec-trum, the firm can focus on carrying out spot transactions. At the other end, the firm can be fully vertically integrated into production and distribution. In between, the entrant can pursue a variety of contractual alternatives. Licensing brands and technology provides entrants with a way of avoiding practically all vertical integration into production and distribution.

The manager begins by identifying the supplier country or the customer country. The manager then decides how best to structure the company's orga-nization.[22] The company can choose many combinations of entry modes for international sourcing and serving, as shown in table 5.2. The company's sourcing modes can be similar to or different from its serving modes. The manager seeks to coordinate the company's modes of entry to gain a global competitive advantage.

The manager chooses among the options based on the advantages and dis-advantages of international vertical integration. Spot transactions with offshore suppliers or customers represent the least international vertical inte-gration. Growth and M&A represent full vertical FDI. In between, a partner-ship in the form of an alliance or JV reduces the firm's share of FDI required for entry into the country.[23]

Table 5.2. Modes of entry

Options	Sourcing	Serving
Spot transactions	Buy from suppliers	Sell to distributors
Licenses and franchises	Technology and brands from producers	Technology and brands to distributors
Contracts	Purchase contracts with suppliers	Sales contracts with distributors
Partnerships: alliances and JVs	Form alliance with suppliers	Form alliance with distributors
Growth	Establish manufacturing unit	Establish distribution unit
M&A	Merge with or acquire supplier	Merge with or acquire distributor

Market knowledge is an important consideration in the decision to enter into distribution. If a company has greater familiarity with customers than outside distributors it may choose to distribute its own products. When the company decides that its efforts are best employed in distribution, it may choose to exit other activities. A company such as Nike concentrates on design and marketing while outsourcing most of its manufacturing. Conversely, if external distributors have greater knowledge of customers and distribution methods, it may be necessary to contract with those distributors. However, even if the company has greater market knowledge than external distributors it may still choose to contract with others for distribution if the company can add greater value by focusing its efforts on other activities such as R&D or manufacturing.

One of the advantages of vertically integrating into distribution is a closer relationship with final customers abroad: by relying on other companies for distribution, a company obtains information about customer preferences only indirectly. Some manufacturers survey their final customers to better understand how customers use their products. Companies that rely on outside distributors attempt to overcome this information problem by distributing some portion of its output directly to obtain a window on the market. After an early period of separating their Internet sales strategies from catalog and store sales, many companies moved to an integrated strategy. Staples, for example, folded their Internet unit Staples.com back into the company after discovering that sales per customer were much higher for shoppers that visited the company's three channels (in-store, catalog, and online) as compared with customers that visited only the store or used both the catalog and the store.

The international business may change its mode of entry over time. The key is learning about new foreign markets. Early entry may take the form of spot transactions or short-term contracts, avoiding the risks associated with capital investment. Later, the firm may learn more about the target market and partner with local suppliers or distributors. With sufficient knowledge of local market conditions, the firm then may choose a full FDI commitment by establishing greenfield production or distribution facilities, or by acquiring a local business. Often, international firms acquire their local JV partners as they learn more about the host country.[24]

Alliances and JVs avoid the need for the partners to integrate vertically, they are able to coordinate their activities through contracts and informal agreements. In deciding whether to enter into an alliance or a JV, companies take into account the transaction costs of forming and maintaining these relationships. International alliances and JVs have higher management costs than partnerships within the same country, and involve greater risk of contractual difficulties. Still, such alliances do allow companies to share market knowledge and combine complementary skills in a new market.

Hutchison Whampoa based in Hong Kong, Anda based in Shekou, China, and the Tibbett & Britten Group from the UK formed a JV in the People's Republic of China (PRC). The JV, named Hutchison Tibbett & Britten Anda, was created to provide distribution services and was the largest retail logistics contractor in China that provided both warehousing and distribution services.

The partners to the JV offered complementary skills and resources. Hutchison Whampoa provided knowledge of China and Chinese market connections, as well as access to its Yantian Port facilities and Shanghai Container Terminals. Anda provided a trucking network and access to its Shekou Container Terminal. The Tibbett & Britten Group, in turn, provided knowledge of contract logistics services and supply-chain management. The JV shipped products sourced from Chinese manufacturers to retail sector customers in Europe and North America. Hutchison Tibbett & Britten Anda also offered access to the Guanlan Retail Consolidation Centre which, according to the company, was the largest warehouse and container handling facility in South China. The partners already operated a JV that ran distribution for Hutchison Whampoa's supermarket group Park N Shop. In addition to the main partners, the JV was a vehicle for inclusion of other secondary JV partners. In particular, Air Tiger Express added its air freight services and Orient Express Container Co. Ltd supplied ocean freight services.[25]

Companies also can minimize their extent of vertical FDI by international *licensing*. Companies license patents, technology, trademarks, brands, business methods, product designs, software, transaction methods, and business franchises. Companies can choose to license their technology to manufacturers, who are then responsible not only for production but also for sales. By licensing technology, companies avoid foreign investments in production or distribution. Licensing technology is becoming increasingly common in international business, allowing companies to sell their technology abroad without the need to bear the risks of FDI or the need to learn about manufacturing or distribution in foreign markets.

Licensing potentially confers a number of competitive advantages. The company participates in domestic and international markets for IP. Increased sales from licensing technology generate incremental returns to the company's innovation efforts. By investing more in R&D, rather than in manufacturing and distribution activities, the company benefits from scale and scope economies in R&D and gains expertise in creating IP. Conversely, the company lowers its capital commitment to physical plant or marketing, thereby lowering its capital costs. Technology can be adapted to a changing market more rapidly through licensing than through vertical integration, since clients using the technology often are more familiar with specific applications. Companies licensing technology can also provide value added services. IBM, as the leading world supplier of technology for application-specific integrated circuits, emphasizes speed to market for customers. According to IBM, licensees can obtain "the same system-on-a-chip (SOC) expertise, extensive core library, and methodologies that we use in our own products."[26]

Licensing arrangements allow manufacturers and distributors to partner with developers lacking production and marketing capabilities. Pharmaceutical companies outsource R&D by contracting with biotechnology companies. One of the best-selling diagnostic tests in the US, for example, was a blood test for hepatitis C marketed to hospitals and blood banks by Johnson & Johnson and Abbott Laboratories. Johnson & Johnson received a royalty from Abbott and split its profits and the royalty with Chiron Corp., the developer of the test.[27]

Franchising is an important type of licensing that creates a process for rapid growth and lowers the necessary capital outlay by relying on the investment of franchisees. The franchise company benefits from the incentive effects of franchise ownership since small business owners are able to engage in intensive monitoring of performance. Leading franchisers include McDonald's, Burger King, Yogen Früz Worldwide, Subway, Baskin Robbins, GNC Franchising, KFC, and Dairy Queen.

Companies are increasingly turning to international licensing of technology and brands. Among the advantages of international licensing are the avoidance of import and export transaction costs, currency risks, transportation costs and tariffs, and other costs of trade regulations. Companies do not have incur the costs of establishing manufacturing or distribution facilities abroad, where they have less knowledge of the business environment. Licensing can reduce the risks of contracting for manufacturing and distribution with unfamiliar international partners. Moreover, companies avoid investment abroad whose value can be reduced by changes in trade regulations imposed by foreign governments.

Companies engaged in international licensing face various challenges. They face the problem of protecting brand equity overseas where there are additional costs of monitoring the performance of license holders. Licensing also entails transaction costs, including the costs of negotiation and enforcement of contractual agreements and currency risk. Companies also must deal with different levels of legal protection for IP, such as patents and trademarks across countries. Licensing technology abroad can increase the risks of imitation and copying. Companies engaged in international franchising also incur the additional costs of finding franchisees abroad and monitoring their performance.

Overview

Global competitive advantage requires that the firm's managers form a *global investment strategy*. The manager must carefully choose the proper mode of entry into supplier countries and customer countries. FDI puts capital at risk outside the home country, adding political risk to market risks. FDI also reduces long-term flexibility since the firm commits capital to production or distribution facilities in particular country locations and with specific technologies. FDI requires not only an entry strategy but consideration of exit strategies, such as divestiture.

FDI offers substantial opportunities as well, however. Restrictions on foreign investment continue to preserve opportunities abroad for firms with innovative production technologies and distribution methods. Companies can gain global competitive advantage when constructing global production networks that coordinate supply chains across countries. These supply chains take advantage of differences in the costs and quality of labor and the location of suppliers while providing responsiveness to short-run market fluctuations.

Companies that want both vertical integration and offshore production or distribution must have an FDI strategy. Such FDI can generate efficiencies if the costs of coordination within the organization are less than the costs of cross-border transactions with independent suppliers or distributors. Vertical FDI also helps to protect the firm's IP in international markets.

The manager's global investment strategy must be responsive to the gains and costs of international trade. When market forces and government regulations favor arm's-length transactions, the firm must be virtual, reaching out to suppliers, distributors, and partners. When market forces and government regulations favor ownership and control of facilities, the firm must turn to global investment and multinational operations.

6   The global business organization

The great Chicago architect, Louis Sullivan, urged builders to let "form follow function."[1] The same advice holds for managers designing the business organization. As business historian, Alfred D. Chandler observed: "structure follows strategy." After choosing the company's strategy, managers should adjust the *structural design* of the organization to accomplish it. The international business poses important problems in organizational design. This chapter emphasizes the manager's choice of the *horizontal* structure of the firm – that is, the divisions of the organization.

The overall structure of the international organization depends on the company's global strategy. The corporate strategy of a multi-business company refers primarily to the company's choice of what businesses it wishes to operate. Corporate strategy thus entails maintaining some existing businesses, withdrawing from some businesses, and entering new ones. The process of expanding the company's range of business is referred to as diversification. Based on their choices about what businesses the company will operate, managers then establish the company's divisions; these divisions are an important aspect of the *organizational structure* of the company.

A *market-based* divisional structure is the best way to implement the company's global strategy. This organizational structure makes the best use of the information generated by the manager's "Star Analysis." The market-based divisional structure allows the company to take advantage of the best features of the home country, supplier countries, customer countries, and partner countries. The firm is able to develop a global value connection and to pursue a global competitive advantage.

Divisions of the global business organization

The evolution of the international business organization is perhaps best illustrated by Germany's Siemens. In the mid-1990s the company reorganized product-based units into worldwide businesses, moving greater responsibility to the level of individual business units. Within several years, the company reorganized again, with business units reconfigured to give them greater market orientation. According to Siemens, the second reorganization completed the company's shift from being a technology-driven to a customer-driven company.

How should a manager determine the organizational structure of the international business organization? The practical answer is that the firm should be divided on the basis of the international businesses that it operates. The company's corporate strategy thus determines how its managers will choose the divisions of the company and allocate activities across those divisions. Leading corporations enhance their performance by building organizations that respond flexibly to market change and reflect the company's strategic shifts. To transform the company's goals and strategy into action, managers design and build an organization whose divisions are able to address specific international markets.

Companies that operate multiple businesses tend to match the divisions of the company to them. By establishing market-based divisions, international multi-business companies adapt products to customer preferences in target countries and respond more effectively to global competition. Single-business companies tend to be divided along geographic and functional lines (sales, operations, purchasing, human resources). The international business organization must be configured to carry out the company's global strategy – that is, it must allow the company to operate in multiple countries and to transact efficiently across national borders.

Market-based divisions should be chosen to correspond to the manager's definitions of the company's international markets, see figure 6.1. The manager's market definitions are based on the characteristics of the customers being served. For the international business, this requires an awareness of the features of the firm's customer countries.

A market-based division is responsible for creating and capturing value. Because it serves as a profit center, the market-based division is responsible for its revenues and most of its costs, as well as sales, marketing, and purchasing decisions. Market-based divisions operate with considerable autonomy from the central office and so are more responsive to customer needs and competitor actions. The market-based organizational form extends the idea of "strategic business units" (SBUs) to international markets.[2]

The company's organization should allow the company's managers to address the five main drivers of international competitive advantage. The company should be able to obtain the benefits of its home-country location,

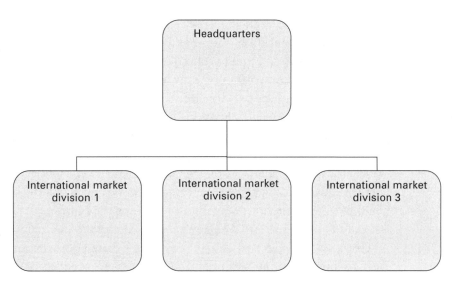

Fig. 6.1   The international business organization

while having the flexibility to transact internationally so as to overcome any home-country limitations. The company should be able to identify suppliers in global markets and coordinate procurement and production in supplier countries. The company should be able to target effectively customers in global markets and sell and distribute its products effectively in customer countries. The organizational structure should provide the company with a platform to form alliances and JVs in partner countries. The organizational structure should help the company implement its strategy and meet competitive challenges around the world.

The manager's market definition is central to the division's strategic plan. A company's market-based divisions are better able to determine the most appropriate strategies to maximize value for their particular market. Depending on the types of markets that it serves, each market-based division may follow a distinct competitive strategy. For large businesses, market-based divisions may house multiple lines of businesses, each serving a segment of a larger market. Each business serving a different market segment may choose a different strategy, with coordination provided at the divisional level.

The manager needs to identify the services that customers receive from the company, either directly or through the consumption of its products:
- What is the customer's opportunity cost of time?
- How can delivery and usage of the firm's products be enhanced?
- How can delivery be speeded up?
- How can the transaction be simplified?

By evaluating and reducing the transaction costs for the customer, the company can create additional value, and bid for the customer without lowering product prices. Getting to know customers is the basis of organizational design, since the company's divisions must follow its market definitions. By not fully distinguishing between home and business use of personal computers, IBM missed out on the booming home computer market, despite having been the originator of the Personal Computer (PC) standard.

The market-based organization helps to create competitive advantage by concentrating the attention of managers on the markets they serve. This increases the company's customer responsiveness and allows the manager to tailor strategies to market conditions. In serving a specific market, each division of the market-based company becomes attuned to the characteristics of its customers; by understanding the customer's preferences, the company can begin to paint a picture of the demand for the firm's products or services.

A market-based organization helps managers to respond to shifts in market demand caused by changes in preferences, income, and general economic conditions. Managers can devote more attention to customer needs. They also can observe the effects of the company's product features on customer demand. Such market information is not simply an input to the firm's marketing and sales efforts. Rather, it permeates the market-based division of the firm, affecting product design and innovation, operations management, and product delivery. Close attention to detail will not occur as easily in a division handling many products and serving widely diverse customer needs; tailoring prices and products to customer needs is enhanced by matching the firm's divisions to its markets.

Defining markets and designing organizations are closely intertwined. Organizations should adapt flexibly to market developments. A market-based organization is more responsive to customers and better able to observe, and even influence, market change. Because it is costly to alter the company's organization, the company's divisions cannot mirror every transitory market change. The manager's market definitions, and the corresponding divisions of the firm, must be sufficiently general to encompass short-term market changes.

The market-based organization improves the firm's ability to monitor and reward performance. Because the company is divided along market lines, the company is able to obtain more accurate measures of performance. The net revenues generated by market-based divisions can be used to calculate their profitability; this allows the corporate office to reduce its command-and-control responsibilities and rely on market-based performance measures for the organization's divisions. One advantage of market-based divisions is that the company's products are designed based on customer needs and competing alternatives. Another advantage is that the company is able to reduce conflicts over shared resources.

Defining the company's global markets is fundamental to the art of management strategy. The organization must adapt flexibly to market developments: it is costly to alter the company's organization, so the company's divisions cannot mirror every market change. Managers must thus define divisions that broadly anticipate market change and allow for adjustment.

International businesses must design organizations that allow them to efficiently transact across international borders. The organization must facilitate sourcing inputs in a variety of countries and serving customers in multiple countries. The international business faces problems of coordinating its sourcing and serving activities in diverse national environments; the organization must facilitate coordination across countries while adapting marketing and procurement activities to the characteristics of local markets.

The market-based organization is best at identifying global value connections. Because each division serves international markets, it can focus on its own suppliers and customers; this allows it to identify the best combinations of customer countries and supplier countries to create gains from trade. Also, because it is a profit center serving international markets, the division can identify the costs of trade that accompany its international transactions. The international market division has every incentive to maximize gains from trade net of costs of trade so that it can capture the value thus created.

The costs of managing an organization are increased significantly when the company operates across international borders. Managers face complex problems in supervising employees in different countries, with the corresponding differences in language, culture, employment relationships, and business practices. Managers also must coordinate groups of employees in different countries so that they work together to carry out the company's goals.

In addition, transaction costs are magnified when companies operate in different countries. Companies face greatly increased organizational costs associated with managing cross-border transaction costs, transportation costs, the costs of tariff and non-tariff barriers, and time costs. Managers must supervise the company's complex buying, selling, and investment activities, often in many countries. The company's organization must provide managers with the means to coordinate these complicated market transactions, and the organization should facilitate the task of harmonizing the company's market transactions and functional activities.

The increased responsibilities of the company's central office tend to increase the size of the company's bureaucracy. However, the difficulties in managing an international business argue against attempts to centralize all decision making in the home-country central office. The complexities of operating in multiple countries suggest that many of the functions carried out by the central office should be dispersed to the company's divisions. For a company organized on geographic lines, this requires dispersing some management activities to country or regional headquarters.[3]

The international business division *coordinates* its sourcing and serving activities across international borders. A global business division is responsible for serving customers around the world; the division arranges to deliver its products worldwide while often tailoring its distribution activities (wholesale, retail, logistics, marketing, sales) to local or regional markets. The division's competitors are both domestic businesses in the markets it serves and other international businesses.

Often the global business division is responsible for sourcing inputs, including purchasing of raw materials, parts and components, and services. The division identifies the best sources of supply that minimize procurement costs, transportation costs, tariff costs, and transaction costs. The division's purchasing choices respond to the needs of the company's global customer markets, which might not be possible with centralized procurement.

Ingram Micro

The world's largest computer wholesaler, Ingram Micro, adopted market-based divisions to take advantage of changing opportunities. It created twelve divisions to address the requirements of manufacturers and resellers. The four key divisions were as follows:

1 A computer supplies and accessories division that offers over 8,000 products from such suppliers as 3Com, Cisco Systems, Intel, Hewlett-Packard (HP), Lexmark, and Microsoft.
2 A consumer markets division that serves retail chains, warehouse clubs, and other merchants.
3 A government division that provides support for resellers, value added resellers, and systems integrators, helping them with contract management, proposal development, technical assistance, and credit options.
4 An education division that provides over 2,000 products from over eighty manufacturers to the academic market.

In addition, there were eight other divisions:

5 An enterprise computing division that supports systems integrators and value added resellers tailored to workstations and client/server products from HP.

6 An export division for international sales not including the North American and European affiliates of Ingram Micro that uses the company's worldwide network of warehouses.

7 A global sales division that provides services to resellers including in-country distribution with 32 worldwide distribution centers and 13,000 multilingual associates, a reseller network that helps resellers locate in-country partners in over 90 countries, and an export operations unit that delivers technology to over 7,000 resellers not covered by Ingram Micro's distribution network.

8 An alliance division that offers resellers access to products from high-volume purchases and helps with bids, sales, and training in alliance with large manufacturers such as Compaq, IBM, and NEC.

9 A Macintosh and Apple Computer division that is the world's largest distributor of Apple and Apple-related products from over 500 manufacturers.

10 An open systems division that carries and supports Sun Microsystems' line of open-network computing products including its SPARC workstations and Internet servers.

11 A telecom integration division that assists resellers in computer–telephone integration and sales while working with a large number of computer and telecommunications manufacturers including Cisco Systems, Bay Networks, Ascend Communications, and Siemens.

12 A technical products division that helps value added resellers obtain products and technical support in UNIX, networking, communications, and interoperability.[4]

Ingram's divisions tended to be market-focused, connecting distributors and resellers with manufacturers and sources of technology. For example, the company's telecom integration division connected a wide variety of suppliers with a particular class of distributors – value added resellers – by creating a technological supermarket. The company was able to foster innovative transactions by close relations to computer and telecommunications manufacturers that kept Ingram current on technological change. Ingram's strong relations with resellers helped the company closely monitor changes in final customer demands.[5]

Evolving organizational structures

Organizational forms have evolved toward increasing decentralization. Many companies have moved from centralized function-based divisions to products-based divisions. By 1980, over 85 percent of large US firms had a multi-divisional structure,[6] and between 70 and 90 percent of large European firms were multi-divisional by the early 1990s.[7] Such divisions offer advantages for organizing purchasing, technology, and operations. Many companies with product-based organizations have attempted to redefine their divisions as individual businesses serving particular markets.

The functional organization

The traditional functional organization is divided by the company's functional areas, including marketing and sales, purchasing, operations, R&D, finance and accounting, and personnel, see figure 6.2. The functional organization is centralized, offering the advantages of central control, but tends to be bureaucratic as the organization grows in size since it allows for only limited delegation of authority. The structure is based on organizational process and procedures, which are the inputs to producing products and services for customers. As a result, the organizational form provides operation convenience rather than customer-focused outputs. The company's operating units are necessarily cost centers, since they generate profit only when they work together.

This organizational structure is generally not useful for larger companies that do business internationally. It has substantial limitations for a multi-business company since each of the businesses are divided along functional instead of along market lines. The marketing and sales unit must divide its attention among multiple businesses. Coordination of marketing and sales with operations or R&D necessarily requires the intervention of top management since units do not communicate directly. For a multi-business company, such a structure would impede addressing change in supplier countries and customer countries because of the bureaucratic delays associated with centralized communication.

Geographic divisions

It is common for companies to make geographic divisions. For example, companies often have regional sales territories or domestic and international sales divisions. This is a reasonable way of dividing the sales force that takes into account regional or country differences. For single-product companies, such geographic divisions are a valuable way of implementing the company's sales and distribution strategies, because for a single-product company geographic divisions generally correspond to the company's markets.

However, for many companies a geographic approach to market segmentation does not capture the important characteristics of the firm's customers. For example, an office products company may serve two distinct markets for corporate customers and small businesses. The office products company might better serve its markets with a corporate division and small business division. Corporate customers might have very different requirements than

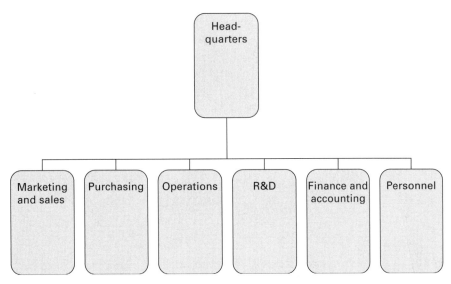

Fig. 6.2   The functional organization

small businesses, and may wish to have a single national or worldwide account, while small businesses may require local services.

To take another example, an IT consulting company may need to create divisions that serve specific industries – such as government, education, financial firms, and manufacturers. Customers within each industry may require different types of services and the company will need personnel with different types of expertise.

The traditional organization of the international business primarily reflected geographic considerations: companies tended to be divided by the specific countries and regions of the world that they served, see figure 6.3. Companies in the US, even if they were organized along product lines for their domestic businesses, often established an international division that offered the company's products and services for export. This constituted a hybrid form of organization with a product basis for domestic markets and a geographic basis for the company's international markets, see figure 6.4.

Geographic divisions make sense for a company selling a single product or a narrow set of products. R&D, human resources, financing, procurement, production, and other activities can then be centralized. The company's marketing and sales activities can be decentralized on the basis of the geographic markets that the company serves. The company's divisions can be matched to specific countries or regions depending on the rate of sales growth and customer characteristics. For companies that sell a single product that is

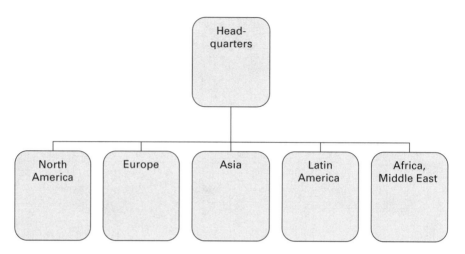

Fig. 6.3   Geographic structure of an international business

produced locally and is costly to transport, geographic organization may be necessary, with some autonomy accorded to local divisions. Companies such as the Mexican cement company, Cemex, although organized geographically, centrally coordinate worldwide manufacturing, technology transfer, and extensive international trading of cement.

However, if the company produces diverse products, geographic divisions often create disadvantages. If a multi-product company is divided along geographic lines, the company will tend to centralize its manufacturing and other operations to achieve scale, resulting in a highly centralized organization. The manufacturing and operations divisions produce multiple products, but are separated from customers by the geographic divisions.

Geographic divisions thus become cost centers rather than profit centers. The geographic divisions in turn become marketing and sales arms of the company, with little interaction with the company's R&D, purchasing, and operations departments. The company's geographic divisions must contact the central office of the company to interact with the company's manufacturing and operations.

Coordination problems are also present for a multi-divisional company that has a separate international division. The international division generally becomes a marketing division rather than a business unit with profit and loss responsibilities. Again, the international division must rely on other parts of the company for various functions, including manufacturing and product innovation. The result is that product managers in the domestic division are not concerned directly with sales abroad. Moreover, international sales cam-

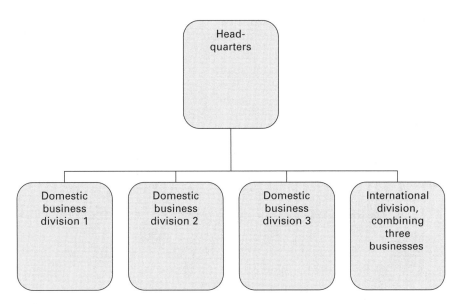

Fig. 6.4   Hybrid international organization with separate international division

paigns and product introductions are delayed until after the domestic divisions have introduced products. By switching to market-based divisions, with each selling products around the world, the divisions can tailor manufacturing, sourcing, distribution, investment, and product features to local requirements.

The separate international division must also communicate through the central office to obtain services from the parent organization. This gives it less clout within the organization since it depends on products and resources from elsewhere in the company. The result is that the international division cannot effectively tailor its offering to its customers since the domestic divisions take priority. The company becomes less responsive to changes in international markets.

The integration of national markets into a global market place has put pressure on companies to reorganize along market rather than along geographic lines. Companies that focus on domestic markets and serve all other markets abroad through a separate international division find it harder to develop a competitive advantage against companies with international market divisions.

Product-based divisions versus market-based divisions

Management definitions of the company's businesses have important implications for the types of business units that the company establishes. The

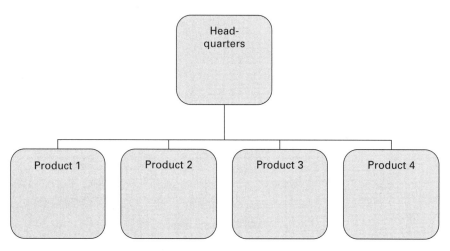

Fig. 6.5   The product-based organization

more appropriate are the business definitions, the better the organizational divisions will be suited to their objectives.

Some manufacturing companies have a divisional structure that is based on both the inputs used in their operations and the types of manufacturing processes that are employed. For example, Archer Daniels Midland Company has among its divisions: Agri Industries (oilseed products), Bioproducts Division, Corn Processing Division, Milling Co. (barley, corn, oats, rice, wheat), and Processing Division (soybeans, cotton, canola). Some companies that were vertically integrated, such as IBM, traditionally had a mixed functional and product structure, with some divisions manufacturing inputs and other divisions serving final customers.

Multi-product companies often are organized along the lines of product-based divisions, see figure 6.5. The problem with this approach is that product definitions are often technology-based. Products can change drastically as a result of innovation and the entry of firms providing substitute products. The characteristics of potential customers that the firm can serve tend to be more stable than product definitions and provide a better basis for establishing divisions of the organization. Moreover, as customer characteristics change, the firm must be prepared to respond. Market-based divisions are organized around the services provided to customers, and can continue to perform well even with product innovation and changes in the company's strategy.

The failure of managers to consider what services the company is providing to their customers is referred to as *marketing myopia*.[8] Managers are focused on product features rather than on customer service so that they fail to anticipate competition from providers of new types of products. The marketing myopia problem can be made worse by the company's organizational design. Myopic managers establish the company's divisions on the basis of easy-to-identify features of the company's products. Paying attention to customer service can lead to a significantly different organizational design.

Marketing myopia creates divisions based entirely on the company's perspective. The company defines its businesses based on its manufacturing technology or the physical features of its products. These narrow definitions can prevent managers from anticipating competitive threats from products with different physical features or from services that address the customer's needs in a new way. Managers can miss products that the customer can use to substitute for its offerings, may fail to perceive entering companies with different types of organization, and may not be alert to shifts in consumer tastes. Finally, managers may have trouble discerning technological change that will make its products obsolete, even to the point of being driven out of business.

Decentralizing the product development function to market-based divisions helps the company's products to be market-driven rather than technology-driven. Depending on the nature of the technology and available investment resources, companies can still choose to centralize basic research. However, because there are so many alternative product configurations the costs of product development limit the company's avenues of inquiry. Moreover, the final product can have only a limited number of possible features and still be competitively priced. Only by adapting product development to market forces can companies respond to changing customer tastes and competitive challenges.

The product-based organization has limited use for international business if the product-based divisions do not match up well with global markets: variations across target customer countries are likely to require corresponding product variations. Organizational divisions that are product-based may not be sufficiently flexible or defined broadly enough to encompass these variations, and their managers may find themselves limited in their ability to generate new products and to adapt their products to local conditions. The divisional structure must have sufficient generality to allow divisions to serve global markets and provide products and services that adapt to the firm's many customer countries.

The product-based organizational structure is better suited for international business than is the functional organization. It is decentralized and divided on the basis of outputs rather than inputs. However, the international "fit" of the product-based organization does not perform as well as the market-based organization. It is less well suited for identifying supplier countries and targeting customer countries. The product-based organization is less adept at coordinating sourcing and serving activities because of its technology focus. Most importantly, it is less able to identify potential competitive advantages since it is stuck with a product-based perspective. The market-based view is more responsive to customer needs and competitor challenges.

General Motors reorganization

General Motors (GM) had long had an international division, even though it had been organized domestically along product lines since Alfred P. Sloan's reorganization of the company in the 1920s. As the market has changed, the distinctions between Chevrolet, Oldsmobile, Pontiac, Buick, and Cadillac (and, later, Saturn) were no longer as good a "fit" as they once had been. The distinction between different makes of automobile had been based on income differences, and the continued division of GM along its traditional business lines restricted its opportunities in automobile markets.

GM faced the difficult problem of repositioning its brand names in a manner that corresponded to current customer preferences and income levels. This was complicated by the range of choices within each division that cut across income lines. The product lines of the different divisions competed with each other. A realignment of the brands would affect the company's organizational divisions.

GM addressed the problem by unifying the marketing staffs of Chevrolet, Oldsmobile, Pontiac, Buick, and Cadillac, while keeping the marketing staff of its Saturn division separate. The intent was to unify the function of interacting with auto dealers and to avoid duplication of effort in marketing. The unified sales force was intended to take a wholesale perspective in relation to the manufacturing divisions, intermediating between manufacturing and auto dealers.

GM recognized the importance of a market-based organization in a different manner, by consolidating its North American and international divisions into a single global unit. The international division operated as a separate unit that designed and sold a full range of cars that were marketed in Europe, Asia, and Latin America. The company blended its International Operations and GM North America into one organization, GM Automotive, in 1998. Jack Smith, GM's chairman, observed that: "As the world opened up to free trade, Sloan's system was not competitive."[9]

GM's intent was to "accelerate our integration and leverage our worldwide capabilities, while improving our responsiveness in all our local markets around the globe."[10] According to the company, GM "interwove global processes like purchasing, manufacturing, engineering, research and development, human resources, and communications across all regions of the world, giving us economies of scale, but also allowing enough local control to meet the needs of local markets."[11] Within GM Automotive, the company retained four regional divisions: North America, Europe, Asia–Pacific, and Latin America–Africa–Middle East. For example, GM Europe, headquartered in Zurich, offered the brands Opel, Vauxhall, Saab, Cadillac, and Chevrolet.

Matrix organizations

Companies using the "matrix" organizational form try to have their cake and eat it too, maintaining both functional divisions and product divisions, which constitute, respectively, the rows and columns of the matrix, see figure 6.6. Yet, this organizational form yields neither effective central control nor the market responsiveness of the divisional form.

The matrix form has been tried with mixed results by many companies, including Digital Equipment Company, Dow Chemical, General Electric, Shell

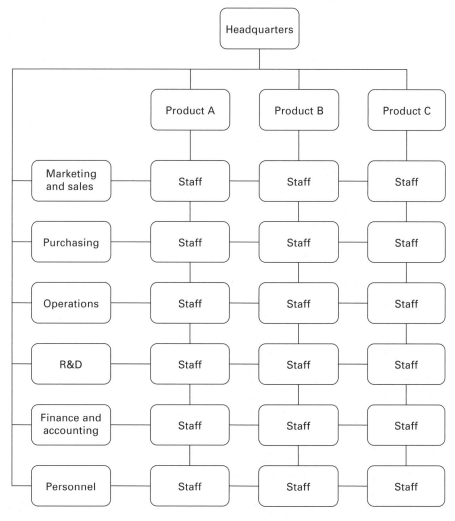

Fig. 6.6   The matrix organization

Oil, TRW, and Texas Instruments. The matrix form can be useful temporarily for the completion of short-term projects. Projects can be moved along by the creation of temporary teams of representatives from functional departments under the overall direction of a project manager; however, this creates temporary SBUs and can be viewed as a variant of that organizational form.

Asea Brown Boveri

The multinational electrical equipment company Asea Brown Boveri (ABB) applied an organizational structure resembling a matrix form by dividing the company along both product groups and by countries. Formed in 1988 by a merger between Asea of Sweden and Brown Boveri of Switzerland, with headquarters in Zurich, ABB employed about 170,000 people around the world. ABB took as its motto "think global, act local," and many MNCs were inspired by ABB's organizational structure.

The company's organization had long emphasized its global business segments over its regional divisions. In practice, the company's organization was not really a matrix because its country managers were actually support staff for its product managers.

ABB's so-called "multi-domestic structure" was established in response to both the necessities of serving multiple markets and those of responding to different political and regulatory constraints in the countries in which it operated, although one would expect market considerations to dominate within the organization. Its product managers served worldwide markets while its national companies served domestic markets. Changes in the global market place required a modification of the matrix form to emphasize a market-based organization.

ABB operated a global engineering conglomerate serving customers in electric power generation, power transmission and distribution, industrial and building systems, and rail transportation. The company was divided into 50 global Business Areas (BAs). For example, the BA for power transformers served 25 factories in 16 countries. The 50 managers of the BAs reported directly to the CEO and the company's executive committee. In turn, the BAs were grouped into eight business segments, resembling an SBU-type structure. For example the Power Generation Business Areas were as follows: Gas Turbine & Combined-Cycle Plants, Utility Steam Power Plants, Power Generation Industry, Hydro Power Plants, Fossil Combustion Systems & Services, Nuclear Power Plants, Environmental Systems, and District Heating.

The country structure had national enterprises that contained all of the local companies within the BAs for that country. For example, ABB's national company in Germany had 36,000 employees. There were 1,300 local companies in 140 countries whose president reported to both their BA leader and the national company CEO. Country managers had responsibility for providing shared facilities and for coordinating the firm's handling of taxes, domestic regulations, and trade restrictions. However, the authority of cross-national product managers tended to dominate that of country managers. Thus, the company was primarily divided in terms of SBUs.

In 1998, the company reorganized to more closely approximate global business divisions. The large Industrial & Building Systems segment was divided into three new segments:

Automation; Oil, Gas & Petrochemicals; and Products & Contracting. The Power Transmission & Distribution segment became two separate segments: Power Transmission and Power Distribution. The Power Generation & Financial Services segments remained unchanged. The company dissolved its regional organizations primarily in the Europe, Americas, and Asia regions while retaining country organizations. The company found that the regional organizations had fulfilled their mission to coordinate ABB's expansion.[12]

The reorganization brought the company's structure into greater conformity with a business-based organization. ABB's then-CEO, Göran Lindahl, said: "This is an aggressive move aimed at greater speed and efficiency by further focusing and flattening the organization. This step is possible now thanks to our strong, decentralized presence in all local and global markets around the world." He further noted that: "This should be seen as a leapfrog move in response to market trends, to make sure we can serve our customers better and build more value for our stakeholders." According to ABB: "The new business segment structure aims at further promoting growth areas where ABB has technology advantages and unique capabilities. It also reflects business opportunities created by deregulation, and provides the new segments with a clear competitive focus."[13] Ultimately, the company was divided into six business groups: Automation; Building Technologies; Financial Services; Oil, Gas, & Petrochemicals; Power Distribution; and Power Transmission.

Faced with competitive challenges in its world markets, the company encountered mounting financial difficulties. According to a Company Press Release Summary from 2001: "ABB becomes the first industry to organize around customers rather than technologies. Its worldwide enterprises are now centered around four customer groups to boost growth in a business environment of globalization, deregulation, consolidation and eBusiness." ABB's management sold off the firm's Financial Services unit, mostly to GE Commercial Finance. The company considered additional divestitures of other businesses as it began to reevaluate whether it should remain as a conglomerate. The company put its Building Systems up for sale and sold part of its Oil, Gas & Petrochemicals unit, while considering other sales of non-core businesses. The company consolidated its divisional structure to focus on two sets of global markets: Power Technologies and Automation Technologies. The restructured company served over 100,000 people in 100 countries.[14]

The problem with the matrix organization is that the lines of supervision, communication, and control cross – staff members are responsible to two managers, the product division manager and the functional area manager. This creates high transaction costs within the firm and confusion about lines of authority. This violates one of the most basic principles of management: that each member of the organization reports to only one superior. The inevitable result of two bosses is conflict, generally between the functional area manager and the project manager. These conflicts could in principle be mitigated by strong central authority, but that undercuts the delegation of authority to the other managers, and increases the central office bureaucracy. Staff positions are duplicated, raising labor costs and increasing internal transaction costs. The matrix form creates inefficiency within the firm, and should be avoided.

Incorporating geographic divisions in the market-based organization

The international market-based business incorporates geographic divisions by incorporating regional subunits within its market divisions. This allows each of the company's market divisions to operate with the desired level of autonomy.

Although the corporation increasingly is likely to be organized into international business units, there tend to be geographic branches within the business divisions. The marketing and sales units of the company's business divisions tailor marketing and distribution to the requirements of country and regional markets. The geographic branches of the product divisions can engage in local assembly, manufacturing, and input procurement. The company may wish to coordinate its marketing campaigns or input procurement in specific countries or regions as a means of attaining scale economies. The company may also coordinate its activities within a country to address local issues involving taxation, law, regulation, and public policy concerns. However, the business unit is responsible for developing global competitive strategies.

The regional definitions may differ across the company's market divisions. The regional divisions reflect the supplier countries and customer countries of the international market that is being served. They also reflect the best configuration for competitive advantage in the specific international market that the company serves.

The main difference between the market-based organization with regional subunits and the matrix form is that geographic units are subordinate to market-based divisions. The company gets its priorities straight – serving international markets. The regional divisions are the means of addressing the needs of customers in its markets.

A common objection to the organizational design shown in figure 6.7 is that the regional structures of each division involve some duplication of effort, particularly in marketing and sales. Could not the company achieve economies of scale by centralizing marketing and sales, or other functions such as purchasing?

The answer to such an objection is that designing an organization always involves trade-offs. It is likely that companies forgo some economies of scale when they decentralize functions, particularly such functions as marketing and sales. However, the company benefits from the flexibility and market responsiveness that come from decentralizing these functions.

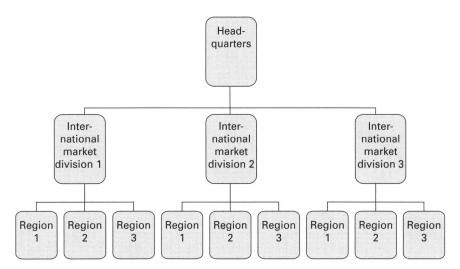

Fig. 6.7   The international market-based organization with regional divisions

The influence of international market managers has increased substantially relative to country managers.[15] Each global business division is responsible for serving the worldwide market for a specific product or related group of products. Managers of the global business divisions are responsible for international procurement, manufacturing, sales, and marketing. Thus, many of the functional tasks of the company are the responsibility of the business divisions rather than being controlled by the central office.

Procter & Gamble

Procter & Gamble (P&G), with 110,000 employees, was traditionally organized in four geographic business groups. Such a geographic organization conflicted with the company's strategy of selling through major retailers such as Wal-Mart and Carrefour, whose operations crossed international borders. The geographic organization made dealing with such major retailers difficult, since it required coordinating any given product line across the four geographic business units. The lack of responsiveness of an international division is illustrated by P&G's experience with the introduction of new products outside the US. Initially, the company offered a new product known as Febreze only in the US market, delaying for some years its introduction abroad. Febreze is a liquid that is sprayed on fabrics to eliminate odors. According to P&G, the company's delayed product introduction may have caused it to miss about $300 million in sales overseas, many times its initial annual US sales.

Under CEO Durk I. Jager, the company undertook a major reorganization along product lines. The company was divided into seven global business units. The seven product lines were: Baby Care, Beauty Care, Fabric & Home Care, Feminine Protection, Food & Beverage, Health Care & Corporate New Ventures, Tissue & Towel. Moreover, the company decentralized functional areas by moving them into the product divisions. Among the decentralized functions were R&D, Product Supply, Marketing, Information Technology, Finance and Accounting, and Human Resources. The company also moved its Corporate Functions directly into the business units.

To handle geographic coordination, P&G created Market Development Organizations (MDOs) at both regional and local country levels. The MDOs were intended to feed consumer and market knowledge into the global business units and collaborate with them to develop plans for brands in local markets. The eight regional MDOs were: North America, which includes the US, Canada, and Puerto Rico; Western Europe; Central & Eastern Europe; Middle East, Africa & General Export; Japan/Korea; Greater China; ASEAN, India & Australasia; and Latin America. The company also created a Global Business Services unit to provide a range of services, such as accounting, payroll, and order management, and MDOs at both regional and local country levels.

Alan G. Lafley, who succeeded Durk I. Jager as CEO, changed the strategic direction of the company by sharpening its focus on high-margin brands. He sought to emphasize health, beauty, and fabric care. He expanded hair care by purchasing Clairol from Bristol-Myers Squibb, adding the hair care brands Clairol, Aussie, Infusium, and Herbal Essences, and adding the hair coloring brands Nice 'n Easy, Natural Instincts, Miss Clairol, and Hydrience. According to Lafley: "With the acquisition of Clairol, we'll become one of the two leaders in hair care worldwide."[16] He further planned to shed the Jif peanut butter brand and the Crisco cooking oil business, while spinning off Pringles chips brands in a JV with Coca-Cola Co.; the company's only remaining food line would be Folgers coffee.[17] According to Lafley: "Strategies and action plans we put in place in the last year are getting P&G back on track."[18] What implications do these strategic shifts have for the company's organizational structure?

Conglomerates and holding companies

Management decisions about what businesses the company should establish are a fundamental part of a company's corporate strategy. Some companies operate a single business and others operate multiple businesses. Some companies operate businesses that are very similar to each other: P&G, for example, has many *related* consumer product businesses, such as household cleaners. Other companies operate very different or *unrelated* lines of businesses: Siemens, for example, operates groups of distinct businesses – information and communication systems; automation and control; power generation, transmission, and distribution; transportation; medical equipment; and lighting.

A common strategic recommendation is for companies to focus on the business that they know best. This suggests that multiple-product companies should engage in *related diversification* – that is, the companies should expand only by offering products and services that are similar to the products that the company already offers. The company can serve its existing customers with products that are complementary to its existing products. Microsoft, for example, expanded from offering computer operating systems software to offering suites of software applications such as word processing and spreadsheets. The company can also develop products that employ related technologies and skills. Honda, for example, offers motorcycles, automobiles, and lawnmowers that use its engine technology.

A line of business involves much more than the products that business offers. Practically all companies sell multiple products. However, there is a difference between the range of products offered by the company and the number of businesses that it operates. The corner grocery store sells many items, but it operates a single retail business. The local restaurant offers a wide range of selections, but it operates a single restaurant service. An airline serves many geographic routes, but it is in the airline business. A company may turn out a range of suitcases, but it is still in the luggage manufacturing business. It is useful for managers to define a line of business by the general type of service the company provides to its customers.

To maintain its focus, a company following market opportunities sheds existing businesses that no longer conform to its corporate strategy. Corporate managers concentrate their efforts on businesses that are expected to yield the greatest return to those efforts. Moreover, the performance of the company reflects its key businesses, providing a clearer picture to both managers and investors.

One advantage of operating multiple businesses is that the company can *share resources* across the businesses, thus achieving economies of scale and scope. The decision to enter or exit a market is significantly affected by what businesses the company already operates. If the entry decision were entirely independent of the company's existing businesses, then the new business might be better carried out by a separate company. The management could establish a separate company from scratch or spin off part of the existing company.

Shared resources are important for companies that operate *related* lines of business. An advantage to be gained from multiple related lines of business is that the company shares engineering and R&D resources. The company benefits by spreading knowledge across its activities. Another advantage of operating related lines of business is sharing assembly and manufacturing facilities, allowing for greater capacity utilization and economies of scale and scope at the plant level. Companies also derive advantages from common procurement of resources, parts, and components. Common sourcing not only raises the company's bargaining power with suppliers but also allows for economies of scale in the design and manufacture of parts.

Marketing and sales advantages can be obtained by sharing a common brand across multiple types of products. A company such as P&G puts its brand on a wide variety of products so that it realizes greater value from the brand. There are also transaction costs benefits from related lines of businesses. Companies such as Nestlé offer products that are in every aisle of the supermarket, from coffee to frozen dinners to petfood, thus reducing their transaction costs of selling through supermarket chains. Companies with related lines of business benefit from cross-marketing products, with the company's lines of business selling to each other's customers. Citigroup operates a financial supermarket that tries to take advantage of cross-selling to customers of its banking, brokerage, and insurance businesses.

Another advantage of multiple lines of businesses is sharing the services of the central office, including corporate management, corporate efforts in raising financial capital, accounting services, recruiting and managing personnel, and legal and regulatory services. For corporations that operate *unrelated* businesses, these types of shared services are generally the main reasons that the businesses are located within the same company. If a company operates many unrelated businesses without a significant amount of shared resources, managers should explore whether the businesses should be divested and operated as separate companies.

Companies that operate many different types of businesses are referred to as *conglomerates*. Holding companies and leveraged-buyout (LBO) partnerships are conglomerates that function as collections of individual companies. The key question is whether the whole is greater than the sum of the parts. When investors, or corporate management, cannot distinguish the individual performance of the businesses, separations through divestitures, then spin-offs, or bustups, are called for. Conglomerates at their best represent a group of companies that take advantage of the management talent and capital-raising abilities of the parent corporation. These companies benefit from an internal capital market and a common pool of management talent.

Common resources are at once the advantage and the drawback of conglomerates. Because resources are shared, the corporation may encounter difficulties in distinguishing the performance of individual businesses. It is necessary for each business to enhance the performance of the corporation as a whole. The danger is that managers of the individual businesses have an incentive to draw upon the collective resources of the firm, thus raising the total costs of the corporation. Each manager will seek to enhance the performance of his or her own business by attempting to divert resources from the corporation, and the corporation must constantly make sure that individual businesses within the company are not subsidizing others.

Another problem with multiple business companies is the need to provide incentives for the company's divisions to operate their businesses efficiently since profit and loss responsibilities are sometimes complicated by shared resources. Unless managers are rewarded based on the performance of their individual business, there is a tendency for management to be internally focused more on organizational politics and less on the markets of the individual business. However, the company's divisions must also work together to increase the overall value of the company. The divisions can become a random collection of businesses that gain little in value by being within the same corporation. Corporate managers face the difficult job of coordinating the activities of diverse businesses to maximize the company's shareholder value. When the costs of coordination outweigh the advantages of shared resources, it is time to divest businesses.

The purpose of a conglomerate is *not* to hold a financial portfolio of businesses. Financial portfolios are valuable to individual investors as a means of reducing overall risk through diversification. However, the benefits that an individual investor obtains from owning a diversified financial portfolio do not apply to corporations. The reason is that individual investors can efficiently assemble their own portfolios of securities to reflect their investment objectives and the risk profile of each security. It is far less costly for individual investors to create portfolios of securities than for a company to assemble diverse businesses under the same roof. Moreover, investors benefit from monitoring the performance of each individual stock and from assembling a portfolio to meet individual investment needs.

A conglomerate's choice of businesses should be based only on the benefits obtained from jointly *operating* those businesses. Thus, coordinating the businesses and sharing resources justify joint operation, not ownership of assets yielding financial returns. Financial markets seek information about the performance of individual businesses so that combining returns on the balance sheet does not add value for investors and may even reduce the value of the publicly held company by obscuring information. Businesses should be operated jointly only for strategic reasons – that is, only if the businesses create more value together than they do separately.

The performance record of many conglomerates has been decidedly mixed. ITT shed over 250 companies through the 1980s, including its telecommunications business. The company was divided into industry groups including defense and electronics, financial services, communication and information services, automotive, fluid technology, ITT Sheraton Corp., and Hartford Fire Insurance. In the mid-1990s, ITT announced a breakup into three separate companies, separating insurance, industrial, and hotels and entertainment. Referring to Harold Geneen, who was CEO for two decades beginning in 1959, the move was hailed as the end of conglomerates, and the "death of the Geneen machine."[19]

Another conglomerate, Westinghouse Electric Corporation, lost billions and approached bankruptcy by the early 1990s, until CEO Michael H. Jordan began a turnaround. Like ITT, Westinghouse was organized into seven business groups: defense and electronic systems, environmental services, power generation, energy systems, Thermo King Corporation (mobile refrigeration units), Westinghouse Broadcasting Company, and The Knoll Group (office furniture). Seeking further growth, Westinghouse announced a $5.4 billion acquisition of the CBS television network to complement its own successful cable networks and broadcasting operations. Yet, the acquisition was a substantial change of direction for the company. Primarily a manufacturer, Westinghouse derived only 10 percent of its $8.8 billion in revenues from broadcasting; with CBS, Westinghouse's broadcasting business would be ten times larger. The combined companies would have eleven TV stations, thirty-nine radio stations, and TV, radio, and cable networks. In evaluating the merger of the Westinghouse Broadcasting Company and CBS, managers needed to find a connection between the broadcasting business and nuclear power plants, hazardous waste disposal, or office furniture.

General Electric (GE) is often used as the example of a successful conglomerate. Jeffrey R. Immelt, who succeeded Jack Welch as chairman of GE, sold its electronic commerce unit, Global eXchange Services, and contemplated selling its lighting and appliances businesses.[20] Tyco, a conglomerate with over 250,000 employees that had tried to copy GE's organization, spun off its finance unit. According to the company: "Tyco is the world's largest manufacturer and servicer of electrical and electronic components; the world's largest designer, manufacturer, installer and servicer of undersea telecommunications systems; the world's largest manufacturer, installer and provider of fire protection systems and electronic security services; and the world's largest manufacturer of specialty valves."[21] Faced with financial difficulties, Tyco considered breaking up its set of manufacturing companies.

Large conglomerates in the form of industrial groups are common in many countries: the large industrial conglomerates in Japan and Korea, the Grupos of Latin America, the Hongs of Hong Kong, and the Business Houses of India and Malaysia. Tarun Khanna and Krishna Palepu suggest that focused strategies may not fit in emerging markets if the large, diversified industrial groups fill institutional gaps that result from incomplete financial markets, imperfect information in product markets, and inadequate legal systems. If financial markets do not function adequately, industrial groups raise capital from earnings and from domestic and international investors and allocate the funds through internal capital markets.[22] However, as financial institutions strengthen in emerging economies, the value added by the formation of such industrial groups is likely to diminish substantially. The economic problems encountered in many developing countries can be traced to inefficient capital allocation within the industrial conglomerates.

In developing countries, when buyers and sellers lack market information, there may be a need for branding across industries by large conglomerates.[23] In India, the Tata Group extends its brand to a wide range of activities, including airlines, telecommunications systems, IT, automotive components, metals, chemicals, energy, tea, and management consulting.[24] In Korea, Samsung's brand appears on about twenty-eight companies offering a wide range of products, including consumer electronics, microwave ovens, chemicals, shipbuilding, construction, military aircraft, and financial services.[25]

Japan's technology conglomerate Toshiba applies common brands to a wide range of electronic products. The branding of unrelated products poses risks for conglomerates since it is difficult to maintain a consistent quality of service or brand image across many industries. Competition from international companies may force these diversified industrial conglomerates to separate their businesses and to create market-specific brands. Responding to such intense competition, Japan's five big technology conglomerates – NEC, Toshiba, Hitachi, Fujitsu, and Mitsubishi Electric – entered into far-ranging corporate restructurings and divestitures based on the concept of "selection and focus."[26]

Holding companies take diversification and organizational separation to the limit by operating their businesses as separate companies. This corporate form has advantages over conglomerates as a means of monitoring managers. Because individual companies account for all their earnings and costs, managers can be rewarded on the basis of individual company performance. Moreover, the member companies cannot draw on common resources, avoiding free rider problems. In contrast, managers within conglomerates draw salaries that can imperfectly reflect the performance of the units they manage. This reduces their incentive to compete aggressively and increase the earnings of their units.

The independence of the units is a strength of the holding company. It is a decentralized form of organization with minimal involvement of the central office in the day-to-day affairs of the business units. This allows unit managers to respond quickly to market changes and to adjust their strategies to competitive imperatives, rather than to central office directives.

The question is: Why have a holding company at all if the member companies operate independently? Holding companies can create value in a number of ways. Most importantly, the holding company is a financial intermediary. Successful holding companies are skilled at raising capital from creditors and shareholders; to complete the intermediation, the holding company allocates the capital within the organization, by selecting investment projects, evaluating company expansion plans, and monitoring management performance. With perfect information, such a task might be performed by outside investors, but it is costly to gather such information. The holding company parent provides these services at a lower cost, and with greater effectiveness.

Next, the holding company is an intermediary in the market for corporate managers. They hire and fire the heads of companies. Because the holding company has a stake in the performance of the companies, its monitoring is far more active than many corporate boards; it can take action quickly. The parent holding company builds expertise at recruiting managers and then allocates managerial talent within the organization. Monitoring the managers to improve company performance builds up the value of the company for the holding company as owner or prepares it for future sale.

The holding company is an intermediary in the market for buying and selling companies. The parent company develops contacts and expertise in the market for acquiring and divesting companies. The holding company has contacts with owners and managers of companies to identify prospective takeover targets. It develops skills in reviewing company balance sheets and assets. IT has market contacts that are useful in selling off companies. The holding company is often used by family-controlled businesses; see figure 6.8 for the holding company structure of India's Tata Group, which includes over ninety operating companies in seven major business sectors.

To pursue strategic focus, an international holding company must divest unrelated businesses. For example, as a holding company, DaimlerBenz shed its non-core businesses to focus on automobiles. It divested its rail systems to Canada's Bombardier, it placed software and IT services in a JV with Deutsche Telekom, and sold some of its holdings in the European Aeronautic Defense and Space Company (EADS), that includes the Airbus consortium. Through its merger with Chrysler and its partnership with Mitsubishi, the company focused its strategic attention, and its organization, on global automobile markets.

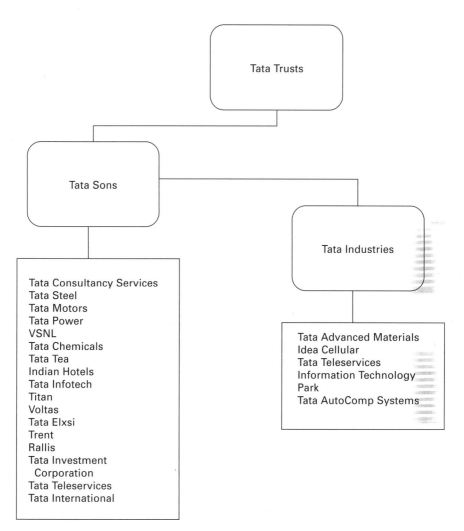

Fig. 6.8   Holding company organizational structure for India's Tata Group
Source: www.tata.com/0_aboutus_us/business/promoter_companies.htm+group_holding.

Overview

The company's corporate strategy determines how its managers choose the divisions of the company. A focused strategy suggests that managers should operate only related businesses. There must be substantial returns to shared resources for companies to engage in unrelated diversification. The divisions of the companies should be based on the businesses that the company operates. The market responsiveness of the company is enhanced by decentralizing functions within the company's business-based divisions. Multi-product international businesses have become organized around global markets rather than on a geographic basis.

To carry out market-based strategies, many company organizations have progressively evolved from function-based to products-based to business-based organizations. In an increased focus on being responsive to customer characteristics and needs, organizations have adjusted the boundaries of their divisions to match up with the markets that the firm is serving. As global integration of the market intensifies, companies have formed global market-based divisions rather than organizing the company along geographic lines.

The market-based organizational form establishes divisions that reflect closely the firm's business strategies. The firm's markets are defined in terms of the characteristics of the customers that the company is trying to serve. The company's divisions interact directly with the customers they serve. The market-based organization decentralizes functions to the division level, allowing the company's divisions to interact directly with their suppliers of finance, labor, manufactured inputs, and technology. The structure of the company also facilitates communication within the organization about customer and supplier markets.

The advantage of market-based divisions is flexibility in adjusting to changes in customer characteristics and actions of competing companies. To enhance the ability of divisions to adapt to changing markets, companies have decentralized many corporate functions by moving them into divisions. In some cases, hybrid organizational forms can serve strategic objectives. The expansion of the Internet and its use in business-to-business transactions has facilitated the decentralization of business activities within organizations, and the outsourcing of functional services.

The growth of international business has resulted in the reorganization of major companies, moving from a geographic orientation to a product focus. Companies such as Wal-Mart, General Motors, GE, Nestlé, and ABB rely on international markets for a major portion of their sales. These types of companies have shifted from geographic divisions to global business-based divisions. The divisions are responsible for selling specific products or groups of products worldwide, competing with other global companies as well as local and regional companies.

7   Lenovo: entering global competition

The shock in international business circles was palpable. The *New York Times* asked "Lenovo. Who?" under a headline that read "An Unknown Giant Flexes Its Muscles."[1] China's Lenovo Group had purchased IBM's personal computer (PC) business for US$1.75 billion in cash, stock, and debt. The acquisition created shock waves in part because the purchaser was a Chinese company, and perceptions in developed economies had not fully adjusted to the growth of Chinese businesses or to the technological progress taking place in China. Some were startled by IBM's exit from the PC business, despite having pioneered its development in the early 1980s. Known as "Big Blue," IBM had played a key role in establishing PC industry standards through its alliances with Intel in microprocessors and with Microsoft in operating system software.

Lenovo vaulted from being the eighth-largest PC maker in the world to the third-largest, after Dell and Hewlett-Packard (HP). At a stroke, Lenovo gained an internationally recognized brand name, access to customers, skilled managers, advanced technology, and a powerful partner. Buying IBM's PC division transformed Lenovo from a leading domestic player in China to a major global company:

- How did Lenovo make such a great change so quickly?
- How did the acquisition fit into Lenovo's overall strategy?
- How would Lenovo adapt its strategy and organization to become an effective global competitor?

Yang Yuanqing took the helm of the Lenovo Group (formerly the Legend Group) as the PRC (hereafter, China) prepared for its accession to the WTO. He was concerned about the company's prospects for the future in the face of intensified competition from global computer companies. Foreign computer giants such as Acer, Dell, HP, IBM, Samsung, Sony, and Toshiba were already establishing plants in China and making deals with local partners for a renewed run at Chinese consumers and business customers. Dell Computer opened a large-scale manufacturing plant in Xiamen, Fujian Province, and brought its direct-sales approach to China.

Computer companies operating in China had been cutting their PC prices and Lenovo expected further price pressures. How should the company adjust its pricing strategies and distribution policies to handle competition from world-class marketers? Could the company maintain its domestic leadership position in an environment of rapid cost-cutting and technological change? What mix of cooperation and head-to-head competition would continue the company's successful performance? The company's managers considered competing against global computer companies in overseas markets and weighed the costs and benefits of expanding outside of China. Yang believed that Lenovo could meet the challenges and become a successful global player.

Lenovo's founder and then-Chairman, Liu Chuanzhi, observed: "Legend Group is a young and dynamic enterprise born amidst the tidal wave symbolizing China's reform and open door policy. We have grown in a market of intense competition, and witnessed the vigorous speed at which China's information industry has developed."[2] Lenovo's corporate culture statement emphasized that the company was: "Achieving greatness with ambition and determination." Yang told *BusinessWeek* that the company planned to be among the global top ten of PC makers.[3] Within a year of Yang's announcement, Lenovo had effectively achieved its objective thanks to its acquisition of IBM's PC business. Many new challenges lay ahead as a transformed Lenovo entered into the global arena.

Birth of a Legend

At the beginning of the twenty-first century, Lenovo found itself the leading computer supplier in China, the fastest-growing market for computers in the world. Housed in new, high-tech facilities, the company had some time ago passed a major milestone, producing its millionth computer. Majority-owned by the Chinese government at its foundation, the company operated with considerable flexibility and was listed on the Hong Kong Stock Exchange, quoted on the London Stock Exchange, and traded in the US through ADRs. How did Lenovo become China's leading computer company?

Lenovo emerged from academia with a rocky start. Originally named Legend, the company began in 1984 as an experimental state-owned enterprise housed in a small bungalow at the Chinese Academy of Sciences (CAS). Liu Chuanzhi and ten colleagues started Lenovo with 200,000 renminbi (approximately US$24,000) in seed money from the CAS; the company would be privately operated despite government ownership. Engineers and scientists at the CAS had focused on designing microprocessors for military applications and on developing satellites, rockets, and heavy machinery. Lenovo initially sold and distributed computer products of companies such as IBM and HP.

In the company's early years, the greatest challenge faced by its managers was learning basic business concepts. As Liu admitted: "I won't say that we became successful straight away, in fact we went through a very difficult period between 1984 and 1988." Liu observed that:

The major reason for our success is our background in the CAS – our background in research. But since 1984 the focus of our efforts was on marketing and management. When we started, the main focus was not so much on research but on how to manage an enterprise. Much of our efforts went into researching management. This might sound strange to Westerners but, for us, the major issue was how to open up the market and how to finance our production, so it was very important to study strategy.[4]

According to Liu, in understanding marketing and the organization of sales channels, "HP was our earliest and best teacher."[5] Liu applied this knowledge to establish an intricate and entrenched distribution network that helped Lenovo gain its substantial market share.

Because Lenovo had initially distributed foreign companies' computers, Liu had to convince government officials that it was capable of making computers. Lenovo's first products were digital watches and Chinese-language computer input devices. Lenovo did not have its own brand of computers until 1990.

Although the Chinese government had a controlling ownership share and provided funding, the company had sufficient autonomy to compete as an independent entity. A division of the company, Legend Holdings Limited, was incorporated in Hong Kong in 1988 and listed on the Hong Kong Stock Exchange in 1994.[6] Still, for Liu, government reforms that made independent state enterprises possible were a basis for the company's success:

The CAS provided an ideal environment in which to develop. We received money from the state and were given freedom in terms of personnel management training and financing. In addition to salaries, we were able to give bonuses or shares to our staff. These incentives are an important factor in employee motivation.[7]

Lenovo focused on training and attracting qualified personnel. Liu noted that: "At Legend, we try to merge the goals and ideals of personal development with that of the company. Since we are a listed company in Hong Kong we are allowed to set aside 10 percent of the group's shares for stock options for staff members, this gives staff a real incentive to see the company perform well."[8]

The focus on diligence and effort was summarized by an early company motto: "We are making progress every day."

The company developed and manufactured a wide range of computers, including laptops, desktop PCs, servers, and workstations. In the 1990s, the company also distributed computer products from over twenty foreign vendors, including Cisco and Sun Microsystems. Lenovo offered successful computer products for the home market, and its computers included the Happy Family software for consumers and My Office software for commercial users.

Lenovo experienced rapid growth in sales and by 1997 had the leading share of the computer market in China. The company's PC sales of 1.8 million units in 2000 represented an increase of almost 90 percent from the previous year.[9] Under CEO Yang, the company launched a variety of new products including PCs aimed at four different age groups of home users: Tianhui for children; Future Pioneer for high school students; Tianlu for adults; and Tianle for the middle-aged and the elderly.[10]

Lenovo and other companies in the high-tech sector continued to benefit from association with the CAS. The Chinese government announced in 1998 that it would send 400 researchers from the CAS to conduct R&D at Lenovo.[11] Domestic competitors had similar ties, with Founder Electronics associated with Beijing University and Great Wall having been established by the Ministry of the Electronics Industry.[12] Lenovo also benefited from its association with the Chinese government: some 25 percent of Lenovo's sales were to the Chinese government during the mid-1990s.[13] However, by 2001, the company's sales to corporate customers, including state-owned enterprises, accounted for less than 25 percent of Lenovo's sales as Lenovo increased its focus on the consumer and commercial markets.[14]

Lenovo also benefited in its early years from Chinese government trade restrictions, which included quotas, tariffs, value added taxes (VAT) on imports, restrictions on foreign companies' access to distribution, and restrictions on ownership and investment. These restrictions conferred potential competitive advantages on Chinese computer makers. For various economic reasons, including the relative costs of production in China versus the rest of the world, exports of computers far exceeded imports, see table 7.1.

Yet, trade liberalization in China took place as part of the process of being considered for WTO membership. Beginning in 1992, there was a reduction in average non-agricultural tariffs from over 42 percent in 1992 to 17 percent by 1998. For microprocessing equipment, the tariff for those countries with whom China had exchanged most-favored-nation (MFN) trading status was

Table 7.1. China's imports and exports of computer equipment, 1997-2001 (Product group 752) (US$000)

	1997	1998	1999	2000	2001
Imports	1,135,129	1,821,250	3,253,327	4,516,388	4,980,964
Exports	5,361,766	7,066,626	7,921,950	10,994,084	13,093,809

Source: Data from International Trade Centre (UNCTAD/WTO).

15 percent by 1998. At that time, the VAT, which was levied on the combined value of imported products plus tariff charges, was 17 percent, which magnified the effects of tariffs.[15] In 2000, tariffs on US IT products imported by China averaged 13 percent.

Greater international competition in China's IT market accompanied these reforms. Chinese imports of US high-tech products expanded by 500 percent between 1990 and 1998,[16] and further changes in trade regulations had additional impacts on the Chinese market. In 1998, the US and China concluded an Information Technology Agreement with important implications for the Chinese IT market. In November 1999, the US and China negotiated a trade agreement that helped to pave the way for China's accession to the WTO in 2001. The agreement granted foreign IT companies rights to engage in distribution by 2003, including wholesaling, retailing, transporting, warehousing, and servicing. The agreement also reduced Chinese IT tariffs by two-thirds before 2003 and fully eliminated them by 2005, and abolished IT import quotas upon accession to the WTO. The agreement further opened Chinese markets to investment and services while providing IP protections.[17] Upon joining the WTO, China began the relaxation of trade barriers. According to the Office of the US Trade Representative: "China's elimination of tariffs on the products covered by the Information TechnologyAgreement (ITA) – semiconductors and semiconductor manufacturing equipment, computers and computer parts, software, telecommunications equipment and computer-based analytical instruments – began upon accession and is to be completed by 2005." China maintained various tariff and non-tariff barriers such as preferences for domestic producers in government procurement, but these practices came under increased scrutiny.[18]

Lenovo continued to compete effectively with global firms entering the Chinese PC market. Lenovo's sales growth coincided with declining sales of well-known international competitors, see table 7.2. In 1994, Lenovo had only 6 percent of the Chinese market, with AST, Compaq, DEC, and IBM having a combined market share of 56 percent. In 1997, Compaq, HP, and IBM had a

Table 7.2. Selected market shares of PC suppliers in China, 1994–2003

Market shares of PC companies (1994)[a]	Market shares of PC companies (1998)[b]	Market shares of PC companies (2001)[c]	Market shares of notebook computer companies (first half of 2003)[d]
AST	Lenovo	Lenovo	Lenovo
25%	14%	28%	20%
Compaq	IBM	Founder	IBM
16%	7%	10%	18%
IBM	Compaq/Digital	Qinghua Tongfang	Toshiba
8%	6%	6%	12%
DEC	HP	Dell	Dell
7%	6%	5%	11%
Great Wall	Tontru	IBM	Founder Electronics
6%	3.5%	4%	9%
Lenovo	Founder	TCL	Compaq (HP)
6%	3.5%	3%	8%
Acer	Great Wall	Acer	Tsinghua Unisplendour
4%	2.5%	3%	5%
Langchao	Acer	Great Wall	ASUSTek
3%	2%	3%	4%
Changjiang	Toshiba	Hisense	Acer
2%	1.5%	2.5%	4%
Other imports	NEC	HP	Tongfang
4%	1%	2.5%	4%
Other producers	Other producers	Other producers	Other producers
19%	53%	33%	5%

Note: Market shares are only approximate to indicate market rank.

Sources: Data from:

[a] Yadong Luo, 2000, *Multinational Corporations in China: Benefiting from Structural Transformation*, Copenhagen: Copenhagen Business School Press.

[b] Approximate market shares based on news reports, company data, and Morgan Stanley Dean Witter, *Asia/Pacific Investment Research*, "Legend Holdings, Leader of the Chinese PC Revolution," December 7, 1998, p. 15, which uses data from *PC AsiaDat Bulletin*.

[c] Approximate market shares based on news reports, company data, and Deutsche Bank, *Legend Holdings Limited*, February 6, 2002, figure 18, p. 15, which uses International Development Corporation data.

[d] Approximate market shares based on news reports, company data, and CEINet Market Research, Beijing CEINet Corporation, September 30, 2003, which uses data from Huicong International Information.

combined share of 21 percent of the Chinese market and that share fell below 10 percent in 2000, while during that same period the Chinese market grew at the rate of 25 percent per year, reaching 9 million units. Lenovo's market share rose to over 25 percent in 2000 and surpassed 30 percent by 2002.[19] Overall, Liu felt fortunate that: "Legend Group was operating in an era of continuous progress, and participating in an industry characterized by innovation and transformation."[20]

Lenovo was reorganized into six business units in 1995:

1 Legend Computer Systems, which engaged in R&D, manufacture, and distribution of Legend-brand PCs
2 Legend Technology, which distributed foreign-brand computer-related products
3 Legend Advanced Systems, which provided systems integration solutions in China
4 Legend Quantum Design International Corp. (QDI), which manufactured and distributed motherboards
5 Legend Techwise Circuits, which manufactured and distributed printed circuit boards
6 Legend Expert Systems, which provided system integration services in Hong Kong.

Lenovo's managers decided to spin off its contract manufacturing unit as a 50/50 JV in 2003. Lenovo had engaged in contract manufacturing of QDI-brand motherboards, and had merged its QDI motherboard manufacturing facility with its Lenovo Computer company after the business encountered losses due to intense competition in its export market. QDI had R&D centers located in Beijing, Shenzhen, Hong Kong, and Silicon Valley. QDI's motherboard brand was ranked fifth in the world and in the top three in Europe.[21] The spinoff would help Lenovo's management to concentrate on the company's core businesses.

Lenovo also spun off Digital China Holdings Ltd in 2001 and the company was listed on the Hong Kong Stock Exchange. Digital China included three units of Lenovo: Legend Technology, Legend Advanced Systems, and Legend Network. Digital China was ranked as the largest IT products distributor and services company in China (see www.digitalchina.com.hk). The spinoff eliminated any potential conflict of interest for Digital China, which could then sell various domestic and foreign brands on an equal footing. Lenovo no longer distributed foreign brands but concentrated on its own branded PCs, and the managers could focus on the company's own product manufacturing and distribution business.

The company manufactured PCs in three facilities – Beijing, Shanghai, and Guangdong Province. Production capacity was expected to reach over 5 million units per year. Lenovo had a turnover of HK$20.2 billion in fiscal 2002–2003, an increase of 5 percent over the previous year, and profits rose by 21 percent to HK$1 billion. Although Lenovo had shown a profit, the domestic market for home PCs was shifting toward laptops rather than desktops: laptops were not only more costly to manufacture but faced intense competition from the branded products offered by Dell, HP, and IBM.[22]

Lenovo's domestic strategy

The success of Lenovo and other domestic computer companies in China went against the expectations of many market analysts. According to *BusinessWeek*: "It wasn't supposed to happen this way. A few years ago, most analysts were convinced that the global powers would gobble up the Chinese market, with locals like Lenovo stuck in second-tier status – at best."[23] Reduced trade barriers had created opportunities for global companies, but the outcome of market competition in China was not easily predictable – both global companies and domestic companies had potential competitive advantages. The company benefited from both its pricing and distribution strategies.

Pricing and costs

Lenovo offered customers a blend of affordable prices, technical efficacy, and patriotism. A consumer purchasing educational software produced by Lenovo explained why he chose it over competing foreign brands: "It's cheap, it works and it's Chinese."[24]

The company priced computers above cheap clones made in China but still competitively low in comparison with international imports. Lenovo recognized that income levels in China would remain low for some time and that penetration of PCs in the household market was limited by income levels. Lenovo and the other top Chinese brands had substantially undercut imported PCs by around 20 percent; some models undercut IBM and Compaq by 30 percent in the mid-1990s.[25] However, projected prices for PCs were expected to decrease by 10–20 percent, putting pressure on the company to keep cutting costs and enhancing quality. Lenovo positioned itself as the high-quality domestic brand, and its pricing strategy was to stay above the prices of competing domestic brands and below the prices of global brands. Price differences narrowed substantially in the following years.

The Legend brand was well known to Chinese consumers. As Liu observed: "The reason we are number one in the China market is because of brand advantage."[26] Lenovo's sales continued to exceed those of lower-priced domestic brands such as Founder Electronics, Great Wall, and Tongfang. In competing with global brands, Lenovo had the advantage of an exclusive focus on the China market, with specialized applications for specific market segments such as state enterprises, banks, and small businesses.

Many foreign companies, such as HP and IBM, had encountered difficulties in trying to break into the Chinese market, contrary to confident early predictions. International companies benefited from established global brands, economies of scale, substantial financial resources, access to technology, and relationships with hardware and software providers. However, the market share of imports in PCs had declined steadily. A PC represented two to three years' salary for an average Chinese household, so the low cost and relative quality of Lenovo's computers allowed the company to capture over 27 percent of the Chinese market by 2003.[27]

The international companies were aware of the difficulties in serving the market, but the rapid growth of the Chinese economy proved attractive. China was the world's fastest-growing market for information and telecommunications technology, with a "compound annual growth rate of 27 percent, approximately 4.5 times greater than the US."[28] Much of the 200 percent annual growth in PC sales in China in the early 1990s, however, was concentrated in the low-end market segment.[29] In computers, MNCs operating in China missed out on some of the opportunities provided by this growth because of their focus on the high-price, high-quality end of the market, and their orientation toward wealthier urban consumers.[30]

Chinese consumers were initially unfamiliar with computers or the Internet, see table 7.3 on Internet usage in China. International companies were accustomed to dealing with consumers in developed economies and so did not offer sufficient information and training to new computer buyers. In 1999, only one out of every 175 Chinese owned a computer.[31] Lenovo provided sales assistance and tutorials on how to operate a computer and how to use the Internet. While international companies offered well-known international brands, Chinese companies such as Lenovo offered brands that were well known and popular in the domestic market.

International businesses found it hard to distribute their computers in China because of ownership restrictions in wholesale and retail and limited

Table 7.3. PCs, Internet, and telephone usage in China, 1998 and 2001

	1998	2001
PCs (per 1,000 people)	8.9	19.0
Internet users	2.1 million	33.7 million
Fixed lines and mobile telephones (per 1,000 people)	88.6	247.7

Source: Data from World Development Indicators Database, August 2003, Washington, DC: World Bank.

experience operating distribution channels. Lenovo had already established its far-reaching domestic distribution network. Moreover, while Lenovo sold through traditional dealer and retail outlets, Dell planned to bring its direct-sales business model to the Chinese market place. Liu expected that the direct-sales model would encounter difficulties in China because of the limited use of credit cards, inadequate independent delivery, and preference by Chinese consumers for face-to-face interaction with sales personnel. Company founder and CEO Michael Dell reacted to these doubts by noting: "That's even what they told us in the United States."[32]

Foreign competitors had faced tariffs and VAT when they shipped computer components to China for assembly and imported computers that they manufactured abroad.[33] International firms also incurred transportation and transaction costs when they imported parts or finished products. These costs created advantages for domestic producers that initially allowed them to undercut the prices of international brands.

Distribution

Lenovo's growth in China was anchored to its strong domestic distribution network. Lenovo sold through about 3,700 distributors and resellers.[34] Given that Chinese consumers required substantial amounts of information, Lenovo's distribution system conferred a distinct competitive advantage;[35] customers relied on demonstrations and advice from retail sales personnel.

Lenovo's specialty shops further enhanced its market position with consumers. Lenovo established its own 1+1 Home PC Specialty Shops located in Beijing, Shanghai, and Guangzhou, and also targeted small and medium-sized cities, with over 1,000 stores established by early 2003.[36] Liu Chuanzhi noted that with a retail marketing channel, the company would be "in a better position to understand customers' needs and to better fulfill the demands of home

PC users."[37] These shops provided consumers with training seminars and also computer demonstrations that showcased Lenovo's computer capabilities such as the ability to handle digital photography, film, and also how Lenovo's PCs could be linked in a home network. The specialty shops also featured Lenovo products and innovations.

In a Press Release of August 1999, Liu discussed the reason for creating these specialty shops: "These . . . shops will provide more thorough support in the area of application to computer users in China. Through this direct marketing channel, we will also be in a better position to understand customers' needs and to fulfill the demands of home PC users. They will also help to enhance the popularity of home PC products and users' knowledge in their applications."

Yet Lenovo's distribution system had to adjust its operations in response to competition. Dell's centers needed to keep only six days' inventory due to their direct-sales process. According to Ma Xuezheng, CFO and senior vice president, the twenty-day stock of inventory that Lenovo kept in September 2002 was one-third less than it had been in 2001. Also, because Lenovo expected to see a great increase in demand for made-to-order computers, the company changed three of their six production lines to accommodate the shift in demand.[38]

Lenovo had plans to continue expansion of its distribution network even within China itself. Instead of focusing all of their resources on Beijing, Shanghai, and Guangzhou, Lenovo's assistant president and head of corporate marketing, Alice Li, stated that the company's "sales team will shift a bit to the second- and third-tier cities."[39]

Another important facet of Lenovo's success was its service network. In 2003, the company had established nearly 600 Legend brand service stores and planned more openings. Owners of Lenovo computers could come to these stores and have their computers repaired. Yang believed that Lenovo's service network provided a competitive advantage in serving Chinese consumers, stating that: "Some foreign companies don't provide service by themselves; they hand this over to the others. But we think the service should be provided by ourselves."[40] The service stores also retailed cell phones and other Lenovo products.

Product diversification

Yang Yuanqing set a goal of product diversification for the company. Lenovo entered into markets for handheld computers and mobile phones, and also started providing IT services. Yang believed that these markets would grow quickly in China and that computer makers such as Lenovo were the natural suppliers: "In China a lot of customers haven't known what exactly they want or what they need in terms of information technology and software. The PC manufacturers can help them."[41]

The company issued a four-part mission statement. Lenovo would try to make the home a more digitized place for consumers through its offering of IT products and services. The company would make shareholders' long-term benefits a top priority. The company would provide its employees with an exciting environment leading to personal growth both inside and outside of the workplace. The company would help to bring its community into the modern age.

The company established four business areas: corporate IT, consumer IT, handheld devices, and IT services. The corporate IT division engaged in R&D, manufacture, and distribution of Lenovo's commercial PCs, Notebook PCs, servers, and peripherals. The consumer IT division revolved around the company's consumer PC and digital products. The handheld devices division manufactured various palm devices and mobile handsets. The IT services division provided services in such areas as system security, system operation, IT consulting, and applications in the finance, telecom, manufacturing, and government sectors. These four business areas corresponded to the company's main target markets.

According to Yang, the Lenovo Group planned: "to accelerate business development, with server, notebook, mobile handset and digital products as the major growth drivers. We will also continue to pursue our transformation strategy, strengthening our ability to provide quality professional services and speed up the pace of our technological innovation."[42] Lenovo's system integration business specialized in financial and banking systems as well as government agencies such as the Ministry of Posts and Telecommunications. Lenovo was poised to provide services for the eventual computerization of Chinese companies and government agencies; however, market growth in this area got off to a slow start.

International entry into China's computer market

Chinese public policy and economic conditions provide an essential context for the strategic decisions of Lenovo's managers. Starting with the opening of the Chinese economy to trade in the late 1970s and continuing to the turn of

Table 7.4. Indicators of FDI to and from China, 1985–2003

Year	1985	1987	1989	1991	1993	1995	1997	1999	2001	2003
Investment										
FDI inflows ($million)	1,956	2,314	3,393	4,366	27,515	37,521	45,257	40,319	46,878	53,505
FDI outflows ($million)	629	645	780	913	4,400	2,000	2,563	1,775	6,884	1,800
Cross-border M&A sales (number of sales)	0	1	1	5	26	58	65	72	79	214
Cross-border M&A sales ($million)	0	0	0	125	561	403	1,856	2,395	2,325	3,820
Cross-border M&A purchases (number of purchases)	0	1	6	2	28	13	30	13	22	73
Cross-border M&A purchases ($ million)	0	0	202	3	485	249	799	101	452	1,647

Source: Data from UNCTAD, Foreign Direct Investment Database, www.unctad.org.

the millennium, China's economy experienced a rapid rate of growth of its GDP. China officially opened its economy to FDI in 1979, with additional liberalization of regulations occurring in 1986 and progressively from 1990 onwards.[43] As can be seen from table 7.4, FDI inflows grew substantially after 1991. FDI inflows substantially exceeded FDI outflows, equaling thirty times outflows in 2003. US FDI into China equaled $1,540 million in 2003.[44] China government policy makers reduced economic controls, allowing the development of competitive markets in many sectors while seeking the reform of the large and inefficient state owned enterprises. Although partly owned by the government, Lenovo was subject to the forces of competition from domestic and international companies operating in China.

The cost advantages of domestic producers in China's computer market had eroded substantially in the 1990s, and these advantages would be further reduced with the elimination of tariffs and other trade barriers under the WTO and related agreements. Moreover, transportation and transaction costs associated with imports would be eliminated because the international companies had entered into manufacturing JVs or established manufacturing facilities in China. By manufacturing in China, international companies further benefited from reduced production costs, particularly the lower costs of labor. Lenovo and other domestic Chinese producers could not count on cost advantages in competing with international companies.

International competitors complained that Chinese companies such as Lenovo benefited from government connections, or *guanxi*. The Chinese government had assisted Lenovo not only through tariffs, financial support, and technology, but also through direct purchase of its products by government agencies. Lenovo's CEO Yang thought that these criticisms were not well founded: "It's because the operations staff of those multinational players in China have no other excuse to report to their bosses overseas."[45] Although government purchases had played an initial role in Lenovo's growth, the company had diversified its customer base substantially, becoming reliant primarily on product sales to households and commercial customers and expanding its services to business.

International businesses also faced significant transaction costs associated with distribution because of their limited knowledge concerning consumer characteristics, local business practices, and government regulations. With the opening of the Chinese market as a result of China's WTO accession, these cost advantages would also be lowered. International businesses would be able to establish their own distribution networks or partner with Chinese distributors.

Dell, HP, IBM, and Toshiba cut prices and saw their sales surge.[46] Domestic players such as Founder Electronics and Great Wall responded with their own price reductions. Price competition took its toll on Lenovo's market share and profits,[47] and the company faced the possibility of being stuck in the middle of price wars, with international players at the high end and competition from domestic brands at the low end.

Dell in China

Michael Dell founded Dell Computer Corporation in 1984 in his college dorm room in Austin, Texas, with an initial investment of about $1,000; a year later, the company was making its own line of computers. By 1987, Dell had become an international company by opening a subsidiary in the UK and by 1990 the company had opened a manufacturing plant in Limerick, Ireland, to provide computers to Europe, the Middle East, and Africa. In 2003, Dell had around 40,000 employees worldwide and was the largest PC maker in the world.

Dell's success depended in large part on its versatile direct-sales model that allowed its consumers to order customized products for delivery. Michael Dell argued that the company could succeed internationally because: "In a lot of these markets the computer companies think that their customer is the dealer. Our customer is the end user."[48] Dell's well-known strategy was first to target corporate customers and then to expand into the consumer market. Dell was Lenovo's primary international challenger in the Chinese market, and in late May 1999 Liu met Michael Dell in Hong Kong.

Because of the high rate of growth of the Chinese computer market, Dell felt that there was room for international competitors to obtain a share of the market. Moreover, Dell planned to address the higher-margin business market for desktop computers and servers, where the nature of purchasing decisions differed from that of households. Dell projected that China would be the company's main revenue generator outside of the US within five years. Asia-wide, Dell's operations sales in the region grew by 48 percent in 1998, double the industry rate.[49] Dell's efforts were noticed. Lenovo's Yang remarked: "We pay attention to all our competitors, but especially Dell."[50] In contrast, John Legere, head of Dell's Asian operations said: "We don't have to beat Legend to be successful in China."[51]

Dell made several moves to overcome the potential competitive advantages that Lenovo and other domestic manufacturers had over international entrants. In November 1998, the company opened a 135,000 ft^2 assembly plant in Xiamen, Fujian Province. Dell avoided import costs and lowered transportation costs and some of its manufacturing costs by making its computers in China, and its direct-sales method also allowed the company to reduce inventory costs relative to competitors in China.[52]

Dell's direct-sales approach allowed the company to bypass retail and wholesale intermediaries and avoid establishing a costly distribution network. The direct-sales method offered Chinese customers the ability to customize their computers, and the company introduced toll-free help lines to provide advice.[53] To address the Chinese consumer's need to have hands-on access to products, Dell set up displays in shopping malls. Because of limited credit card usage in China, the company allowed customers to pay with debit cards and provided Chinese banks with Dell bank accounts that customers could use to deposit their payment for a Dell computer. Dell continued to encounter the problem of limited Internet usage, however; in 1999 less than 3 percent of Dell's sales in China were online.[54]

Since the opening of their plant in 1998, Dell's market share in China grew steadily. By June 2003, Dell had 10 percent of the PC market, and 20 percent of the high-end computer server sales.[55] However, Dell sales were concentrated mostly in the niche of the Chinese market served by other foreign companies.

HP in China

In 2002, HP merged with Compaq Computer Corporation, which expanded the company's global market reach to over 162 countries. The combined companies had more than 88,000 employees and revenues of around US$45 billion. Formerly, HP had directed its efforts in China to selling to the commercial market, but in 2003, the company shifted its marketing toward consumer PCs.[56] As Adrian Koch, senior vice-president at HP's personal systems group in the Asia-Pacific and Japan, acknowledged: "We have never been as active in China's consumer space as we have been in its commercial PC space."[57]

The company planned to penetrate the consumer market in several ways. First, HP offered a variety of its Pavilion desktop PCs ranging from models for middle-class consumers to those for high-end consumers.[58] Second, HP offered PCs through both direct-sales and retail distributors.[59] According to Koch: "Our blended go-to-market model was built around the belief of providing customers more than one way to buy our products and receive technical support."[60] Third, HP introduced a range of digital imaging products tailored to Chinese consumers as well as a low-priced multi-function printer.

HP planned a roll out in six major cities – Beijing, Shanghai, Guangzhou, Chengdu, Shenzhen, and Hangzhou. HP also planned to sell its PCs and printers through the two largest home appliance retailers in China: Dazhong and Gome. The company also entered into a program of direct investment and establishment of R&D facilities in China.[61]

IBM in China

IBM, founded in 1914, assisted the Peking Union Hospital in installing a business machine in 1934. After a hiatus due to civil war and political change, IBM returned to China and later opened offices in Beijing and Shanghai in the mid-1980s,[62] establishing relationships with government agencies and supplying an IBM 38 mainframe to the State Planning Commission.[63]

IBM established its Greater China Group to oversee a variety of its businesses. The Group included mainland China, Hong Kong, and Taiwan, employing 13,000 employees in 17 cities, and including 12 JVs in manufacturing, IT services, and software development.[64] Among IBM's JV partners were the

China Great Wall Computer Group, the Ji Tong Company, Tsinghua University, and Shenzhen University. IBM earned JV revenues in at least fifteen Chinese provinces and had customer service centers in many Chinese cities, including Beijing, Shenyang, Shanghai, Nanjing, Guangzhou, Shenzhen, Chengdu, Wuhan, and Xian. IBM operated regional support centers in Beijing, Shanghai, and Guangzhou and invested substantial effort in establishing its brand among Chinese consumers.[65]

IBM saw China as a potential source of technology, made substantial donations of software and computer equipment to Chinese universities, and formed a partnership with the Chinese national education system.[66] These investments would serve to stimulate demand for IBM's products and services but would also attract potential employees and create opportunities for cooperative research. In 1995, IBM established the China Research Laboratory (CRL) in Shangdi in the Northwest of Beijing, one of IBM's eight major research laboratories around the world. The CRL was IBM's first research laboratory in a developing country.[67]

IBM planned a shift in its China marketing strategy to a focus on the rapidly growing software sector. IBM had based most of its activities on hardware manufacturing but it was the leading software company in China, with a market share of over 6 percent.[68] The CEO and Chairman of the IBM Greater China Group, Henry Chow, said: "The rest of the world has grown to a point where software and services exceed 50%, 55%, even 60% of the market . . . But if you look at the China market, probably around 65% to 70% is hardware, although that percentage is coming down." The move echoed IBM's global strategy, which included a worldwide shift toward software and services. Chow continued: "I see that my role is to integrate IBM China into the global IBM, to leverage some of the competitive advantages of China."[69]

Evolution of Lenovo's international strategy

The Chinese economy had passed that of Japan to become the world's second largest market for computers, and with China's accession to the WTO competition from both foreign and domestic computer makers would intensify further. Dell and IBM were the largest foreign firms in the Chinese market and were seeking ways to expand their market shares. Lenovo would have to find ways to defend its home market and to address the challenges posed by international competitors. Lenovo's managers reviewed the company's goals, competitive strategy, and organizational structure.

There were two major alternatives, other than abandoning the PC market altogether or seeking to be acquired. Lenovo could *stay the course* that it had followed since its founding, by focusing on the Chinese market and defending its domestic market position against incursions from other Chinese manufacturers and international competitors. Alternatively, it could *expand internationally*, by developing its marketing and sales outside China, launching its brand in international markets, and seeking alliances with foreign partners. In 2000, Lenovo chose to expand internationally.

Intense competition with international companies for the home and business computer market lay ahead. The company's domestic distribution system had provided a competitive advantage but faced challenges from direct sales over the telephone and over the Internet. The costs of R&D, distribution, and development of the company's brand would potentially affect Lenovo's profit margins in the years to come. The company's pricing strategy of staying above domestic competitors and below international rivals was under pressure as the price of components continued to fall and as international firms built production facilities in China.

Lenovo did not sell the cheapest computers, but instead relied on having a brand that was well known domestically and represented high quality. The computers featured the latest Intel processors and up-to-date software from IBM and Microsoft. As Ma stated: "We don't want to establish Legend as a brand of cheaper, lower quality."[70] In its domestic market, Lenovo faced competitive pressures from lower-priced domestic brands and higher-priced global brands. As Yang Yuanqing said: "We're not interested in waging a price war at the cost of profits."[71]

In 2000, when Yang became CEO of Lenovo Group, he noted that: "We are adapting ourselves to unfavorable conditions in the market. We have prepared ourselves for springtime."[72] He identified international expansion as a major goal for Lenovo. This required reaching beyond the company's traditional computer markets into IT markets in other countries. Overall, Lenovo would attempt to become a leading international IT provider. The company's managers faced the difficult task of building on Lenovo's domestic success while providing a launching pad for international growth.

Yang observed that:

the Group's traditional personal computer business continued to record remarkable growth, and our corporate IT and consumer IT businesses continued to sustain significant rises in operating profit. Our advances in technology and value-added services have also helped us to achieve important breakthroughs in our newly developed businesses.[73]

However, Yang's strategy was ambitious: "We want to take ourselves to an international scale, to the scale of a world first-class enterprise."[74] As Yang formulated the company's international strategy, he planned to carefully target markets with particular products with a five–ten-year progressive roll out: "We won't invest rashly abroad on a large scale."[75]

International expansion would require creating a global brand; as Yang said: "Our goal is to become a famous international brand."[76] The company's first step was to change its brand name in English from Legend to Lenovo. The company's Chinese brand, Lian Xiang, which means "imagination," would remain the same. Yang later observed that:

Having made reference to the successful experience of well-known international brands, we decided to choose a single branding structure, which would facilitate us to concentrate our resources on the accumulation of our brand value . . . We believe this would greatly enhance the brand image of Legend and pave the way for our brighter future.

The new name is a combination of the old brand name of Legend and the Latin word "novo," representing innovation and renewal.[77] The existing brand name of Legend would have posed a barrier to international expansion because other companies in many other countries were already using the name as a registered trademark. As Yang stated: "We had no choice."[78] The new brand name clearly signaled the decision to develop an international presence.

The company identified a number of strategies for achieving these goals. It would continue to serve the IT market in China, while considering how to expand abroad. It would seek to further strengthen Lenovo's brand image with a series of new product introductions, and would devote R&D investment to creating high-margin IT products and Internet-related products and services. International expansion would entail developing international distribution channels and incurring substantial marketing and sales costs. The company would have much to learn about customers outside its home market.

Lenovo's global expansion began with a move into Hong Kong, with plans to enter the US in the next five–ten years and Europe after that.[79] Yang cautioned: "To go straight into the US market – in this industry, the four major brands, HP, IBM, Dell, Gateway, they are all there, they cast their big shadows there, so this may not be your best market."[80] The company faced the challenge of devoting resources to international expansion while simultaneously competing with entry in its home market.

Arguably, Lenovo's most powerful attributes in China were distribution and service networks. To expand successfully outside its domestic market, the company would need to address international distribution. One approach would be to acquire foreign companies with distribution capabilities, while another would be to rely on wholesalers and retailers for distribution. Lenovo's CFO Ma noted these options: "Acquisition is one of the possibilities and hopefully we can go through other people's distribution channels, or partnerships."[81] Another would be to emulate the direct-sales approach that Dell employed so effectively. The company would need to compare the costs and benefits of alternative distribution channels.

In order to stay competitive with the technology of foreign competitors, Lenovo planned to increase its spending of revenue on R&D from 1.8 percent to somewhere in the range of 3–5 percent.[82] Lenovo viewed its ability to tailor IT products to the needs of Chinese consumers as one of its core competencies.[83] The company was a fast follower in applying product innovation incorporating technological innovations, and the company also explored contracts and partnerships with innovative international computer companies to access particular necessary technologies.

Product development was essential if the company was to apply its new Lenovo brand and address the needs of consumers and businesses outside China. Half of the company's home-PC sales in China during 2002 were of their "dual mode" PCs.[84] These were multi-functional in that they allowed users to skip the desktop screen and instead go directly to a screen display for an audio player or a movie player. Such products could prove attractive to consumers in many other countries.

Expansion abroad would also require marketing expenditures to promote the Lenovo brand: managers would need to weigh the investment costs of developing the brand against the potential returns. The company would need to invest in identified target countries and learn about customers and competitors outside its traditional domestic market. Managers would also have to evaluate whether their products were suited to customer needs in developing and developed economies, and whether the company should focus on specific geographic regions.

Substantial expansion of sales abroad would have the advantage of lowering unit production costs if the company could take advantage of economies of scale, particularly in manufacturing. Moreover, production in China would result in labor cost savings that could provide advantages in international markets. However, the company would have to balance these cost economies against the high cost of transportation. Cost economies would also need to be balanced against the potential advantages of locating product design and manufacturing close to customers.

These cost trade-offs existed even within the Chinese market. In July 2003, Lenovo opened a US$7.23 million computer manufacturing plant in Pudong, with the capacity to assemble 1.5 million desktop units and 360,000 laptops. The plant added to the company's manufacturing facilities in Beijing and Huiyang, Guangdong Province. According to Yang: "The plant's setup marks a complete supply chain for Lenovo in Shanghai, including research and development, manufacturing and a marketing network." The plant could serve both the domestic Chinese market and the export market since it was located in the Jinqiao Export Processing Zone. Although the costs of land and labor in Shanghai were the highest in China, the advantages of the plant's location was proximity to larger markets, since Lenovo made about a quarter of its sales in east China. Yang observed that the plant "will bring us big profits from economies of scale." In evaluating the relative costs of manufacturing in Shanghai, where the costs of renting industrial space (1.1 yuan per m^2 per day) are multiples of lower-cost alternatives, Yang noted that: "The priority of our strategy is to produce close to our market. We believe the lower transportation costs for product delivery will offset the increase in other sectors."[85]

Another advantage of producing in Shanghai was the ability to cooperate with international partners. By manufacturing notebook computers in Shanghai, Lenovo planned to work with Taiwanese partners First International Computer, MiTAC, Compal, and Acer, who had advantages in R&D and chip design. Yang noted that: "Legend will use the new assembly plant in Shanghai as a strong foothold from which to develop the market with Taiwan partners."[86]

Competition in the Chinese market for notebook computers intensified. Lenovo and international companies such as Dell, IBM, Sony, and Toshiba maintained or increased their market shares. Matsushita began to produce notebook computers in its factory in Xiamen, Fujian Province. Domestic companies such as Great Wall, Langchao, and Hisense left the notebook market.[87]

To strengthen its R&D and software capabilities, Lenovo partnered with many international companies including HP, IBM, Intel, Microsoft, Siemens, and Toshiba. Lenovo's partnerships, particularly with Intel and Microsoft, provided much-needed access to R&D as well as funds for marketing. In 2001, Lenovo entered into a US$200 million joint venture with AOL Time Warner that involved bundling AOL's Internet services with Lenovo's computers and use of Lenovo's websites. Lenovo's Ma said that Lenovo wanted to have a strong partner when China joined the WTO.[88]

Lenovo launched its "Legend World" technology convention in 2002, the first Chinese IT company to host such an international convention. The conference was attended by the full range of international IT firms, including Intel, Microsoft, Oracle, and Texas Instruments. The meeting was intended to give IT companies in China greater access to international technology while providing greater information about the Chinese market to international companies. Lenovo introduced its concept of "collaborating applications" that allowed different consumer, commercial, and corporate IT products to work together, reflecting Yang's vision of technological innovation and the company's technology strategy in relation to developing global IT standards.[89]

Lenovo, through its Technologies Development Company, contracted with IBM, Lotus, Microsoft, and Oracle to act as their software dealers.[90] Lenovo signed a deal with Microsoft to develop set-top boxes that allow users to access the Internet and email through their television and telephone. The low-cost boxes would use Microsoft's Venus operating system, a Chinese-language version of its Windows software.[91] Lenovo agreed to jointly develop software with Computer Associates. In cooperation with Toshiba, Lenovo established a marketing college, with training sessions to be conducted in Beijing, Shanghai, Guangzhou, and Chengdu to train technicians and sales personnel from Lenovo, Intel, and Toshiba.[92]

Lenovo entered into a number of manufacturing agreements. The company contracted to manufacture HP's Inkjet printer. Lenovo's contractual alliance with Siemens involved production of Siemens computers in Lenovo's Huiyang plant: Siemens was the leading PC seller in Germany and one of the top ten worldwide, and the companies planned long-term cooperation in production, research, development, and marketing.[93] Other global entrants found local partners: HP partnered with the Stone Group and the Star Group, IBM partnered with Great Wall, and Toshiba with Tontru.[94]

In 2003 Lenovo formed the Digital Home Working Group with sixteen other companies (Fujitsu, Gateway, HP, IBM, Intel, Kenwood, Matsushita Electric/Panasonic, Microsoft, NEC CustomTechnica, Nokia, Philips, Samsung, Sharp, Sony, STMicroelectronics, and Thomson). The working group would attempt to standardize formats for digital equipment to give their consumers interoperability between their devices – including, for example, Lenovo PCs and Nokia phones. The working group also sought to develop products that could share information, allowing customers to have a networked household. Devices would share digital content such as music, photos, and video. In addition, the working group would share some types of marketing costs. The working group strengthened Lenovo's lines of communication with international companies, improved its access to technology, and enhanced its international brand recognition.

The IBM acquisition

The IBM acquisition represented a rapid acceleration of Lenovo's plans for international expansion:

- What were the strategic motivations for the acquisition?
- What were the potential complementarities between Lenovo and IBM's computer business?
- What obstacles lay ahead for the company?

By divesting its PC business, which required high volume and economies of scale, IBM could concentrate its efforts on R&D and the high-end corporate market. Also, according to a filing before the US SEC, IBM's personal computing division had steadily made losses for the three and a half years preceding the sale to Lenovo: $397 million in 2001, $171 million in 2002, $258 million in 2003, and $139 million in the first six months of 2004, on total sales of about $34 billion over the period.[95] Although IBM gained from the sale and divestiture of an unprofitable business unit, what would be the benefits for Lenovo in acquiring the PC division?

Lenovo stood to gain scale from the acquisition, potentially adding IBM's $10 million in annual sales. IBM already manufactured its ThinkPad laptops outside the US, see table 7.5. By consolidating some production of the combined company in China, particularly assembly, Lenovo might benefit from economies of scale in manufacturing. By consolidating purchasing of components with its own sourcing, Lenovo could reduce the transaction costs of procurement. Through standardization of parts and price concessions from suppliers receiving a greater volume of orders, Lenovo could reduce procurement costs. Joint management of the supply chains for the combined company might improve productive efficiency and reduce logistics costs. To achieve these gains, Lenovo would need to effectively integrate its worldwide manufacturing and component sourcing activities.

The acquisition potentially offered marketing synergies. Lenovo increased its world market share from 2.3 percent to 8.3 percent, as against Dell's 18 percent and HP's 16 percent, edging out Acer, Apple, Fujitsu, Gateway, NEC, and Toshiba.[96] Lenovo would gain access to US and European markets for its products, such as multimedia PCs, by employing the knowledge of former IBM employees concerning consumer preferences, marketing techniques, and sales distribution channels. At the same time, Lenovo could apply its Chinese distribution network and knowledge of Chinese consumer preferences to market and sell IBM laptop ThinkPads and ThinkCenter desktop PCs. The

Table 7.5. The components for an IBM ThinkPad X31 that sells for $2,349 (2004)

Input	Location	Manufacturers	Approximate cost
Assembly	Mexico	IBM	NA
Memory	S. Korea	10 manufacturers	512 megabytes $60
Case and keyboard	Thailand	NA	$50
Wireless card	Malaysia	Intel	$15–$20
Battery	Asia	NA	$40–$50
Display screen	S. Korea	Samsung and LG Philips	15-in $200 17-in $300
Graphics controller chip	Canada and Taiwan	ATI and TSMC	$30–$100
Microprocessor	US	Intel	Centrino chip $275–$500
Hard drive	Thailand	NA	$1.50–$2.00 a gigabyte (typical drive 40 gigabytes)

Source: Barbosa, *New York Times*, 2004, *ibid.*

company would need to coordinate its international sales and distribution efforts, integrating the IBM business with its Chinese business. Combining IBM's Chinese business with Lenovo's domestic distribution would likely prove straightforward. However, outside China, growing the business might present substantial difficulties, given IBM's prior concentration on business customers and Lenovo's combination of consumer and business sales.

Lenovo gained the use of IBM's brand name, and would use it for the ThinkPad and ThinkCenter PCs for up to five years. This would ease Lenovo's entry into the international market place where IBM's brand was well known. By associating Lenovo's brand with that of IBM, the company would improve recognition for its own brand; this would reduce the marketing costs required to launch a new brand. The challenge would be to hold on to customers who had purchased IBM's ThinkPad as a high-end laptop. Lenovo would have to weigh the effect on IBM's former customers of changes in marketing, product design, and types of components.

In addition to IBM's products, Lenovo stood to benefit from IBM's technological knowledge in two ways. First, Lenovo would obtain the technology owned by IBM's PC division. This included the design of the ThinkPad laptop, which would prove useful given the shift toward mobile computing in PC markets. Second, Lenovo would gain from the technical knowledge of IBM's computer division employees. In addition, Lenovo's existing technological partnership with IBM would be potentially enhanced and lead to cooperative R&D and other JVs.

Yang Yuanqing relinquished the post of CEO and became Lenovo's Chairman. Initially, Stephen M. Ward, Jr., the senior vice president and general manager of IBM's Personal Systems Group, was named CEO of Lenovo. The new company retained top IBM managers, placing them in leading positions. The company would be headquartered in the US but Lenovo would benefit from the knowledge and experience of the managers and employees of IBM's PC division. IBM had over 10,000 employees with about 2,500 in the US and the rest working abroad, about 4,200 of whom were already working in China. These employees would join Lenovo's 9,000 employees and would bring distinct and complementary technology skills. IBM employees would also bring experience in managing an international business and operating in developed economies. Training and international teamwork would be needed for Lenovo to effectively transfer the skills of IBM's employees across the company.

The acquisition of IBM's PC division also represented a partnership with the parent company. IBM had agreed to provide customer service, financing, and leasing. IBM would also have an 18.9 percent share of Lenovo. This meant that IBM would have an interest in Lenovo's success and would be likely to partner with the company in other areas, including R&D. Lenovo could partner with IBM in serving large businesses and government agencies in China; both Lenovo and IBM already served such businesses and agencies, and there were clear benefits from partnering in those efforts. IBM had extensive experience in serving corporate and government customers and offered products and services for large-scale customers. Lenovo brought connections and knowledge of corporate and government customers in China. In July 2003, Samuel J. Palmisano, IBM's CEO, approached a senior official in the Chinese government, seeking approval for the potential sale of its PC unit to Lenovo. Such approval was desirable not simply because Lenovo was partly owned by the Chinese government; it also provided the basis of a partnership between IBM and the Chinese government that could potentially translate into corporate and government sales. Although there was no specific deal, Palmisano observed: "It's a much more subtle, more sophisticated approach. It is that if you become ingrained in their agenda and become truly local and help them advance, then your opportunities are enlarged."[97]

After the IBM acquisition, William J. Amelio moved from Dell to the Lenevo Group, to become the company's president and CEO. Amelio had been Dell's senior vice president for strategy and operations in Asia-Pacific and Japan. Prior to joining Dell, Amelio held senior management positions at NCR, Honeywell, and Allied Signal. He had previously worked for IBM for almost eighteen years and for a time had managed worldwide operations for IBM's PC division. Amelio said: "I am very excited to lead this ground breaking global enterprise."[98] Yang Yuanqing noted: "With our integration of IBM's PC Division on track and our organizational integration complete, we are accelerating our planning for our next phase of growth . . . Bill Amelio's combined experience – in our industry, in emerging and mature markets, in senior operational roles and with IBM – gives him the perfect profile to lead Lenovo from the important stability we have achieved in the first phase of our integration, to the profitable growth and efficiency improvement to which we are committed in our next phase."[99]

Overview

Lenovo's acquisition of IBM's PC division set the stage for the company's entry into global competition. However, the challenges confronting Lenovo were only just beginning. One difficulty would be integrating the organizations of the two companies. Lenovo had concentrated its efforts in China before the acquisition; the company moved its headquarters to the US, first to Purchase, New York and then to Raleigh, North Carolina. Now, the company would need to coordinate its international managers and employees in the US and China. They would face the challenge of integrating diverse corporate cultures that many companies with cross-border mergers have encountered.

Lenovo's experience illustrates the importance of the home country for an international company. In addition, Lenovo's merger presents a rare instance of a global company changing its headquarters to take advantage of technology, management, and customer relationships in another country. With a strong presence in both countries, the company would derive significant production and sales advantages. At the same time, the company would need to synchronize its executive offices in Raleigh, Beijing, and Singapore.

Lenovo had successfully defended its domestic market against both local competitors and global players. Now, the company would need to take on the global competitors in head-to-head competition in many markets. The company would have to make a smooth transition from a domestic powerhouse to a global company. Although IBM's PC unit had served global customers, Lenovo would need to adapt to operating in over sixty customer countries.

Another difficulty would be integrating the product lines of the two companies: the high-end IBM ThinkPad would complement the existing computer products offered by Lenovo as well as the company's other electronics products. The company would have to integrate its manufacturing operations, which would be facilitated as IBM's PC unit already had manufacturing facilities in China. The company's manufacturing was concentrated in China, with manufacturing centers in Shenzhen, Xiamen, Beijing, Shanghai, and Huiyang, with another center in Pondicherry, India.

The combined company faced considerable opportunities to enhance its purchasing power by combining its procurement of computer components. The merger offered significant complementarities in marketing, sales, manufacturing, and technology, but achieving those benefits would require substantial integration and coordination of the company's activities across many countries.

Lenovo faced the difficult and costly task of transforming a domestic brand into a global brand. Acquiring the ThinkPad brand provided instant recognition, especially in developed economies. Although Lenovo could use the IBM label for five years, it chose instead to begin promoting its Lenovo brand as soon as possible. Almost immediately, the company's advertising and marketing avoided mentioning IBM, although IBM still appeared on the ThinkPad. Deepak Advani, the chief marketing officer of Lenovo, stated that in computers: "there is a tight association between the company and the product, so we have to make sure it is clear that it is really Lenovo selling it to you, and not IBM."[100]

By acquiring IBM's PC division, Lenovo heightened its rivalry with Dell and HP. The company would need to address the cost efficiencies of Dell's direct-sales model and HP's strong consumer retail sales in the US and Europe. Computer prices continued to drop and other competitors were expanding their international activities. Fujitsu–Siemens, the leading computer company in Europe, offered both consumer and corporate IT products, drawing on the strengths of its two large parent companies. Japan's Toshiba would continue to build on its strengths as a large diversified electronics company with expertise in mobile computing, design and manufacturing of components, and industrial electronics. Taiwan's Acer had significant experience in global operations. Building on its position as the leading laptop computer seller, Acer planned to expand its sales in the US and China. Although Lenovo had become the third-largest PC company in the world, in many ways the company's entry into international competition was only just beginning.

8   Cemex: making global markets

Lorenzo Zambrano, Chairman and CEO of Cementos Mexicanos (Cemex), once observed that "we had to become an international company to survive."[1] From its home country, Mexico, Cemex created an international business by extensive acquisition of other cement companies, construction of capacity, and international sourcing from independents. Extending its operations from emerging markets to developed economies, Cemex was rated as one of the most admired companies in the world.[2] The company sought to reduce volatility of earnings by pooling risk across a wide range of geographic markets, in the Americas, Europe, Asia, Africa, and the Middle East. To Zambrano: "It is standard portfolio theory."[3] For the long term, Zambrano's objective was to ensure that no one market would account for more than one-third of its business, to find new markets with significant and rapidly growing demand.[4] As a result of its many acquisitions and geographic diversification, the company faced high debt, significant currency risk, many sources of market demand risk, and various types of supply-side risk.[5] The company's strategy of delivering value as a global producer and market maker would be tested to the full.

Cemex and the Mexican market for cement

Cemex was created in 1931 through the merger of Cementos Hidalgo, founded in 1906, and Cementos Monterrey, founded in 1920.[6] Growth through acquisition and plant construction was significant in the postwar period and by the mid-1970s the company had achieved a national presence and become the country's leading cement producer.[7] Acquisitions of rivals in its home country continued apace well into the 1980s, a period characterized by trade liberalization,[8] culminating in the purchase in 1989 of Mexico's second largest producer, Cementos Tolteca. Early consolidation in the Mexican cement industry enabled Cemex, then only a local business, to become one of the ten largest cement companies in the world. That period also saw Cemex integrating forward and beginning to acquire or set up ready-mix concrete firms.[9]

In line with other developing markets, the Mexican cement business was largely a "retail" operation, with cement being dispatched in bags to resellers (retailers) who then sold on to "do-it-yourself" buyers and small contractors. The bulkiness, fast turnover, and short shelf life of the product led producers to set up extensive distribution networks, reaching far "down the trade" via direct-from-plant deliveries and distribution terminals. Cemex sold to as many as 6,000 resellers. Only a small portion of the business was shipped in bulk to large buyers, such as ready-mix concrete firms (including Cemex's own), large construction firms, and producers of concrete aggregates (such as concrete blocks, roof tiles and precast concrete products).

Cemex's Mexican operations were highly profitable. This was due, in part, to Cemex's pricing power in its home country. According to the *Wall Street Journal*: "Cemex's cement prices in Mexico are the highest found in any major market around the globe."[10] Despite the removal of trade barriers from the late 1980s, domestic cement producers benefited from Mexico's rugged terrain and the fact that its main consumer markets were far removed from both the East and West coasts, making the penetration of cement imports more difficult. When it was already the market leader in Mexico, Cemex merged with the number two cement producer, Cementos Tolteca, thus gaining additional domestic market share without encountering antitrust restrictions.[11] Cemex also believed that by investing in logistics and superior customer service it could sustain its home country profits. In 2003, following a decade of international acquisitions, Mexico still contributed 70 percent of the company's profits, although it accounted for just 37 percent of sales.[12]

Cemex's international expansion

Cemex rapidly grew into the largest cement company in the Americas and the third largest worldwide, behind Lafarge of France and Holcim of Switzerland. By 2004 the company had reached a productive capacity of 97 million metric tons (mt), distributed across twenty nations in the Americas, Europe, and Asia, and sold directly to customers in more than fifty countries. Headquartered in Monterrey, Mexico, it was a market leader in Mexico, the US, Spain, Venezuela, Panama, and the Dominican Republic, and enjoyed significant market share in numerous other countries. The company was not only a major manufacturer and distributor of cement and its intermediate clinker (the main component of cement), but also of specialty cement-based products (concrete aggregates), ready-mix concrete, and gravel, among other products.[13]

Cemex's stock first began to be traded on the Mexican Stock Exchange in 1976. That same year, the company starting exporting its products, primarily in response to tight capacity in its northern neighbor, the US. Cemex's American Depositary Shares (ADS) began trading on the NYSE in 1999.

Despite some opportunistic foreign venturing in the form of exports, Cemex was essentially a local company in 1985, when Lorenzo Zambrano became CEO. Under Zambrano, who is both an engineer and an MBA, Cemex embarked on a series of international acquisitions. Cemex expanded its international operations in part to compete effectively with other companies that were taking advantage of Mexico's removal of protectionist trade and investment barriers. In 1992, the company purchased the two largest cement producers in *Spain*: Valenciana and Sanson. Two years later, Cemex acquired Vencemos in *Venezuela*, Cemento Bayano in *Panama*, and the Balcones Plant in Texas, *US*. In 1995, Cemex bought Cementos Nacionales in the *Dominican Republic* and the next year acquired a major stake in Cementos Diamante and Cementos Samper in *Colombia*. Through purchases in 1997 and 1998, the company obtained a 70 percent interest in the *Philippine* company Rizal Cement. In 1998, Cemex purchased a minority interest in PT Semen Gresik, the largest cement maker in *Indonesia*. In 1999, the company purchased APO Cement in the *Philippines* and the *Costa Rican* company Cementos del Pacifico. Also in 1999, Cemex ventured into Africa, snapping up Assiut Cement, one of *Egypt's* leading producers. In 2000, Cemex entered a distributorship agreement with Universe Cement of *Taiwan*, and began the construction of a grinding mill in *Bangladesh*, to process clinker imported primarily from the company's fully integrated cement plants located elsewhere in the region.

Arguably the company's boldest foreign acquisition was formalized in late 2000, with the purchase of *US*-based Southdown, Inc., promoting Cemex to the position of largest cement producer in North America. The two following years saw acquisitions in *Thailand* (Saraburi Cement, in 2001) and in the *Caribbean* (Puerto Rican Cement, in 2002). In 2005, in another bold move, Cemex acquired the British-based RMC Group, a large building materials supplier (including ready-mix concrete and concrete aggregates) with assets across both important developed markets (such as the *UK*, the *US*, and *Germany*) and growth markets (Eastern European countries such as *Poland*, *Hungary*, and the *Czech Republic*).

As a result of its acquisitions in Mexico and abroad, around four-fifths of its total productive capacity was purchased rather than constructed. Cemex's major intermediate holding companies, its key subsidiaries, and ownership in these

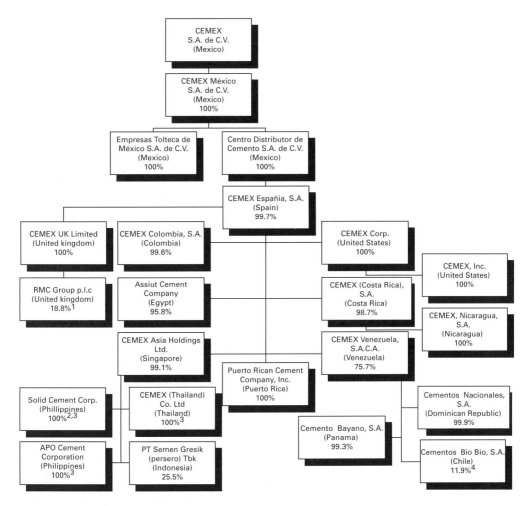

1 Represents the 50 million RMC shares acquired by CEMEX UK Limited on September 27, 2004. On March 1, 2004, CEMEX UK Limited acquired the remaining 81.2% of RMC's shares.

2 Formerly, Rizal Cement Co. Inc. Includes CEMEX Asia Holdings' 70% economic interest and a 30% economic interest held by a wholly-owned subsidiary of CEMEX España, S.A.

3 Represents CEMEX Asia Holdings' indirectr economic interest

4 Sold April 26, 2005.

Fig. 8.1 Cemex's corporate structure as of December 31, 2004
Source: 2004 20-F.

subsidiaries are shown in figure 8.1. In 2004, prior to the acquisition of RMC, sales by region were 60 percent in North America, 15 percent in South America and the Caribbean, 20 percent in Europe, and 5 percent in Asia, Africa, and the Middle East. The acquisition of RMC in 2005 balanced the distribution of sales across North America and Europe, with North America's share falling from 60 percent to around 40 percent and Europe's share rising from 20 percent to

Table 8.1. Cemex, company operations at the close of 2004

	% of total sales	% of total assets	Product. capacity mt/year	Cement plants owned/ min. part.	Ready-mix plants	Land distrib. centers	Marine terminals
Mexico	36	33	27.2	18	211	68	8
US	24	23	14.3	17	97	48	6
Spain	17	17	11.0	8	77	11	19
Venezuela	4	4	4.6	3	35	12	4
Colombia	3	5	4.8	5	22	2	0
CAC[a]	8	7	4.0	11	36	12	10
Egypt	2	3	4.9	1	3	4	1
Philippines	2	3	5.8	3	0	7	3
Indonesia	1	2	4.4	4	9	25	10
Thailand	0	1	0.7	1	0	0	0
Others	3	2	0.0	0	0	0	0
Total	**100**	**100**	**81.7**	**71**	**490**	**189**	**61**

Notes:
Does not include the effect of the RMC acquisition in 2005.
[a] Central America and Caribbean.
Source: Cemex *Annual Report* 2004.

approximately 45 percent. The importance of the company's home market would continue to shrink, with the RMC acquisition leading to a drop in Mexico's share of company sales from over one-third in 2004 to under one-fifth.[14]

With over four-fifths of sales abroad, Cemex was a leading example of the new class of Latin American companies called "*multilatinas*" that do not depend on government trade protection but instead seek growth abroad.[15] Somewhat protected in its highly lucrative home market, Cemex could well have focused all its energy on defending its internal operations. There were precedents for this; the Brazilian cement leader Votorantim Cimentos had focused on its home market until 2001, when it first ventured abroad. Instead, Cemex chose to pursue a global strategy. The company's geographic distribution of sales, assets, and other activities at the close of 2004 are listed in table 8.1.

Spain (1992)

Cemex's purchase of Valenciana and Sanson marked the company's first foray into international terrain. The company inaugurated its international investment strategy by acquiring *leading assets* (the two largest cement makers) in a country of some *cultural familiarity* (such as sharing a common language and having had a prior colonial relationship). Such a pattern was to be repeated over and over again. Spain was the largest and fastest-growing cement market in Europe. Spain's cement users acquired cement largely in bulk, with bagged shipments accounting for only around one-fifth of the market. This high proportion of bulk shipping stood in contrast to the Mexican market and was typical of a developed market.

Southdown, Inc. (2000)

Zambrano had stated countless times his ambition of propelling Cemex to the number one industry position in the Americas. The company's entry into the large country north of the Mexican border had initially been through the back door, via cement exports from Mexican plants with surplus capacity to US-based distributors (including a JV that Cemex entered into in 1986 with the US-based producer Southdown, Inc., which the partners dissolved a few years later[16]). Struggling against a backdrop of constrained domestic capacity and growing imports, US-based producers (Southdown, Inc. included) filed dumping charges against foreign suppliers, including Cemex, in an attempt to limit entry and sustain higher prices. The company's determination to establish a dominant position in the US remained unwavering. Following its 1994 acquisition of the Balcones Plant in Texas, in 2000 Cemex announced the acquisition of Southdown, Inc.

RMC Group (2005)

The acquisition of the RMC Group not only enabled Cemex to expand its presence in the US and Western Europe, but also catapulted the firm to prominence in Eastern Europe's growth markets. Cement producers commonly integrated forward to acquire or set up ready-mix concrete and other concrete distribution businesses. RMC was an unusual example of a building materials powerhouse whose origins lay downstream and that had integrated backward into cement, owning twenty-one cement plants. Cemex's successful bid represented, in some sense, the reestablishment of the typical forward-integration pattern. The $5.77 billion acquisition, the largest ever by a Mexican company, doubled Cemex's revenues and made it the world's largest maker of concrete, more than tripling its number of ready-mix facilities. It also quadrupled Cemex's aggregates business. However, investors were concerned by the debt the company had to take on to finance the deal, and by the hefty premium paid over the preceding period's share price. CEO Zambrano sought to reassure the financial markets by vowing to "be quiet for the next year to year-and-a-half" in order to bring debt levels back to where they had been prior to the RMC acquisition.[17]

Brazil: not in sight?

While Cemex's acquisition of Southdown, Inc. was conceivably a reaction to growing protectionism in the US, a move which Jagdish Bhagwati first called "*quid pro quo* FDI," the contrast with events in Brazil was intriguing.[18] Cemex's absence from the Brazilian cement industry remained a puzzle. Brazil was Latin America's largest cement market and its vast housing deficit and infrastructure needs suggested tremendous growth potential. In a similar vein to Cemex's initial entry strategy into the US some decades earlier, around the mid-1990s Cemex began to supply some markets in the North and the Northeast of Brazil from its plants based in Venezuela and Mexico. Following successful lobbying by domestic producers, Brazil's government enacted antidumping measures directed against specific exporters such as Cemex.

Following the US experience, and given Brazil's physical and cultural proximity to the company's home country, Mexico, one might have expected to see renewed determination on Cemex's part. But the company appeared to retreat. Cemex was unable – or chose not – to grab any of the numerous and attractive productive assets that exchanged hands in the second half of the 1990s. By contrast, among the list of active buyers were Cemex's global rivals Lafarge and Holcim, already experienced players in Brazil, in addition to the market leader Votorantim Cimentos. Industry observers would ponder, upon every round of the spate of cement mergers, at the absence of Cemex. Even Portugal-based Cimpor, a so-called "second-tier" multinational cement producer with no previous activity in Brazil, was able to acquire strategically placed cement plants (first in 1997, and then in 1999).[19]

The international cement industry

Operations

Cement is produced largely from limestone and clay in a weight proportion of roughly 5:1. The mixture is burned (calcinated) at a very high temperature in a rotary kiln producing cement *clinker*. The clinker pellets – once cooled – are then ground and mixed with a retarding agent (gypsum) and varying types of additives to form different formulations of cement. These different types of cement, however, are substitutes in most types of user applications. Moreover, each type of cement must conform to legislation that specifies its (physical and chemical) properties. Thus, product differentiation based on formulation is limited. Product differentiation by branding is also limited, particularly among large, better-informed buyers.

Cement plants can be of two types. Fully integrated plants comprise a clinker-producing kiln and a grinding mill. These integrated facilities can require vast capital outlays (as much as $200 per ton of capacity), tied up in the kiln, the largest single piece of industrial equipment in the world. The second type of plant consists of a grinding operation only, sourcing clinker from a fully integrated plant located elsewhere (internal to the company, or purchased from other producers). Such capital considerations typically lead producers attempting to enter markets to pursue a two-step strategy:

1 Begin by setting up relatively inexpensive grinding and distribution operations, sourcing clinker from outside the plant
2 Subsequently, adding clinker capacity by investing in a kiln, resulting in an integrated plant.

Barriers to entry are further compounded by an integrated plant's need to access reserves in close proximity to a limestone quarry,[20] and to meet its huge energy requirements (fossil fuel for the kiln and electricity for grinding).

The low value of cement in relation to its weight also makes the business highly dependent on logistics. While transportation by road, and to a lesser extent by rail, is very costly, the development of specialized waterborne handling and transportation equipment beginning in the 1970s made feasible the ocean shipping of cement (clinker) over vast distances.[21] Such developments in the international shipping of cement were to transform the face of the global cement industry, as discussed further below.

Increased returns to scale also affected the competitive landscape. The energy price shocks of the 1970s had led the industry to convert over the following decades from the "wet" process kiln system – which required huge amounts of energy to evaporate water – to the "dry" system. With the energy crisis in the foreground, companies had incentives to invest in larger-scale, more energy-efficient kilns. Maximum kiln capacity in the industry had been increasing steeply, see figure 8.2.

Other technological developments focused on preheating systems (which in turn enabled the construction of larger kilns) and grinding systems (with ball mills being replaced by vertical mills), with a view to further reducing

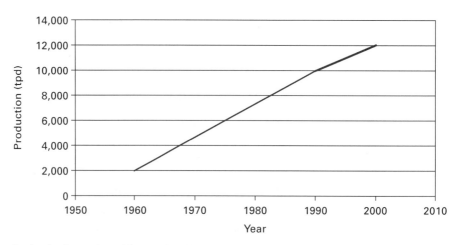

Fig. 8.2   Tendencies for maximum kiln capacity, 1950–2010
Note: tpd = Truck loads per day.
Source: Fuller Company, *World Cement*, January 2000.

energy consumption and addressing environmental concerns.[22] Other areas of technological progress were control systems (computer-integrated manufacturing) and the use of alternative fuels, such as waste materials with residual heat content, including hazardous waste.

Process innovation in the cement industry was largely outsourced to a handful of equipment suppliers with global reach, such as ThyssenKrupp and FLSmidth. While cement producers worked closely with equipment suppliers, it was the latter that undertook process R&D for the cement industry. R&D spending by cement producers themselves was limited: operating at the forefront of cement-production technology, the Japanese cement producer Taiheiyo spent less than 1 percent of sales revenue on R&D. "Turn-key" plants could be ordered from suppliers, though the larger firms chose to be closely involved in the specification of plants and equipment. Nevertheless, access to production technology was not a differentiating factor between cement producers.[23] It is rather the way in which individual plants were *integrated into a distribution system* that enabled some cement firms to gain a competitive edge. Cemex would pursue international competitive advantage through the design of its supply chain, its distribution network, and through its market making activities.

Consolidation of the global cement industry

World demand, estimated by Cembureau at 1,940 mt in 2003, had been growing at an annual rate of around 3 percent. Growth was concentrated in emerging markets – Asia, in particular – while demand in North America and Western Europe was growing slowly.

Since the mid-1980s, a significant process of consolidation had been running its course in the global cement industry. While family-run and state-owned firms[24] had been put up for sale, a few MNCs had been on a buying spree, aggressively moving into new markets or expanding in markets where they had previously operated. The combined production share (excluding China) of the world's six largest firms in 2000 was 35 percent, up from 23 percent in 1995 and 14 percent in 1985.[25]

Consolidation had occurred in waves. During the mid-to-late 1980s, several of the major European producers which were generating substantial cash flows, yet saw limited growth opportunities in their home markets, acquired firms in the US, where profits were under pressure owing to tight capacity stemming from environmental concerns and competition from imports. With the collapse of communism in the early 1990s and the privatization that ensued, there was a burst of acquisition activity in Eastern Europe. Attention then turned to Latin America, with one-third of total capacity changing ownership between 1994 and 1999. After the Asian financial crisis from 1998 onwards, many foreign-currency debt-laden Asian producers sold off their assets to the large global firms. There had also been significant consolidation within Europe; among the Mediterranean countries the combined capacity share of the six largest producers increased from 33 percent in 1993 to 48 percent in 2000. In France, for example, of the twenty firms operating in 1970, just four remained in 2000.

The international expansion of Cemex, with its first foreign acquisition taking place in 1992, thus began relatively late. Arguably, it was only after having expanded through acquisitions to a dominant position in the Mexican market that the company was in a position to expand abroad. Through its highly profitable Mexican operations, stemming in part from the high cement prices it was able to command, Cemex was able to attract the capital needed for its acquisitions through its high cash flow and guarantees offered to investors from expectations of continuing domestic cash flow.[26] The company's late start to expansion, let alone its developing market origin, made Cemex's rise to the top of the industry league, behind rivals Lafarge and Holcim, all the more fascinating.

Top global rivals: Lafarge and Holcim

Cemex's two main rivals, Lafarge and Holcim, had been international businesses for many decades. Lafarge had leapt ahead of Holcim in 2001 when it acquired the British-based producer Blue Circle, along with over 50 mt of cement capacity. Lafarge was also more diversified than Holcim, with a major presence in concrete (ready-mix and aggregates), and its Roofing and Gypsum divisions accounting for 20 percent of the group's sales.

Founded in 1833, Lafarge's first important international contract was in 1864 for a large shipment of lime to be used in the construction of the Suez Canal.[27] The company made its entry into the Americas with a manufacturing plant in Canada in 1956 and operations in Brazil several years later.[28] Lafarge became the leading building materials company, ranked first worldwide in cement, second in aggregates and concrete, and third in gypsum. Headquartered in Paris, the company employed 77,000 people in seventy-five countries.[29]

Holcim employed 61,000 in seventy countries. The company was founded in the Swiss village of Holderbank and was headquartered in Zurich, Switzerland.[30] Compared to Lafarge and Cemex, which exercised substantial control over regional operations from their global headquarters, Holcim's management structure was more decentralized.[31] Holcim's trading company managed from Madrid traded cement and clinker, while operating cement ships and floating terminals.[32] The company's corporate procurement department coordinated supplier relations worldwide, and the company operated regional procurement offices in Holderbank, Miami, and Singapore.[33]

Table 8.2 provides some statistics regarding the global industry's "Big Three." Lafarge had an annual cement production capacity of 175 mt distributed across 134 plants, followed by Holcim with 154 mt (129 plants), and Cemex with 97 mt (92 plants). Through the RMC acquisition, Cemex overtook Lafarge as the world's leading seller of ready-mix concrete, leaping from shipments of 24 million m³ to 75 million m³, now twice the size of Lafarge's ready-mix business.

In terms of geographic reach, the RMC acquisition raised the number of countries in which Cemex operated to fifty. Holcim's geographic sales distribution was the most even of the three: in relative terms, Lafarge was more dependent on Europe, at the expense of South America while Cemex was more dependent on North America, at the expense of Asia. Lafarge's overall profit margin, as measured by EBITDA, was the lowest of the three, in large part because of its product mix: concrete and aggregates were a lower-margin business as compared to cement. Cemex's acquisition of RMC, with its predominance in downstream businesses, would thus lead to a reduction in its EBITDA margin.

Table 8.2. The global industry's "Big Three" in 2004

	Lafarge	Holcim	Cemex[a]
Cement production capacity (mt/year)	175	154	82 (97)
Cement/clinker shipments (mt)	119	102	66 (80)
Aggregates shipments (mt)	234	104	37 (170)
Ready-mix concrete shipments (mill. m³)	37.0	29.3	23.9 (75.0)
No. of cement plants (incl. grind. only)	134	129	71 (92)
No. of ready-mix plants	1,105	763	490 (1,700)
Geographic reach			
Volume of cross-border trade (mt)	NA	17	10
No. of countries with operations	75	70	30 (50)
No. countries with trade relationships	NA	NA	60 (90)
Proportion of sales by region			
North America	27	21	60 (41)
South & Central America & Caribbean	4	18	15 (8)
Europe	47	37	20 (45)
Asia/Pacific	10	13	3 (3)
Africa & Middle East	12	11	2 (3)
EBITDA[b] Margin (%)	**21**	**27**	**31**

Notes:

[a] Figures for Cemex in brackets include the actual or estimated effect of the RMC acquisition in 2005.

[b] EBITDA = Earnings before interest, tax, depreciation, and amortization.

Source: Annual Reports; Quarterly Earnings Reports; Form 20-F submitted to the SEC; Cemex Fact Sheet ("Building the Future"); authors' calculations.

The Chinese market

The Chinese cement industry was vast, and unlike any other. Chinese production of cement, estimated by Cembureau at 863 mt in 2003, amounted to a staggering 44 percent of world cement production. China's production was directed almost exclusively to domestic consumption, which took 857 mt in 2003. As such, China's presence in the international trading of cement had so far been negligible.

The entry of international firms into China had also been timid. While both Lafarge and Holcim had set up JVs with domestic producers (notably with Shui On Cement in Southwest China, in the case of Lafarge, and with Huaxin Cement in Hubei Province, in the case of Holcim), Cemex's absence from the Chinese markets was conspicuous. Citing government interference in the form of price controls and an awkward tax system, CEO Zambrano summed up his company's absence to date from China: "The industry isn't profitable."[34] Though beginning to modernize, the Chinese industry was indeed a completely different animal. With a highly fragmented industry, the country was notorious for producing low-quality cement in energy-inefficient and environmentally unfriendly "backyard" mini-cement plants. In a 1999 report, Flemings Research estimated the number of producers in China at approximately 6,000, with the largest firm accounting for only 0.6 percent of nationwide production. Analysts were unanimous in pointing out that China's integration into the global cement industry would change the face of the industry.

Cemex and international market making

International trade in cement and clinker in 2000 amounted to 115 mt (7.1 percent of global cement consumption), of which 91 mt was seaborne. The high-fixed-cost, low-marginal-cost nature of the business, coupled with the typical demand fluctuations facing the industry, meant that shipping cement from markets with surplus capacity to markets where demand was outpacing supply could make economic sense, if only trade costs could be contained.

The rise of international trade in cement

During the 1970s, investments in cement shipping technology and facilities by traders (both producers and non-producers) led to rapidly declining seaborne transport costs. During the same decade, heavy import requirements in the Middle East had led a Saudi firm, in association with a Norwegian shipbuilder, to develop a new cement silo ship that could be used as a floating terminal. By 1987, forty-two cement vessels were in operation around the world, 62 percent of which were controlled by non-producing traders.[35]

The US typified the potential of cement imports from distant regions in disrupting competition in coastal markets. In the 1970s, capacity shortfalls led domestic producers to import cement and to invest in specialized terminals and handling equipment in deep-water ports. Independent ready-mix concrete firms, in a vulnerable bargaining position against producers, also organized themselves and began to import cement. By the mid-1980s, imports had captured a sizeable proportion (15–20 percent) of the US market. The setting up of trading networks and infrastructure proved irreversible. The rise of arbitrageurs in the global industry had permanently changed the competitive rationale in coastal markets such as Florida, California, and New York. Imports have remained high ever since, amounting to about one-quarter of domestic consumption in 2004.

While many cement producers around the world resisted the rise in international trade, others saw it as an opportunity. By the 1990s, with consolidation of the global industry already in full swing, the top cement producers were acquiring assets and taking leadership positions in the trading process. In 2000, Holcim's CEO, Thomas Schmidheiny, summed up his company's investment rationale:

We are looking for markets where we can supply into using our own marketing and trading organization. As an example we have recently bought into a plant in Azerbaijan. This market can also be supplied with cement and clinker from our plants in Russia. What we plan is a global network . . . In our view trading levels will grow.[36]

International market making by Cemex

Championing international trade was central to the emergence of Cemex on the world stage. The company became the archetypal example of the logistics-driven international cement business, bent on achieving greater capacity utilization over rivals and competing on service, with improved availability and shortened delivery times. An industry analyst commented on the company's strategy in 2000:

The company's worldwide cement distribution network allows Cemex to smooth demand and price fluctuations across its various markets and to take advantage of imbalances between capacity and demand in different parts of the world. Thus Cemex has been able to maintain high capacity utilization even when local markets are depressed, as has been true in Venezuela recently.[37]

Cemex became "one of the world's top traders of cement and clinker," trading more than 10 million tons in 2004.[38] Approximately 60 percent of this volume derived from Cemex's own production facilities around the world; the rest came through intermediation with third-party suppliers. According to Cemex: "our trading operations help us to optimize our worldwide production capacity, direct excess capacity to where it is most needed, and explore new markets without making significant initial capital investments." CEO Zambrano explained that: "[O]ur aim has been to create a diversified portfolio of high-growth cement assets and to do this we have to have a global reach complete with economies of scale and related synergies as well as benefiting from diversified economic cycles."[39]

Market makers help financial and commodity markets operate smoothly by standing ready to buy and sell. Market makers encourage sellers to participate in a product market because they know that they will be able to sell the good when they need to sell because of inventory, production, and business conditions. Firms that are market makers encourage buyers to participate in a product market because they know the good will be available when it is needed. Market makers earn returns by helping markets operate more efficiently, in contrast to a situation in which buyers and sellers deal directly with each other.[40]

By *standing ready to buy* cement on the world market, Cemex provided other producers and intermediaries with a distribution outlet for their output. For example, the 1998 economic downturn in Asia led to overcapacity and lower prices for cement there. Cemex took advantage of this situation to purchase low-cost cement from China for customers in California, improving profits by more than $10 million.[41] That year, the company also sourced from Bulgarian, English, Greek, Romanian, Russian, Thai, Tunisian, Turkish, and Ukrainian suppliers. Cemex carried out this arbitrage through its global presence and the resulting knowledge of both customer markets and sources of supply. Zambrano pointed out that: "You don't buy when you feel like it, but when someone else is selling."[42]

Cemex also *stood ready to sell* cement on the world market, finding additional buyers for its own output and developing outlets for its cement purchases. Cemex stood ready to serve other producers and distributors located in countries where Cemex did not own operations. In all, as table 8.2 shows, while Cemex ran operations in fifty countries in 2004, it "maintain[ed] trade relationships with approximately 90 nations."[43] The vision was that customers anywhere around the world, whether producers, distributors, or end users, could count on sufficient supplies to carry out construction projects. In planning its operations, Cemex intermediated between numerous suppliers and customers of cement. These suppliers and customers of cement could be either internal or external to the company: for example, cement plants owned by Cemex or by other producers, and ready-mix concrete operations owned by Cemex or by third parties. These suppliers and customers of cement could either be located in the same country or in different countries: see figure 8.3 for a depiction of Cemex's role in the value chain.

Cemex facilitated the movement of cement products by coordinating these various sources of supply and sources of demand. As already mentioned, by combining its production capability and relationships with outside suppliers, Cemex could move cement from markets with excess supply and meet

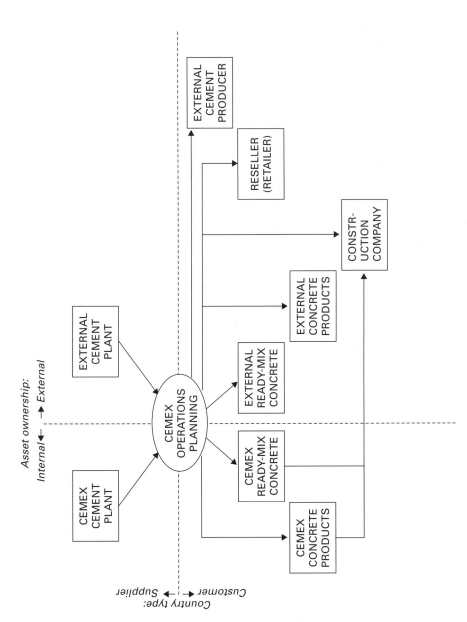

Fig. 8.3 Cemex's intermediation role in the value chain, by ownership, by country type

customers' needs in markets with excess demand. The company's reaction to the Asian crisis in 1998 provides an example: "In the wake of the Mexican peso devaluation, [Cemex] shipped cement and clinker from Mexico to the then-booming Asian economies. Today, however, [Cemex is] helping Asian trading partners to place their cement surpluses to meet North America's growing construction needs."[44] According to the company's *Annual Report* in 1998, Cemex's "market knowledge, flexibility and international trading infra-structure, [made it] one of the largest cement importers in the United States, accounting for over 20 percent of the country's imports."

Cemex's international trading provided additional management efficiencies. As a result of the company's trading activities, each of Cemex's internal operations would always be subject to passing a *market test*. For example, if an internal plant could not deliver cement to a given local market at a competitive cost, other Cemex plants or plants owned by other cement producers would be candidates for supplying that market. In explaining Cemex's capital budgeting process, Hector Medina, executive vice president for Planning & Finance, stated: "Operations compete against each other for [the] discretionary capital expenditure basket."[45]

The company's operations around the world gave it a trading presence in virtually every time zone. Its operations were organized into four regional groups – North America Region; Europe Region; Iberia, Middle East, Africa and Asia Region; South America and Caribbean Region – with an executive in charge of each. The president of the North America Region was also responsible for overseeing the company's Trading unit. The global reach of Cemex enabled it to profitably connect suppliers and customers across great distances; given the relatively low cost per weight of cement, this capability was critical to Cemex's role as an intermediary. "Because [Cemex] understand[s] the realities of the shipping business, [it] maintain[s] good relationships with suppliers and shippers; these relationships translate into lower costs."[46] Moreover, cost reductions also stemmed from "the centralization of [its] contracts with suppliers and the volume discounts that Cemex was able to negotiate from them."[47]

Cemex's Center for Logistical Operations (CLO) Division brought together the company's buyers and its sellers, both within countries and across national borders. The CLO was responsible for maintaining long-term distributor and end-user relationships, negotiating contracts, and informing other Cemex divisions of its customers' needs and contract terms and conditions. The CLO managed cross-border transactions, including purchasing and contracting, and carried out back-office processes (bills, invoices, orders, receipts, and payments).

The CLO Division processed orders, coordinated shipping, and executed delivery. The Order Processing unit took orders; revised the client's credit status; declared commitment to the client's order; generated invoice orders; informed clients in the event of consultations; and tailored service to the client's needs: restrictions and requirements in regard to capacity and unloading procedure, warehouse capacity and inventory status. The Shipping unit carried out shipping agreements with clients (external and internal); administered and monitored the client's inventories; adjusted shipping decisions based on trends, economic forecasts, and customers' consumption rates; generated shipping orders (allotment and procedures). The Shipping Execution unit received shipping orders; assigned transport (depending on product availability, cement's variable cost, and shipping capacity); monitored shipping performance and anticipated and solved execution problems.[48]

Cemex's focus on customer service

In the construction industry, customers placed a high value on timely delivery of products. Cemex used advanced IT to provide value added services to its customers. Cemex focused on optimizing its logistics system so that its delivery trucks were in the right place at the right time. The company's placement of cement factories and delivery networks ensured that it would be able to provide its products where demand for them was greatest.

By establishing an effective logistics system, Cemex delivered to customers with a high degree of reliability. Location of plants close to customers helped make supplies readily available for shipment. In Mexico, Cemex had many more plants than its nearest competitor. The plants were geographically dispersed, so that Cemex could efficiently supply most locations in Mexico with lower transportation costs than competitors. It replicated this advantage in many of its other markets; for example, it was the market leader in the US and Spain, and the second largest producer in the Philippines.

According to *BusinessWeek*: "Timing is of the essence in the cement business."[49] Construction companies could optimize construction plans to lower the variability in delivery time. They placed a premium on timely delivery to avoid construction delays. Early delivery was costly for customers as well, because of the space required for storage; early delivery also was costly for Cemex, because trucks would be tied up and there were added risks of inventory loss or spoilage.

Cemex used sophisticated techniques to ensure that it maintained a competitive advantage in timely delivery. The company studied the operations of Federal Express and the Houston 911 dispatch center. From Federal Express, Cemex learned the value to customers of guaranteed timely delivery. The 911 dispatch center showed Cemex that although individual calls are random, it was possible to forecast call patterns and have emergency vehicles ready to be dispatched.[50] Cemex used this knowledge and technology to develop a network that assured delivery within a 20-minute window in Mexico City, with much shorter lead times than competitors offered. This response time was often superior to the capabilities of Cemex's competitors in emerging markets. Cemex profited from providing timing flexibility, reliability, and precision for its customers.

Early on, Cemex adopted a high-technology strategy to lower transaction costs and at the same time provide a higher service level. According to one senior analyst: "not only is Cemex among the most technologically advanced companies in Latin America, it's one of the most advanced worldwide."[51] Cemex expanded its computer system to connect suppliers, distributors, and customers online. This innovation served a dual purpose: it increased efficiency, thereby substantially lowering costs; and it strengthened working relationships between Cemex and its customers and suppliers.[52]

The use of technology extended to Cemex's transportation and distribution network, increasing flexibility and further reducing transaction costs. Each truck in Mexico, for example, was equipped with a Global Positioning Satellite (GPS) unit, so all trucks were always accounted for and could be dispatched efficiently. The company used "dazzlingly complex computer systems to keep its fleet of trucks minutes away from customers in one of the world's most congested cities," giving it a profound service advantage at reduced cost.[53]

Whereas the company used to require long lead times and assessed penalties for changing orders, Cemex subsequently "resolved to embrace the complexity of the marketplace rather than resist it, to do business on the customer's terms, however zany those terms may be." The company eliminated many work rules for drivers so they could focus on satisfying customers. With respect to delivery operations in Mexico, Francisco Perez, Operations Manager, observed that:

Instead of delivering concrete, our people are delivering a service. They used to think of themselves as drivers. But anyone can deliver concrete. Now our people know that they're delivering a service that the competition cannot deliver.[54]

The emphasis on customer service and timely performance inspired comparisons with pizza delivery.[55] Pizzas are delivered when customers want them, not when delivery is convenient for the company. Pizzas are dispatched upon demand with short lead times.

Cemex faced the problem of sustaining its competitive advantage in customer service. The company attempted to understand the needs of its customers in a way that competitors did not. For example, Cemex's practice of offering delivery within a very narrow time frame showed both the company's transformation and its new customer focus. To the extent that Cemex had closer relationships with customers than its competitors, it gained an informational advantage over them. Second, Cemex embarked on a technological and logistical improvement path that was intended to outdistance rivals, particularly in the area of logistics. Finally, Cemex developed long-term relationships with suppliers and customers that could be difficult for competitors to replicate.

Cemex's computer system provided real-time information on inventory, delivery schedules, and quality records. The company's e-commerce site linked clients, suppliers, customs agents, and Cemex managers around the world, a system that allowed Cemex to anticipate costs and plan product shipments. Moreover, the company's information system shared information with customs agents concerning the status of arriving and departing shipments and of customs duties to be paid.[56]

The company's proprietary Internet-based system informed clients, such as distributors, not only when they should expect specific shipments but also the current location of the shipment as obtained from the GPS unit aboard each delivery truck. This assisted the client in planning the reselling or the cement-pouring process. Cemex could monitor client payment records and determine whether the customer had received shipments on time. By compiling the information gathered from customers and suppliers, Cemex provided them with value added services.

Knowledge transfer in Cemex's organization

Cemex's stated mission was "to meet the global building needs of its customers and build value for all stakeholders by becoming the world's most efficient and profitable multinational cement company." The company's success at improving efficiency was demonstrated by achieving higher cash flow margins than competitors. Cemex's initial expansion strategy took advantage of its knowledge of Mexico's cement industry to enter similar markets in other emerging economies.[57] Geographic diversification enabled the company to operate in multiple regions with different business cycles. The *Financial Times* reported in 1998 that Cemex was "the only Latin American company to feature in the world tables . . . In less than a decade, Cemex has turned from a local operator into the world's third largest cement producer."[58]

According to Cemex, the fundamentals that drove its business were management expertise, its core cement, ready-mix concrete, and aggregates base, and its low operating costs. In addition, the company emphasized its state-of-the-art management information systems and production technology; innovative and resourceful financial management and capital structure; and the company's experience in developing markets.[59] The company created proprietary IT to carry out these tasks.

Cemex's financial performance in the decade leading up to 2004 suggested the effectiveness of its strategy. Over that period, the company achieved compounded annual growth rates in sales and free cash flow of 15 percent and 19 percent, respectively. Between September 1999, when its shares were listed on the NYSE, and the end of 2004, Cemex's stock delivered a total compounded annual return in excess of 13 percent.[60] In September 2005, Cemex had a market capitalization value of $17.3 billion.

Cemex realized the importance of a supporting culture for its intermediation activities:

To become a truly world-class company, Cemex worked hard to break down geographic borders and cultural barriers. Cemex's people would need a multinational, multi cultural perspective to succeed in the global marketplace. Accordingly, the company brought together executives and employees from its offices all over the world to exchange ideas, present problems and discuss issues of concern to the entire organization.[61]

Within the company, Cemex successfully transferred knowledge acquired through international operations and acquisitions across the markets it served. For example, with regard to inventory management: "Southeast Asian suppliers look to Cemex because of its ability to manage cement supplies on a long-term basis across the globe." Cemex's "Dominican Republic [applied] the best practices from various Cemex subsidiaries to improve the warehouse area; bar code technology for inventory control (from Mexico); electronic remission for warehouse consumption (from Venezuela); and Spain's inventory replacement model."

Another example of fast knowledge transfer was the company's acquisition of Spain's Valenciana. In the early 1990s, Valenciana had figured out how to burn petroleum coke (pet coke), a relatively low-cost fuel, in its kilns. Cemex was quick to redeploy the technology across its plants and signed contracts for the long-term provision of pet coke from suppliers. By 2004, pet coke accounted for half of Cemex's fuel needs. According to Ben Ziesmer, an energy consultant and editor to the *Pace Petroleum Coke Quarterly*: "Cemex was the first cement company to use pet coke as a key strategy for gaining competitive advantage. They recognized it early, spread the use of pet coke throughout their organization, and others have started to follow." According to the *Wall Street Journal*, in an industry where individual plants traditionally ordered their own fuel supplies, Cemex's Houston subsidiary arranged for pet coke to be shipped to Cemex's plants around the world, even making a small profit on selling any surplus pet coke the company did not need.[62]

Cemex's IT was intended to

allow different business divisions to create "virtual communities," where they will have real-time access to their colleagues in similar departments around the world; to prices, business plans, news reports relevant to their business, and daily information on commodity prices that might affect their bottom line.

The company also used IT to provide accurate timing estimates for international shipments. Cemex's ships were tracked by computer, and their destinations could be adjusted *en route* as market conditions required. Cemex's IT also helped it to lower its international transaction costs. For example, when trading across borders, Cemex provided Internet-based software to communicate with its customs brokers so they could share data about inbound and outbound shipments. By exchanging such information in real time, Cemex minimized delays and complications in the customs-clearing process and lowered transaction costs. Cemex also used its head start in technology to improve the efficiency of its operations through better information flow and responsiveness to customers.

BusinessWeek noted that: "High technology has helped make [Cemex] one of the lowest-cost producers anywhere."[63] Cemex's size and presence in multiple emerging markets ensured that the company enjoyed economies of scale for its inputs. Upon acquiring assets, Cemex's foremost objective was to reduce input costs:

To turn around its acquisitions, Cemex stated that it pursues lower costs with a fervor that could come straight out of the top US business schools from which its executives are plucked. It dispatches a hit squad of company experts to new plants to negotiate lower prices from energy suppliers, job cuts and improved marketing strategies.[64]

Furthermore, the company's comprehensive knowledge of demand patterns for its outputs, achieved through IT, helped Cemex to schedule the production of its products. More importantly, such information enabled Cemex to optimize its own production process, minimizing input costs (through efficient scheduling and utilization), and thus enhancing profits. Finally, Cemex's technology-enhanced knowledge of its customers' requirements enabled the company to command a premium price for higher value added services. According to the company, its reluctance to lower prices in the face of competition in Mexico led to the current technology agenda.[65]

Overview

Cemex's rapid expansion of productive capacity plants in Latin America, the US, Europe, Africa, and South-east Asia entailed substantial debt. Cemex relied on superior customer service to distinguish itself from both local competitors and other international companies. Keeping down costs required the right combination of low-cost production and external sourcing, and careful management of inventory and international logistics. The company faced competition in its customer service and trading operations as rivals upgraded their information systems. As the company considered the advantages and drawbacks of further expansion, its international market making strategy seemed pivotal.

The Cemex experience illustrates the role of the international business in establishing and organizing international markets. Cemex offers a striking and vivid example of how a company can take leadership of the process of globalization. In an industry where high trade costs had historically held back international trade flows, Cemex was quick to perceive how shifts in distribution technologies would reshape the global cement industry, bringing previously segmented regional markets closer together. Rather than merely reacting to the threat posed by such forces to its profitable home business, this previously local company took decisive action to use the falling trade costs to its own competitive advantage.

Within a decade, Cemex had established operations spanning all continents and was in an enviable position to arbitrage across its many buyer and seller markets thanks to its world-class international trading platform. The success of Cemex clearly demonstrates how a business established and operated in an emerging market can become a leading global business. Responding to the global challenge, Cemex shows how a company can seize the opportunity to transform its business. The company surpassed many of the global competitors who were once threatening it in its home market. Rather than being overwhelmed by global competition, Cemex took advantage of global opportunities to increase the scale of its operations and grow its company.

Cemex employed geographic diversification to select many supplier countries and many target customer countries. International markets in cement were subject to substantial fluctuations in both demand and supply. Cemex coordinated its transactions and activities, using its global network to optimize its purchasing, manufacturing, delivering, and sales. Cemex became a global market maker in cement, bringing buyers and sellers together through its international trading and operations.

9 Dairy Farm: regional retail strategy

The supermarket revolution was sweeping through Asia. Consumers were switching from traditional street stalls and outdoor markets for fresh food, known as "wet markets," to supermarkets and hypermarkets. From India to China to Indonesia, buying patterns were changing, powered by economic development, rising incomes, urban growth, and improved transportation.[1] Supermarkets offered consumers the transparency of posted prices instead of bargaining and the convenience of one-stop shopping instead of a search among many specialized vendors. Supermarkets also featured packaged goods, branded products, imported foods, modern sanitary conditions, refrigeration, and prepared foods.

Dairy Farm was perfectly positioned to participate in this supermarket revolution. The company had withdrawn from operations in Australia, Europe, and New Zealand to focus on Asia. The company had divested distribution and other businesses to concentrate on supermarkets, hypermarkets, drugstores, and convenience stores. Having weathered the earlier Asian financial crisis, Dairy Farm braced itself for increasing costs and intensified competition. CEO and managing director, Ronald J. Floto, noted at that time: "We have been picking the low hanging fruit and it's going to get tougher rather than easier . . . Every one of our markets is troubled; that represents another challenge."[2]

Dairy Farm, headquartered in Hong Kong, was a unit of the conglomerate Jardine Matheson Group. Despite the forces of the supermarket revolution, the company still faced tenacious competition from traditional wet markets and mom-and-pop grocery stores, as well as from domestic supermarket chains in its target country markets. Moreover, major global retailers such as Wal-Mart, Carrefour, and Tesco were rapidly entering Asian markets. Floto and Dairy Farm's senior managers would need to determine which Asian countries provided the best opportunities for future growth. The company's regional retail strategy would be tested strongly.

Dairy Farm and Hong Kong

Company history

Dairy Farm was established in Hong Kong in 1886 and the company's history was connected intimately with events on the island. Dairy Farm became part of the holding company Jardine Matheson, the oldest of the island's diversified trading companies, known as "hongs."[3] From Britain's annexation of the small island off China's western coast in 1841 until the return of the territory to the People's Republic of China (PRC, hereafter, Mainland China) in July 1997, Hong Kong's politics, wars, and geographic location affected the fortunes of Dairy Farm.[4] The great success of Hong Kong in international trade and its role as a gateway to China were reflected in Dairy Farm's growth.

Sir Patrick Manson, a Scottish surgeon, arrived in Hong Kong in the late 1880s following his tour of duty aboard Great Britain's Chinese maritime fleet. Manson joined a local physician Dr James Cantlie in investigating milk products. As Manson wrote:

This is a serious matter . . . for the young children and the sick, with whom milk is the principal and often the only food, and is indeed the staff of life. It is felt . . . a public company with an adequate capital, a Dairy Farm . . . shall supply a thoroughly reliable article that may become what milk ought to be, one of the principal elements in the food of the poor in all communities.

Seeing a dearth of safely drinkable milk in Hong Kong, Manson proposed to "start a dairy of 100 head of cows on a capital of HK$25,000 and . . . gradually increase the herd so as to meet the requirements of the Colony." Dairy Farm imported eighty cows, hired cowboys, and purchased land. It chose a grazing range that was far enough from town to limit bovine disease (rinderpest) but close enough to customers to keep transportation costs down.

The company's growth halted dramatically when plague swept through both Mainland China and Hong Kong in 1894. An outbreak of pleuropneumonia devastated the cattle herd at almost the same time. Dr Manson had returned to Scotland a few years earlier, and the surviving investors assumed control of the company.

The French were building a railroad from Vietnam to Yunan and acquired a lease on certain Chinese ports during the latter part of the nineteenth century. The British, threatened by French advancement, leased the New Territories region of China (off the coast of Hong Kong) in 1898 for ninety-nine years.

The prosperity of British Hong Kong companies increased with the improve-ment in the health of the colony. The population recovered dramatically from the plague devastation and grew to 528,000 residents in 1916. During the pop-ulation boom, Dairy Farm was lauded for its strict adherence to the rules of hygiene and sanitation on which it had been founded. Pasteurization processes began in 1902 and residents of the region generally considered Dairy Farm to be the most reliable source of milk products.

The company established its first retail store in 1904 at its Central District depot, now a Hong Kong landmark.[5] It purchased Australian cattle in antici-pation of the end of the First World War. In 1917, moving to become the dom-inant cold storer in Hong Kong, Dairy Farm purchased the Hong Kong Ice Co. The newly named Dairy Farm, Ice & Cold Storage Company Ltd acquired a virtual monopoly of facilities for cold storage in the colony and contributed toward the Company's goal of self-sufficiency. The Company opened its second store in Kowloon and began producing ice, much of which was used by Hong Kong's fishing boats.[6] By 1924, the cattle herd increased to 1,073 cattle, the most in the company's early history. By 1928, diversification was a key element of the company's success. The company operated six retail stores, benefiting from a growing Chinese demand for milk products. It now raised pigs and turkeys as well as cattle to provide a food range from bacon to ice cream and special milk for infants. The population of Hong Kong grew sub-stantially between 1918 and 1939, and Dairy Farm also continued its expan-sion in the inter-war period.

After the Second World War, Dairy Farm faced devastation: employees had died, company ships were wrecked, cows and pigs had been lost, and all records from 1920 until the war had been burned. Despite these problems, Dairy Farm, which had cut "Ice & Cold Storage" from its name, was one of the first firms to resume business in Hong Kong. The company acquired cattle and a crane for lifting them out of boats and ammonia for restarting the pasteur-ization process.

The company's growth in the postwar years included an expansion into the airline catering business in the mid-1950s. In 1960, Dairy Farm merged with Lane Crawford. The new company, Dairy Lane Ltd, made arrangements with Woolworths of Australia to sell frozen foods there. The Company established a supermarket in Thailand along with shrimp exportation facilities. In 1964, the company purchased Wellcome, a China-based grocery chain, and Scott's Provisions of Australia. By the end of the 1960s, no company on the island could compare to Dairy Lane's breadth of dairy services and distribution channels.

In November 1972, Hongkong Land carried out a hostile takeover of Dairy Farm by purchasing almost 60 percent of its shares. This was the first important corporate takeover in the history of Hong Kong.[7] Dairy Farm would continue to operate as an "independent and autonomous company with its own board, management, and staff," according to the operational directive issued at the first meeting of the new board of directors.

Thanks to Hongkong Land's property acquisitions, the company was able to build nineteen supermarkets in Hong Kong and on mainland Kowloon. In 1979, the Dairy Farm leadership, with the financial backing of Hongkong Land, purchased the seventy-five-store Australian grocery chain Franklins. Uniting its various stores under a single name, the name Dairy Lane was changed to Wellcome. In 1980, Dairy Farm became the first company to enter into a JV contract with the Mainland Chinese government, for the operation of a flight catering service at Beijing International Airport.[8]

Jardine Matheson

As a result of the Hongkong Land takeover, Dairy Farm became a subsidiary of Jardine Matheson (hereafter, Jardines). The parent company Jardines had its origins as one of the British diversified trading companies that operated out of Canton, Hong Kong, and Macao. Still British-owned, Jardines had been established in 1832 in Canton by Scotsmen William Jardine and James Matheson, and relatives of William Jardine would continue to run the firm. The company was a major participant in Britain's South China trade in the nineteenth century, with its complex and problematic history. Jardines built the first Chinese railway in 1876, which ran from Shanghai to Woosung.

Jardines was the first foreign company to enter Japan and among the first European companies to operate in Shanghai and China. Jardines viewed Shanghai as its headquarters beginning in 1912, but returned to Hong Kong in the 1950s. On land it had acquired in 1841, Jardines established operations on Victoria Harbour, which was to become Causeway Bay. There, it built workshops to service the company's fleet of clipper ships, warehouses (godowns) to store trade goods, and the winter residence of the Taipan, as the head of the company was called.[9] Today, the land on Causeway Bay is part of a reclaimed area in Hong Kong's highly developed business district. Jardines' early structures have been replaced by shops, high-rise buildings, the Excelsior Hotel, and Hong Kong's World Trade Center.

Jardines continues to fire the Noonday Gun in Causeway Bay, a tradition originally honoring the comings and goings of the Taipan. The company's colorful history was allegedly the inspiration for James Clavell's trio of novels; *Tai-Pan*, *Gai-Jin*, and *Noble House*.

Headquartered in Hong Kong, Jardines was a major conglomerate with a wide range of business interests. The company employed over 200,000 people and operated in more than thirty countries. In addition to Dairy Farm, these businesses included automobile distributor Jardine Motors Group, insurer Jardine Lloyd Thompson, hotel development and management company Mandarin Oriental Hotel Group International, and the commercial real estate owner and developer Hongkong Land. Jardines also owned the Singapore-listed Jardine Cycle & Carriage, which was an automobile distributor. Jardine Cycle & Carriage also owned a 50 percent stake in their major Indonesian conglomerate Astra International, the largest independent automotive manufacturer in South-east Asia with businesses in infrastructure, IT, agribusiness, heavy equipment, and financial services.[10]

Jardines was well acquainted with Dairy Farm, having in 1879 helped to establish the ice making factory in Hong Kong that Dairy Farm purchased in 1917. Jardines made investments that helped to establish Hongkong Land in 1889, and substantially increased its ownership share after 1980.

Hongkong Land's offer for Dairy Farm's shares identified a number of expected benefits from the merger. It mentioned that Hongkong Land would provide "valuable property expertise" and that the companies would be part of a diversified conglomerate "with resources invested in three of the most rapidly growing industries in this area – property, leisure and catering," creating one of the most important hotel, catering and provisions groups in the Pacific Basin.[11] Jardines' knowledge of property markets in Asia would be valuable to Dairy Farm's retail operations, as would the parent company's capital investments.

Developing a regional focus in Asia

Owen Price, who took over the management of Dairy Farm in April 1981, noted that: "The public's perception of Dairy Farm in Hong Kong was that of an old and trusted company, but a conservative and old fashioned one." Price decided to concentrate the company's resources on its core businesses of retailing, wholesaling, food and ice manufacturing, and catering.

Changes in Dairy Farm's activities

After a few years, a price war broke out between Wellcome and its rival Park N Shop. Park N Shop cut prices dramatically, forcing Wellcome to do the same; Wellcome rapidly increased traffic from its 4.5 million customers to 7.5 million customers. Dairy Farm's catering business also faced stiff competition after the entry of the Swire Group, which offered catering and a range of other services to airlines on a reciprocal basis. Dairy Farm sold its catering interests and its few stores in Singapore. The company signed a new JV contract with the Chinese government named International Food Corporation Limited (IFCO), with Dairy Farm controlling 70 percent of the equity. Owen Price predicted that: "The new frontier for Dairy Farm will lie in China."

Dairy Farm marked its centenary year in 1986; the company had over 300 retail outlets, and was relisted on the Hong Kong Stock Exchange after having been separated from Hongkong Land. Dairy Farm continued its expansion over the next decade with acquisitions of retail chains in Britain, Spain, and New Zealand, and the establishment of a JV in Japan. The company opened supermarkets in Taiwan and acquired the 142-store Cold Storage chain in Singapore. Dairy Farm bought the 228-store 7-Eleven chain in Hong Kong and opened additional 7-Eleven convenience stores in Shenzhen and Guangdong, China. Malaysia also provided fertile ground, as the company established a 50/50 joint venture with Cold Storage to develop supermarkets in that region.[12]

A significant change in course took place in 1997 with the appointment of Ronald J. Floto as CEO. Floto, a graduate of West Point and the Harvard Business School, had served eight years in the US Army. He brought over twenty-four years of retail experience in the US where he had been the executive vice president of Kmart Corporation and the president of Super Kmart. He also held positions with Kash N'Karry Food Stores and Jewel Companies.[13]

Floto emphasized Dairy Farm's competitive advantages in the Asia–Pacific region. The same year that he became CEO, Dairy Farm sold its Spanish supermarket subsidiary Simago, comprising sixty-one supermarkets and fifty-six discount stores. Dairy Farm had a minority interest in Kwik Save, one of the UK's leading low-cost grocers with 850 stores nationwide. When British grocery retailer Somerfield merged with Kwik Save, Dairy Farm received shares in Somerfield, which it subsequently sold off. Dairy Farm's sales of Simago and Somerfield shares essentially completed Dairy Farm's exit from Europe.

Then, in 2001, Dairy Farm resolved what it considered a major problem by selling its Australian supermarket chain Franklins with its 287 outlets.[14]

Although it was Australia's third largest supermarket chain, Franklins had become "stuck in the middle": it was neither the low-cost leader nor the high-quality firm. The chain pursued a low-cost "no-frills" strategy, selling basic groceries and frozen foods, leaving meat and fresh produce to independent sellers. Such reliance on independent butchers and greengrocers caused problems for the company when competition led to extended hours of operation, since the independent butchers and greengrocers kept to limited hours.[15]

Franklins emphasized price discounts and promotions over store layouts and presentation of merchandise. Customers had to bag their own groceries and to make their way through aisles cluttered with unpacked stock.

Franklins faced tough competition from market leaders Woolworths and Coles-Myer. Franklins had a retail margin of 1 percent compared to 3 percent for its competitors. The Franklins unit sustained substantial losses – $27 million in 1999 and $71 million in 2000. The Woolworths chain, based in Sydney, began offering its customers larger stores with a better shopping experience than Franklins. Woolworths sold higher-margin meats and fresh produce, combined with lower-priced groceries and frozen foods. Thus, customers found Woolworths to be both lower priced and a more pleasant place to shop than Franklins. Franklins responded by adding fresh produce and a new store format called Big Fresh, a concept brought in from Dairy Farm's New Zealand operations. By this time, Dairy Farm found it hard to close the gap with its competitors. The new format was not rolled out in many stores and years of losses followed.[16]

Franklins also tried to achieve additional supply chain efficiencies. The company attempted to reduce the cost of business by closing a warehouse and outsourcing transport operations in New South Wales. Dairy Farm operated large-scale distribution centers in New South Wales, Queensland, Victoria, and South Australia. The company introduced modern warehousing techniques related to Wal-Mart's cross-docking systems, but these cost-saving moves were not enough to offset the revenue losses from a decreased market share.

Dairy Farm sold many of its newer Franklins stores to Woolworths with its lower-cost and "no-frills" format stores going to other chains. The following year, Dairy Farm sold off its supermarket business in New Zealand (coincidentally named Woolworths). This completed the company's exit from Australia and New Zealand.

Dairy Farm further trimmed its holdings in Asia to concentrate more on retail activities. The company sold its dairy products manufacturing JV in Hong Kong and China to its partner Nestlé. It sold off its Oliver's Super Sandwiches (with twenty-two outlets in Hong Kong and a small franchise network in Malaysia and the Philippines) to Jardine Restaurants Group (JRG), another member of the Jardine Matheson Group. It closed its Mannings drugstore chain in Taiwan and discontinued its Japanese Wellsave supermarket joint venture with Seiyu.[17] Having made these adjustments, Floto considered targets for acquisition and opportunities for further growth in the Asia-Pacific region.

Strategic lessons

By exiting from Europe, Australia, New Zealand, and Japan, the company gained more than a geographic focus. The divested operations had been in developed economies. Dairy Farm's retail store formats and wholesale distribution operations did not provide competitive advantages over established domestic retailers operating in Europe as well as other international retailers serving the European market. The company's brands and customer shopping experiences were not sufficient to attract customers in comparison with competing retailers.

Dairy Farm did not succeed in developing sufficient benefits from its IT or distribution systems that might have offered cost advantages over rivals in developed countries. Moreover, Dairy Farm did not obtain specialized knowledge about customers in Europe, Australia, New Zealand, or Japan that would convey market superiority over its local and international competitors.

The company's managers shifted the company's efforts to the Asia–Pacific region, a shift that would help managers to identify market opportunities and better position the company to achieve competitive advantages. The company summarized its strategy as follows: "The group is geographically committed to Asia." Ronald J. Floto emphasized that the company would continue to pursue its "strategy for expansion in Asia." In addition to refurbishing stores, Floto identified five key areas for capital investment:

• Opening hypermarkets in South Asia;
• Expanding the Ikea network;
• Growing in Mainland China;
• Bolt-on acquisitions in existing markets; and
• Entering new Asian markets, preferably by acquisition.[18]

Dairy Farm's geographic focus was matched by a narrowing of the company's activities: the company decreased its vertical integration to concentrate on its core competencies. Dairy Farm divested its long-standing ice manufacturing business, its cold storage facilities, and its warehousing operations, all of which were located in Hong Kong. The company strove for economies of scale by sharing infrastructure costs across multiple store formats, thus centralizing its logistics, human resources, finance, procurement, and IT.[19]

Customer countries

Dairy Farm's managers faced a number of critical questions:
- Could the setbacks suffered in Europe, Australia, New Zealand, and Japan be avoided in their target customer markets?
- Would Dairy Farm be able to develop a competitive advantage over domestic rivals in those markets?
- Were its store formats, brands, and food offering sufficient to attract customers?
- Were its procurement methods, distribution systems, and IT sufficiently efficient in its target markets?
- How would Dairy Farm fare in comparison with global competitors that also were entering its target customer markets?

Dairy Farm concentrated on expanding its activities and continuing to improve its performance in its nine major customer countries, see table 9.1. The company operated over 3,000 stores, including supermarkets, hypermarkets, convenience stores, health and beauty stores, home furnishing stores, and restaurants. With more than 60,000 employees and sales topping $5 billion, Dairy Farm was a major regional player in Asia.

Dairy Farm's top managers considered the differences in the company's target markets. They required to evaluate continually what were customer needs in those markets. They would have to observe competitive challenges and shifts in government policy. Dairy Farm's top managers would need to determine what store formats fitted best in the target markets and to find the most promising markets for growing the company. Dairy Farm's presence in South Korea was limited to a JV with 50 percent ownership of Olive Young, a rapidly-growing health and beauty chain. The company's additional targeted customer countries are now discussed.[20]

Hong Kong and Macau

Dairy Farm's largest presence was naturally in Hong Kong, its home base. Compared to all its target markets, the company was most familiar with customer needs in Hong Kong and highly aware of the real estate market and

Table 9.1. Dairy Farm's retail chains and JVs, by location

Hong Kong
- Wellcome supermarkets
- 7-Eleven convenience stores
- Mannings health and beauty stores
- Ikea home furnishings stores
- Maxim's (JV)
    Chinese restaurants
    Fast food/Catering services
    Cake shops/Bakeries
    European restaurants & other
    Starbucks (JV)

India
- FoodWorld supermarkets (JV)
- Health and Glow health and beauty stores (JV)

Indonesia
- Hero supermarkets
- Giant hypermarkets
- Guardian health and beauty stores
- Starmart convenience stores

Korea
- Olive Young health and beauty stores (JV)

Macau
- 7-Eleven convenience stores
- Maxim's (JV), Starbucks (JV)

Mainland China
- 7-Eleven convenience stores
- Mannings health and beauty stores
- Maxim's
    Starbucks (JV)
    Cake shops

Malaysia
- Giant/Cold Storage supermarkets
- Giant hypermarkets
- Guardian health and beauty stores
- Photo Finish stores

Singapore
- Cold Storage/Shop N Save supermarkets
- Giant hypermarkets
- 7-Eleven convenience stores
- Guardian health and beauty stores
- Photo Finish/Handifix stores

Table 9.1. (continued)

Taiwan
- Wellcome supermarkets
- Ikea home furnishing stores

Source: Dairy Farm International Holdings Limited, *Interim Report, Retail Outlets Summary,* June 30, 2005.

government regulations. The Hong Kong market was highly competitive, but customers were affluent and sophisticated.

Dairy Farm operated 242 Wellcome supermarkets, the largest chain in Hong Kong. Dairy Farm was a major convenience store operator with 642 7-Eleven stores, less than half of which were franchised, and 221 Mannings health and beauty stores. Through its 50 percent-owned Maxim's unit, Dairy Farm operated about 370 eateries including Chinese and European restaurants, fast-food outlets, catering services, cake shops and bakeries, and JV Starbucks coffee shops. Dairy Farm began an expansion into furniture as an operator of Ikea home furnishings stores. Dairy Farm also operated 7-Eleven convenience stores and Starbucks in Macau.

Hong Kong, a city-state with over 7 million people, provided a highly attractive retail environment. *Per capita* income was substantial, and population density was significant, approaching 7,000 people per km². Dairy Farm served a demanding urban clientele. Hong Kong offered a highly developed urban transportation and communications infrastructure, continuing to serve as a world trade hub as well as an import–export gateway for Mainland China. This helped Dairy Farm in its sourcing from Mainland China and in operating its retail operations there.

Hong Kong's retail market for food and drinks exceeded US$6 billion. There were over 16,000 wet market stalls and mom-and-pop stores, and hundreds of convenience stores. Supermarkets provided over half of retail food sales. The growth of supermarkets reflected changes in the habits of Hong Kong residents who traditionally shopped daily for fresh food.[21]

Dairy Farm faced intense direct competition from the supermarket chain Park N Shop. The Park N Shop chain was part of the A.S. Watson Group, the retail and manufacturing business unit of the Hong Kong conglomerate Hutchison Whampoa. The A.S. Watson Group was a major international retailer and manufacturer with over 7,000 retail stores in thirty-four countries and more than 88,000 employees. Watson operated 300 stores including supermarkets in Hong Kong. Park N Shop opened the first superstore in Hong

Kong combining a supermarket format with a traditional Chinese wet market with fresh fruits, vegetables, meat, and fish. Park N Shop also operated stores that combined grocery supermarkets with a large-scale discount merchandise format.[22] Park N Shop's scale, innovation, modern stores, and geographic reach posed a challenge to Dairy Farm.

India

India's retail industry was highly fragmented. Dairy Farm's Indian operations consisted of two large JVs with the major Indian conglomerate RPG Group. FoodWorld, with ninety-four stores, was India's first national supermarket chain and became the largest food retailer in India. The company was a 49/51 percent JV between Dairy Farm and RPG Group's Spencer & Co. unit. Floto saw the JV as giving Dairy Farm "an excellent opportunity to establish itself in its key supermarket format in a promising growth market." He noted that "The FoodWorld operations are redefining retailing in India with high standards of customer service, display, and convenience." Dairy Farm and RPG Group also formed a 50/50 JV Health and Glow, a health and beauty chain with over thirty stores.[23]

The Indian government imposed a ban on FDI in retail in 1997. FoodWorld, formed in 1996 and spun off as a separate JV in 1999, and Health and Glow, formed in 1997, were able to continue to operate. However, Dairy Farm and other foreign retailers could no longer enter the retail sector through M&A or new investment.

Retailing in India was the nation's largest employer, after agriculture. Indian retailing primarily consisted of a large traditional sector with street markets, kiosks, and mom-and-pop stores, known as Kiranas. All but 4 percent of India's 12 million stores were less than 500 ft^2 in area. Restrictions on FDI reflected government concerns that entry of international retailers would compete with the traditional sector and reduce retail employment, but the government announced its intention to review its FDI regulations in retail.[24]

India's sales system had three tiers: distributors, wholesalers, and retailers. A national manufacturer might need to use hundreds of distributors; there were approximately 12 million retail outlets for all types. Although the Indian retail market was estimated at $250 billion, the organized Indian retail industry accounted for less than 5 percent of that total, although many observers expected a rapid growth of that share. India's large population of over 1 billion, of which over 30 percent lived in cities, offered potential retail sales growth. Retailers that found ways to overcome logistics and infrastructure limitations could serve the 70 percent of India's population that lived in rural areas in some 627,000 villages.[25]

Wal-Mart, Carrefour, and Germany's Metro had targeted the Indian retail sector for future entry. Wal-Mart's top managers bought $1.5 billion of Indian goods, including textiles and jewelry, per year. Wal-Mart was intensively lobbying the Indian government to open the retail market and its CEO, Lee Scott, met India's prime minister Manmohan Singh when he visited the US[26] The international retailers were making plans for investment in retail stores and distribution systems and assembling local management teams. Meanwhile, domestic retail chains such as Shoppers' Stop Ltd and Provogue (India) Ltd were expanding.[27]

Indonesia

Foreign investment in Indonesia's retail sector began in earnest in 1998 when the Indonesian government lifted restrictions on investment in that sector.[28] Total retail sales exceeded $4 billion and foreign retailers accounted for over 40 percent of those sales within a few years of liberalization.[29] With 220 million people, a GDP *per capita* of about $800, and an expanding middle class, Indonesia offered the promise of growth in retail.

The same year that Indonesia opened retail to foreign investment, Dairy Farm acquired an interest in PT Hero Supermarket, the leading supermarket chain in Indonesia, and PT Hero Pusakasejati. Floto said: "We have worked alongside Hero since 1995 in developing Mitra Toko Diskon's discount grocery store chain. The strategic alliance between our two groups will benefit Hero customers, employees and suppliers, and ensure that Hero enhances its position as Indonesia's premier supermarket chain." Hero operated a total of seventy-one supermarkets located in Java, Kalimantan, Bali, and Sumatra and had fast-food outlets, baking operations, and personal convenience stores.[30]

As Dairy Farm's Indonesian operations expanded, the company addressed many different market segments with various store formats. Dairy Farm's Indonesian operations included 93 Hero supermarkets, 10 Giant hypermarkets, 88 Guardian health and beauty stores, and 50 Starmart convenience stores.[31]

Dairy Farm faced competition from traditional outdoor markets, mom-and-pop stores, convenience stores, and smaller supermarket chains. Dairy Farm also faced the entry of foreign hypermarkets. The French global retailer Carrefour's entry offered shoppers in Indonesia both a greater variety of products and lower prices in comparison with traditional markets.[32] Carrefour's expansion into Indonesia accompanied its entry into Taiwan, Malaysia, Singapore, and China. Before the relaxation of rules limiting FDI in retailing, Carrefour entered the market by partnering with the local distribution company Tigaraksa Satria.[33]

The relaxation of investment rules coincided with the beginning of a period of political transformation from authoritarian rule to an active democracy. Despite the political liberalization, the *Singapore Straits Times* observed that: "Indonesians cannot eat democracy."[34] The growth of the Indonesian economy would improve living standards; the entry of foreign supermarkets and hypermarkets would impact the way Indonesians shopped and ate.

Mainland China

Dairy Farm's extensive knowledge and experience in Mainland China were not matched by its retail presence: it had neither supermarkets nor hyper-markets there. The company operated over 200 7-Eleven convenience stores and nine Mannings health and beauty stores.

In contrast, Park N Shop, Dairy Farm's Hong Kong rival, operated super-markets and hypermarkets in major Chinese cities such as Guanzhou, Shenzhen, and Dongguan, and attracted over 1 million shoppers per week.[35] The apparent success of Park N Shop and the sheer size of the Mainland China retail market suggested a potential opportunity for Dairy Farm to expand its supermarket operations.

With its rapid economic growth and 1.3 billion consumers, China was an attractive market. China's GDP *per capita* had risen to over $1,200 and China's entry into the WTO had lowered barriers to trade and relaxed restrictions on investment in retail. Moreover, China's population had begun a process of migration in which many residents of rural areas sought work in urban locations, motivated by trade and industrial development. China had over 160 cities with populations greater than 1 million.[36]

Increasing income among Chinese consumers would result in increased retail sales overall. Economic development was likely to increase the pace of the supermarket revolution, particularly in rapidly growing cities. Chinese consumers indicated a willingness to spend more on those food products that provided health benefits than on less healthy food products. Chinese consumers also viewed Chinese and Taiwanese food products as offering better quality and value than foreign brands, although this perception was subject to change as younger and more affluent urban consumers tried new products. An exception was beauty products, where foreign brands were well regarded.[37]

Mainland China was a major supplier country for Dairy Farm even though the company had not located supermarkets there. By sourcing in Mainland China for its Hong Kong stores, Dairy Farm benefited from lower transport costs and an absence of tariffs and other trade barriers in comparison with other imported goods. Dairy Farm also sourced in Mainland China for its store operations in other countries, thus achieving scale economies in its procurement efforts and market advantages with suppliers as a result of its large purchases. According to Douglas Brown, Director of Group Procurement for Dairy Farm, the company handled wholesale tasks: "We go direct to the manufacturers and avoid the costs of logistics." In 2004, Dairy Farm's purchasing in Mainland China approached $500 million, making the company one of the world's largest importers from China. Brown observed that: "Dairy Farm has been procuring in China since Southern China started manufacturing and producing the quality of goods that we required."[38]

Malaysia

Dairy Farm had a significant presence in Malaysia with 47 Giant/Cold Storage supermarkets, 15 Giant hypermarkets, 160 Guardian health and beauty stores, and 6 Photo Finish stores. Dairy Farm held a leading position in both food and in health and beauty. Malaysia had a population of 25 million people with GDP *per capita* of over $4,000; the country had been experiencing a period of steady population growth and migration to cities.

The consumer shift from traditional wet markets for fruits and vegetables to supermarkets was exemplified by urban consumers in Malaysia. Consumer purchases from modern retail chains approached two-thirds of total sales for fruits and one-third of total sales for vegetables.[39] According to Floto, the initial acquisition of Giant in Malaysia had given Dairy Farm the merchandising expertise needed to operate hypermarkets elsewhere in Asia.[40]

Retail and wholesale companies needed government approval to establish operations in Malaysia. Foreign companies could own up to 70 percent as long as the remaining shares satisfied various domestic ownership rules. The government imposed various entry requirements on companies making FDI in retail and wholesale, including satisfaction of minimum capital requirements, local incorporation, meeting special zoning regulations, and provision of socio-economic impact studies. These rules were helpful to domestic supermarket chains and restricted international companies to medium-sized and large urban areas.

Supermarkets and hypermarkets were highly popular in Malaysia, with international entrants playing major roles. Although it held the lead position, Dairy Farm was under pressure from international competitors Carrefour, Tesco, Jaya Jusco (owned by Aeon Group of Japan), and Makro Cash and Carry (owned by SHV of the Netherlands). An important domestic competitor was The Store, the largest and oldest Malaysian supermarket and department store chain, which had sixty-four stores and over 10,000 employees.

Singapore

Dairy Farm thrived in Singapore's urban environment with 78 Cold Storage/Shop N Save supermarkets, 7 Giant hypermarkets, 278 7-Eleven convenience stores, 118 Guardian health and beauty stores, and 27 Photo Finish/Handifix stores. Singapore, an island city-state with over 4 million people, had a substantial population density of more than 6,500 people per km^2 and $20,000 GDP *per capita*.

Dairy Farm faced competition from a number of sources, including the government-supported supermarket chain National Trade Union Congress (NTUC) FairPrice Cooperative. Carrefour, the main active global competitor, had entered Singapore in 1997, and operated two hypermarkets there. Dairy Farm was well established in Singapore. The Cold Storage Chain had been in operation since 1903. Dairy Farm's Giant hypermarket chain pioneered the combination of a supermarket and a wet market within the store, featuring fresh fruits and vegetables, fresh seafood, and spices. Their slogan "Ethnic and Fresh" represented Giant's appeal to local tastes and customs.

Taiwan

Dairy Farm operated the largest supermarket chain in Taiwan, with 167 Wellcome supermarkets. Dairy Farm also had two Ikea home furnishings stores there. Taiwan, with a population of 23 million and GDP *per capita* in excess of $12,000, provided a large potential market. Hypermarkets, supermarkets, and convenience stores had been in Taiwan for over twenty years and had grown rapidly in a highly competitive environment.[41] Total sales in the organized retail sector approached $20 billion.[42]

Dairy Farm's Wellcome opened a "Superstore" that combined a traditional wet market with a modern supermarket. They also established a Jasons Market Place that offered imported foods and higher-end groceries.[43] Dairy Farm faced competition from Carrefour, Tesco, Auchan, and Geant of France, and Costco of the US. Carrefour had thirty-four hypermarkets in Taiwan.[44]

International operators of hypermarkets had an 80 percent market share. The hypermarket sector engaged in intense competition in Taiwan, particularly in selected urban areas, although room for additional stores remained elsewhere in the country. Supermarkets expanded and merged to keep up with hypermarkets and to remain competitive with convenience stores. There were over 7,500 convenience stores in Taiwan. In addition, many department stores in Taiwan included a supermarket, often carrying gourmet food; many of the stores were operated by Japanese companies. Taiwan's retail chains were increasingly offering products with private labels and imported goods to differentiate their stores. Traditional wet markets and street vendors continued to provide competitive alternatives.[45]

Global competitors

Dairy Farm's major global competitors in Asia were Wal-Mart, Carrefour, and Tesco. These global competitors benefited from economies of scale in distribution systems, purchasing operations, IT, and corporate functions. They also had the potential to benefit from market power in purchasing and relationships with major suppliers, particularly for branded products and producers of generic products for house brands. The global players had experience in the design, construction, and operation of multiple retail store formats. By operating in multiple countries, they could also share knowledge across markets.

Wal-Mart

Based in Bentonville, Arkansas, Wal-Mart Stores, Inc. (hereafter, Wal-Mart) was the largest retailer in the world with annual revenues approaching $300 billion. Wal-Mart employed 1.6 million people worldwide of which 450,000 were outside the US. The company served 138 million customers per week throughout its global operations. Wal-Mart had 3,700 stores in the US, and 2,250 stores abroad.

The company went international in 1991 with a Sam's Club in Mexico City, and expanded its global operations to fifteen countries other than the US. Wal-Mart's Asian presence was concentrated in China and Japan.[46] Wal-Mart acquired a controlling interest in Seiyu, the fourth largest Japanese supermarket chain with over 400 stores, and planned to add another 200 international stores in 2006. More than 70 percent of Wal-Mart's international sales were through stores that did not bear the Wal-Mart name.[47] Instead, the stores had brands with local recognition such as Asda in the UK or Bompreço in Brazil.[48]

Wal-Mart first entered China in 1996 and within ten years had 51 Wal-Mart supercenters, 3 Sam's Clubs, and 2 neighborhood markets. China was a major supplier country, providing Wal-Mart with $18 billion of all types of goods in 2004. Wal-Mart supercenters in China carried approximately 20,000 items, combining department store goods such as apparel, electronics, and appliances with a full range of supermarket foods. The combination of a department store and a supermarket offered customers the convenience of one-stop shopping, an advantage over specialized department stores and over standard supermarkets. Wal-Mart's supercenter format took advantage of impulse purchasing and in-store promotions. A customer of the department store or the supermarket might be induced to make an unanticipated purchase from the other side of the supercenter.

Wal-Mart's supercenter format offered economies of scope. The department store and the supermarket shared the overhead costs of the store, as well as sharing the costs of procurement, logistics, and IT. These cost factors also gave Wal-Mart a potential competitive advantage over department stores and supermarkets. Just as it had in the US, Wal-Mart's international operations combined cost savings from economies of scale with customer benefits from product variety.

Wal-Mart encountered problems in South Korea, and exited the market after only eight years, selling its sixteen supercenters to Korean rival Shinsegae. The supercenter format was not successful in competition either with specialized supermarkets or with department stores.

Wal-Mart also ran into difficulties in Germany, which it left after eight years. The chain's food offerings were not competitive with grocery stores; and its locations were not sufficiently convenient for customers. Its eighty-five stores in Germany were obtained through its acquisition of two established chains, which it had rebranded as Wal-Marts.[49]

Wal-Mart expanded its operations in China, beginning with plans for the acquisition of the Taiwanese-owned supermarket chain Trust-Mart. The deal would make Wal-Mart the number one operator of hypermarkets in China. Wal-Mart hired Ed Chan, who was Dairy Farm's North Asia regional director and ran the company's retail business in China and South Korea. Ed Chan would become president and CEO of Wal-Mart China.[50]

Carrefour

The largest retailer in Europe, and second largest global player, France's Carrefour had over 430,000 employees, over 11,000 stores, and annual revenues of more than $110 billion. With stores in thirty-two countries, Carrefour received about half of its sales outside of its home country of France and was the market leader in eight countries other than France.[51]

Carrefour was the first global retailer to enter Asia, beginning its operations there in 1989. The company operated in China, Indonesia, Japan, Malaysia, Singapore, Taiwan, and Thailand. Carrefour, which invented the hypermarket format in 1963, opened its first hypermarket in China in 1995, eventually opening seven others there.[52] Half of Carrefour's new hypermarket floor space was located in China. Like Wal-Mart, Carrefour entered and then exited the Korean market.

In all, Carrefour had 896 stores in Asia by the fall of 2005, in various formats: hypermarkets, supermarkets, discount, and convenience stores. According to the company: "The establishment of hypermarkets in a country makes it possible to put in place the tools and processes necessary to future development (relations with suppliers, logistics, marketing, etc.)." Carrefour used its multiple store formats as part of a coordinated multi-stage international entry strategy. Having established the necessary infrastructure through its hypermarket beachhead, the company can extend its offerings "by setting up supermarkets and hard discount stores and, if the country is sufficiently mature, convenience stores."[53]

Carrefour's multiple formats yielded cost economies by sharing procurement, logistics, marketing, and other functions. According to the company, one of its main competitive advantages in Asia was adapting to the local context: "In every country, the Group takes up the position of a local player." Carrefour divided its China operations into four regional markets to address differences in customer preferences.[54]

Tesco

Tesco of the UK was a major global retailer, with 360,000 employees of whom 100,000 were in its international operations. The company operated over 2,300 stores with several hundred more openings planned. The market leader in the UK, Tesco was also the leader in five of its international markets. Half of the company's retail space was outside the UK.[55]

Tesco operated 31 stores in China, 104 in Japan, 6 in Malaysia, 31 in South Korea, 5 in Taiwan, and 107 in Thailand. It anticipated substantial growth in parts of Asia with planned openings of 15 stores in China, 3 in Japan, 5 in Malaysia, 31 in South Korea, and 83 in Thailand. The company sold its Taiwan operations to Carrefour in return for Carrefour's stores in Eastern Europe. Allan Tien, spokesman for Carrefour Taiwan stated that: "It's hard to survive the fierce competition if you're not No. 1 or No. 2." Tien added: "If you find yourself struggling hard to make headway in certain countries, why keep doing it? We're late in breaking into the Czech Republic and Slovakia, and Tesco faces the same situation in Taiwan. I think this new breakthrough will facilitate these two groups' healthy operations."[56]

Tesco pointed out that "over eight million customers every week shop in over 300 stores across Asia." Tesco's growth in Asia was accomplished quickly after its entry there. The company moved into different countries in rapid succession: Thailand (1998), South Korea (1999), Taiwan (2000), Malaysia (2001), Japan (2003), and China (2004).

Tesco identified six elements of its international strategy:

1 "Be flexible – each market is unique and requires a different approach."
2 "Act local – local customers, local cultures, local supply chains, and local regulations require a tailored offer delivered by local staff."
3 "Keep focus – to be the local brand is a long term effort and takes decades."
4 "Be multiformat – no single format can reach the whole market. A whole spectrum from convenience to hypermarkets is essential."
5 "Develop capability – developing skill in people, processes, and systems and being able to share this skill between markets will improve the chances of success."
6 "Build brands – brands enable the building of important lasting relation-ships with customers."[57]

Overview

What were the prospects for Dairy Farm's Asian retail strategy? The target countries addressed by Dairy Farm included well over 2.5 billion people. The supermarket revolution was progressing rapidly, with a promising environment for future growth since the market share of supermarkets in food retailing was still small relative to the US or Europe. Vigorous economic growth in the region was likely to drive up sales from existing customers while stimulating the shift of customers away from wet markets to supermarkets. Greater international trade and industrialization were fostering urban expansion and increased demand for supermarkets.

The supermarket revolution had a strong local flavor. Each country had a different experience, depending on local tastes, culture, public policy, and economic circumstances. In India, the organized retail food sector was in its early stages. China and Malaysia were experiencing a very rapid startup of supermarkets and hypermarkets. The retail sectors of Hong Kong, the Republic of Korea, and Taiwan were more developed: in the Republic of Korea, supermarkets had attained a 60 percent market share. The market share of supermarkets in processed and packaged foods also varied widely: in Indonesia, Malaysia, and Thailand that share was 33 percent as compared with 63 percent in the Republic of Korea and Taiwan.[58]

Supermarkets expanded their share of processed and packaged foods at a faster rate than for fresh foods. Their offerings satisfied the rule of thumb that supermarkets' share of processed and packaged food should be twice that for fresh food,[59] based on consumer perceptions that traditional markets offered advantages over supermarkets in providing fresh food. However, given the different rates of growth, the market shares of processed and fresh foods might change as supermarkets gained a greater share of total retail sales.

Dairy Farm had concentrated its efforts where they generated the greatest economic return, with a focus on Asia. Achieving economies of scale in retail and wholesale distribution was critical to staying cost competitive. Efficient procurement would be essential to keep costs low while providing the product variety demanded by consumers.

Dairy Farm had selected individual formats or combinations of formats to best fit local conditions in its target markets. It had emphasized supermarkets in India, convenience stores in China, and a mix of store types in Indonesia. Dairy Farm's format choices would need to survive political and economic change in the target countries as well as facing the pressures of global competition. Dairy Farm's stores would need to attract customers away from both traditional fresh markets and domestic competitors who were closely attuned to local tastes.

Responding to the entry of global competitors would require Dairy Farm to make substantial investments to update and remodel existing stores and to establish new ones. Dairy Farm's distribution, procurement, and IT would also have to meet competition from major global companies. Would Dairy Farm's considerable experience and regional knowledge be sufficient for it to profit from Asia's supermarket revolution?

Danone: organizing for global competition

Franck Riboud, upon becoming Chairman and CEO of Groupe Danone, began to rationalize the company's organizational structure. The company, then with over 78,000 employees in 150 countries, had diversified extensively under the management of his father, Antoine Riboud. Playing to its strengths, Franck Riboud narrowed the company to three lines of business with a focus on strong global brands – fresh dairy products, beverages, and biscuits – and divested company interests in pasta, sauces, soups, ready-to-serve dishes, and candy.[1]

Franck Riboud announced that: "I don't see why I will not drive Danone as my colleagues are driving their American companies or their Italian companies or their UK companies. If we want to be a worldwide player, we have to play by the rules. We are going to create positive value year after year." In the year after Franck took the helm, the company listed its American Depositary Shares on the NYSE. In the next several years the stock of Groupe Danone (hereafter, Danone or the Group) rose about 65 percent, outperforming Unilever, P&G, and Coca-Cola.[2]

Danone announced three strategic priorities: "[R]efocus on three core businesses where we are already leaders on world markets (fresh dairy products, beverages, and biscuits), expand our international presence, and enhance profitability – and with it shareholder value."[3] Franck Riboud's early success at Danone had resulted from corporate restructuring. Many wondered whether he could maintain the company's momentum in the highly competitive global food market. Riboud observed: "I'm always under pressure to succeed. But you need pressure to achieve. You try harder."[4] The company set out to realize global growth opportunities in the Americas and Asia.

Company history

In March 1864, Jean-Baptiste Neuvesel, the descendent of a family of glass blowers, distributors, and manufacturers, bought a bankrupt bottle factory in the Rhône area. Neuvesel operated the bottle factory for over half a century and made it the market leader in bottle production. Eugène Souchon, the husband of Neuvesel's granddaughter, later bought a minority share in the mineral water company Evian to take advantage of the growing demand for bottled water. The Lyons-based company, renamed Verrerie Souchon-Neuvesel, produced bottles, industrial containers, and table glassware.[5]

Souchon's great-nephew, Antoine Riboud, took over Verrerie Souchon-Neuvesel in 1965. As a youth, Riboud had suffered from tuberculosis. His prospects seemed doubtful when he failed to pass his baccalaureate exam, and friends and family considered him to be informal and flippant. In his later years, he promised to dedicate his autobiography to the naysayers and entitle it *Last in the Class*.

In 1966, Antoine Riboud merged Verrerie Souchon-Neuvesel with Glaces de Boussois to form Boussois Souchon Neuvesel (BSN). Glaces de Boussois, from the north of France, manufactured automobile plate glass and window glass. The combined company was formed to obtain economies of scale in production and distribution to compete in the growing Common Market. In addition, the move toward no-deposit, no-return bottles meant that there would be increased demand for new glass bottles.[6] In 1968 Riboud was unsuccessful in an attempted takeover of France's leading glass maker, Saint Gobain.

At the time of the French Revolution, the Marquis de Lessert discovered the Cachat Spring in the small town of Evian-les-Bains and announced that it had curative powers. In 1826, the Dukes of Savoy granted the first official authorization to bottle Evian Natural Spring Water. BSN acquired La Société des Eaux Minérales d'Evian in 1970. Also that year, BSN bought the brewer Brasseries Kronenbourg and La Société Européenne de Brasserie a year later.[7]

These acquisitions made BSN the leading French manufacturer of beer and mineral water. Through its acquisition of Evian, BSN also became the leading French maker of baby food. The acquisitions could be viewed as downstream vertical integration since Evian, Kronenbourg, and La Société Européenne de Brasserie were major customers for BSN's glass bottles. The acquisitions also represented business diversification into beverages and baby food. As other types of containers including plastic, cardboard, and metal became increasingly competitive with glass, the company's entry into food production would prove profitable.[8]

Continuing its major entry into the food business, BSN in 1973 acquired Gervais Danone, a maker of yogurt, cheese, and pasta, to become France's largest food company.[9] Gervais Danone itself had a long history. In the mid-nineteenth century, Charles Gervais introduced the Petit Suisse soft cheese.

Isaac Carasso, a Frenchman living in Barcelona in 1919, established Danone to promote the healthful effects of yogurt. He named the company after his son Daniel. The Gervais and Danone companies entered into a cooperative distribution agreement in the 1950s and merged in 1967.[10]

Meanwhile, Isaac Carasso had immigrated to the US during the Second World War to escape the Nazi invasion. Carasso continued to sell yogurt, now renamed Dannon yogurt to accommodate American pronunciation. Dannon became the leading US yogurt brand. Beatrice Foods Company bought Dannon and then sold it to BSN Gervais Danone in 1981 for $84 million, thus reuniting the French and American yogurt brands.[11]

BSN Gervais Danone's transformation into a food company continued in 1981 when it withdrew from the plate glass business through the sale of Glaces de Boussois, although the Group's manufacture of glass containers still made up about 7 percent of its sales. Danone formed a partnership with Gerresheimer, the leading German glass maker.[12] Danone also reorganized its BSN Emballage unit and planned a new bottle manufacturing plant close to the wine-producing area of Languedoc in southwestern France.[13] In 1999 and 2003, the Group would complete its exit from glass manufacturing.

BSN Gervais Danone grew through expansion and a series of acquisitions in the food business, and diversified into confectionery, sauces, and condiments. BSN focused its expansion plans on Europe. In baby food, BSN operated through two subsidiaries, Diepal–Jacquemaire in pureed foods and Gallia in infant milk.[14] In 1986, it purchased the French company General Biscuit which made Lu cookies and operated a network of companies in Germany, Belgium, France, the Netherlands, and Italy. Expanding further into cookies in 1989, BSN Gervais Danone bought Nabisco's Asian subsidiary and its European subsidiaries: Belin in France, Jacob's in the UK, and Saiwa in Italy. With the collapse of the Soviet Union in 1989 and the opening of Eastern Europe, BSN Gervais Danone acquired cookie manufacturers Cokoladovny in the Czech Republic and Bolshevik in Russia. In addition, the company purchased cookie makers Papadopoulos in Greece and W&R Jacob in Ireland, and mineral waters Volvic and Mont Dore in France. Danone purchased Italy's leading cheese manufacturer, Galbani, which it would divest again in 2002.

As it entered the 1990s, BSN was the third-largest diversified food group in Europe and market leader in Belgium, France, Germany, Italy, Luxembourg, Portugal, and Spain.[15] The Group created a specialized export unit for determining international brand appeal in 1993. Global growth efforts relied on partnerships and buyouts in Asia, Latin America, and South Africa. The strategy resulted in a better indication of potential sales in target countries and indications of what products might prove most successful. In addition to expanded marketing efforts, the company produced yogurt, beer, mineral water, and cookies in Argentina, Brazil, China, Indonesia, Japan, and Mexico. Danone yogurt was being manufactured in thirty countries.[16]

Having established Danone as a global brand, BSN changed its name to Groupe Danone in 1994. The company chose as its symbol the image of a little boy gazing up at a star, and the Danone brand would link the company's various food products. Chairman and CEO Antoine Riboud turned to the question of succession.

Antoine Riboud's son Franck attended technical school to study engineering. After completing school, he pursued his passion for windsurfing.[17] After success and first-place finishes in windsurfing competitions, Franck decided to pursue his second love: skiing. The French company Rossignol hired Franck to work at a proposed ski factory in Vermont. When the venture was unsuccessful as a result of several warm New England winters, Franck joined BSN in 1981.[18]

Franck assisted in the $2.5 billion takeover of RJR Nabisco's biscuit and snack company in 1992. He also ran the Evian division and held a number of other positions within the company. In 1994, Franck was promoted to the number two position in Danone as Antoine's designated successor. This elevated Franck above other highly qualified contenders, including Henri Giscard d'Estaing, the son of the former French President. The appointment was greeted with derision by shareholders who suspected Antoine of nepotism. Some felt that Antoine's action was motivated by sentimentality; Banque Nationale de Paris's Jean-Marie L'Homé believed that Riboud senior "tried to accomplish through his son what he dreamed of doing, but did not have the chance." Others questioned Franck's youth and inexperience. Antoine responded that he "could not understand why it's a handicap to have the name Riboud."[19] Franck Riboud was elected the new chairman and CEO at a shareholders' meeting in 1996.

Restructuring Danone's organization

Franck Riboud set out to revamp Groupe Danone, challenging such international competitors as Britain's Unilever and Switzerland's Nestlé. He announced that the company would focus its efforts in three areas that represented 85 percent of sales: dairy products, beverages, and biscuits. The company moved to strengthen its brands, particularly Danone yogurt, Evian mineral water, and Lu cookies.

In a series of company divestitures, the company sold off brands and businesses that were not consistent with its three main areas. Beginning in 1997 and 1998, the company sold off several companies in pasta and prepared foods, including Agnesi, Birkel, Panzani, William Saurin, and La Familia. The Group further divested prepared food maker Liebig-Maille-Amora, which specialized in sauces and condiments, including Maille's Dijon mustard. The company spun off Leicht and Cross crispbread and Sonnen Bassermann heat-and-serve foods. The Group also sold off the confectioner Carambar–La Pie qui Chante, maker of the caramel candy bar with jokes inside the wrapper, which were much beloved by European children.

With sales of pasta businesses in France, Germany, Italy, and Spain, the company exited the market for pasta. The company substantially divested its holdings in sauces and all of its confectionery business.[20] Danone Group announced plans to sell its 50 percent interest in leading Italian grocery company STAR to its partner the Fossati family.[21]

Expanding further in its core areas, Danone took over Brazilian cookie manufacturer Campineira, partnered with Sabanci, the leading Turkish manufacturer of mineral waters and dairy products, and entered into agreements with Clover, the market leader in dairy products in South Africa, and Tunisian dairy manufacturer Meddeb.[22] Danone agreed with its JV partner Nestlé to split Cokoladovny into two companies, a chocolate and confectionery company, to be controlled by Nestlé, and a biscuit company, to be controlled by Danone.

Franck Riboud began to revamp Danone's management and established four divisions: (1) Fresh Dairy Products, (2) Water, (3) Biscuits, and (4) Asia-Pacific, see figure 10.1. He brought in Jan Bennink, a former P&G executive, to be the senior vice president of Fresh Dairy Products Worldwide. Pedro Medina would be senior vice president of Water Worldwide. Jean-Louis Gourbin was designated as senior vice president of Biscuits Worldwide. In addition, Simon Israel, formerly of Sara Lee Asia, would build Danone in the Far East as the senior vice president of Asia-Pacific.

This organizational structure was not consistent since three divisions were product-based while the fourth was based on geography. In part, this represented the company's emphasis on international growth, with some of the company's important target markets being in Asia-Pacific. The company's managers would later revisit the structure of the organization.

Franck Riboud's goal of international expansion would mean reducing the Group's dependence on France as well as on Europe generally. Danone obtained more than three-quarters of its sales in Europe, of which more than

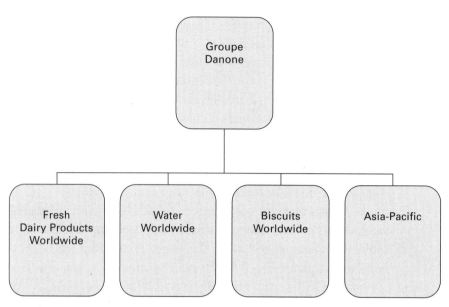

Fig. 10.1   Danone's first reorganization

half were from France alone. Although its business outside Europe had grown from 5 percent of sales to a quarter of sales, the company set a target of obtaining a third of its sales outside Europe.[23]

Franck Riboud's goal of international expansion also would require product innovation, targeting customer tastes outside of Europe. Many of the company's product innovations were introduced in Europe and best suited to European tastes. According to the company:

France was again the main focus of launches that included Danao, Crème de Yaourt, Danette Liègeoise, Charles de Gervais Crèmes Renversantes and Danone et Fruits Recette Crémeuse in dairy products; Lu Ourson, Hello Brownies, Pepito Mini-Rollos and Biscoto in biscuits, and Kronenbourg 2.6º, Kronenbourg Ice and Volvic One-liter bottles in beverages.[24]

The company made a number of Europe-wide product launches including a line of low-fat biscuits named Taillefine/Vitalinea. Crushable plastic bottles, introduced by Evian in 1995, were brought to Spanish and Turkish markets in 1998.[25]

Danone was the global leader in dairy products, including yogurts, cheeses, dairy desserts, and beverages, with a 15 percent world market share. However, three-quarters of its dairy sales were concentrated in Europe.[26]

Danone also was the world leader in cookies or sweet biscuits, with 9 percent of the market. The company also produced savory snacks and crackers, primarily in France, Italy, and Argentina. The company made biscuits in twenty countries and marketed biscuit products in almost seventy countries.[27] The company obtained over 70 percent of its biscuit sales in Europe, with about half of those sales in France. The company experienced its highest growth in operating margins outside Europe from its Bagley brand in Argentina, Danone in Indonesia, and group companies in China and India.[28]

Danone expanded its world holdings in mineral water as the second largest producer in the world behind Nestlé's Perrier. The company identified North America and Asia as its fastest growth areas. Danone paid $112 million in 1998 to acquire AquaPenn, a US mineral water company. The Group bought a 40 percent interest in Indonesia's Aqua and a controlling interest in China's Health water company.[29] Half of Danone's water sales were in France with the rest of Europe accounting for another quarter. The company was the leading brewer in France with Kronenbourg and in Spain with San Miguel and Mahou. The company also had a strong presence in markets for beer in Belgium, China, and Italy.[30]

Danone's Asia-Pacific division was charged with coordinating business development and maintained operations in China, India, and New Zealand, with a presence in Malaysia and Indonesia. The Group employed over 23,000 people in the Asia-Pacific area, almost 30 percent of its total employees. Of Danone's Asian sales, 57 percent were in China, 25 percent in India and Pakistan, 13 percent in Australia and New Zealand, and additional sales in Malaysia and Indonesia. Danone's Wahaha was China's largest beverage company. Danone also operated breweries in Wuhan and Tangshan. Shanghai Danone Biscuits experienced strong growth in sales.[31] Danone expanded its product offerings in Asia. In China, Danone began selling yogurts in plastic cups, a change from glass containers, and offering low-fat yogurt products. In Hong Kong, Danone's ready-to-serve Asian Specialties brand introduced new dim sum products.[32]

Managing Danone as an international business

Danone's transformation into an international business was complete. It had been a decade since BSN had changed its name to Danone and Franck Riboud declared the year 2004 to be a historic one for the company. The repositioning of the company had been a success, sales of dairy products had doubled, and sales of beverages had tripled. Perhaps more significantly, the company had become a truly international business, with the share of its sales outside Europe growing from 15 percent to over 40 percent.[33]

Franck Riboud noted that: "Our growth strategy is clearly founded on the strength of our three core businesses." In addition, Riboud identified three drivers for the company's growth. First, there were the blockbusters – product concepts that achieved double-digit growth and were the result of the company's R&D and focus on health concerns. Second, beverages in Asia were a major force. Third, was the company's geographic expansion.

Franck Riboud observed: "We are building the Groupe Danone of tomorrow in markets that include not only China and Indonesia, but also Mexico, Russia, and, in Fresh Dairy Products, the US." He emphasized that "the potential remains enormous." Noting that the company's sales grew steadily despite headwinds in the company's home market in France, Riboud said: "We are making good progress towards a better geographical balance." Danone moreover also was "consolidating beachheads around the Mediterranean from Morocco to Turkey, a region that will open up new horizons for growth in the future."[34]

Danone's organization was modified so as to give each of its divisions full global responsibilities, see figure 10.2. These three divisions represented over 97 percent of company sales. The company also included some businesses in a smaller global division that included Lea and Perrins in the US (the maker of Worcestershire Sauce), and Amoy Foods in Hong Kong (provider of sauces and frozen foods). The company's headquarters continued to have a regional vice president for Asia-Pacific. However, three executive vice presidents were charged, respectively, with Fresh Dairy Products Worldwide, Water Worldwide, and Biscuits and Cereal Products Worldwide.

The three divisions embodied Danone's quest for a "focused business structure." The Fresh Dairy Products Worldwide division, representing about half of company sales, included yogurt, desserts, and baby food. The Water Worldwide division was primarily bottled water and accounted for 25 percent of sales, and the Biscuits and Cereal Products Worldwide division made up about 22 percent of sales. The company also sought to achieve a "balanced geographic presence," as it tried to move its business in emerging markets from about 30 percent of sales to 40 percent of sales.[35]

The organizational shift, while subtle, was highly important for the company to maintain and extend its competitive advantages. The structure was based on the company's global market strategy, and recognized the success of its expansion strategy in the Asia-Pacific region. It was necessary for the Group to integrate Asia-Pacific into its overall global strategic business units.

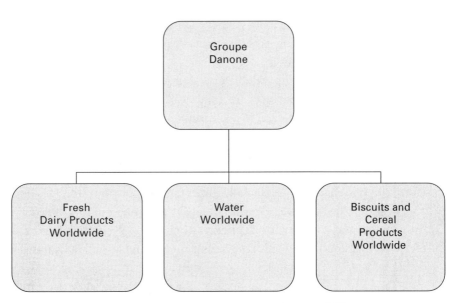

Fig. 10.2   Danone's organization with each business unit assuming global responsibilities

This would allow the heads of Fresh Dairy Products, Water, and Biscuits and Cereal Products to coordinate their efforts within their respective international markets.

The organizational structure contained the company's three main business areas, and also housed the Group's holdings of other companies and international JVs. Fresh Dairy Products contained Danone's acquisition of the US organic yogurt maker, Stonyfield Farm. Water included the company's stake in Wahaha Group, the leading beverage company in China, and various subsidiary JVs. Biscuits and Cereal Products held Griffin's Foods, Danone's wholly-owned subsidiary in New Zealand that made crackers and savory snacks.

According to the Group, its "successful international expansion rewards a strategy focusing on a limited number of countries, selected for their growth potential, where we have the size to achieve significant economies of scale."[36] The company's growth outside Europe was led by its Beverages, which had 47 percent of sales in Europe, 42 percent in Asia-Pacific, and 11 percent in the rest of the world. Dairy and Biscuits each had about three-quarters of their sales in Europe with about a quarter in the rest of the world. The company was able to achieve a number one position in several national markets, see table 10.1.

The company viewed its number one position in various national markets as a foundation for its international leadership position. In turn, the international leadership gave the company a "clear competitive advantage in terms of marketing expertise, industrial efficiency, breadth of product ranges and targeted R&D."[37]

The company operated a global organization with almost 90,000 employees around the world, of which about 56,000 were outside Europe. Managing such an international organization presented a special challenge in itself. Franck Riboud paid particularly close attention to it: "That is something I keep a very close eye on. I don't want us ever to get complacent or feel too comfortable with the way things are." The key for Riboud was geographic decentralization: "it is vitally important that responsibility for doing business should be as close to local markets as possible – that is the only way to preserve our capacity to adapt and anticipate." He emphasized the need for the "rapid circulation of ideas across borders." In particular, Danone has "learned to welcome the influence of the developing countries we work in, because it enables us to take a fresh look at our differences and develop innovative and exciting new ways to move ahead." The company had over 24,000 employees in China alone.[38]

To coordinate management and maintain consistency across the organization, the company instituted its "Danone Way of doing business" program. According to the company, the program "helps the Group build relationships of trust with all stakeholders – suppliers, distributors, industrial partners, employees, consumers as well as local communities."[39] The program provided business units with a set of best practices to promote social responsibility, and the company began to extend it throughout the company's international operating units. A related effort, termed the "Respect Program," was aimed at developing supplier relationships. According to Stephan Arino, the program's head: "The first step is for the manager to visit local suppliers' production facilities and assess working conditions" based on a set of established criteria.[40]

The company instituted an international employee program, that it referred to as "Evolution," designed to address the needs and concerns of non-managers. Tailored to local labor market conditions, the program focused on attracting and training employees. The program provides employees with a "skills passport" that shows the worker's job experience, to aid in job mobility both within and outside the company.[41]

Franck Riboud outlined four concepts based on health benefits of Danone products, with global reach and local brands:

Activia, called Bio in France, favors healthy digestion, while Actimel helps to reinforce the immune system, and Danonino, called Petit Gervais aux Fruits in France, helps

Table 10.1. Leading positions worldwide, by product category and country

Dairy products	Beverages	Biscuits and cereals
Argentina	Argentina	Argentina
Belgium	China	Belgium
Canada	France	China
Eastern Europe	Germany	Eastern Europe
France	Indonesia	France
North Africa and Middle East	Mexico	India
Spain (and Canary Islands)	Spain	Italy
Turkey		New Zealand
US		

Source: The Danone Adventure, Groupe Danone 2004, www.danone.com.

children to grow strong. Finally, Vitalinea, also called Taillefine, Vitasnella and Ser, depending on the country, is a range of diet products for people keeping an eye on their weight.[42]

Ser brought out a popular line of low-calorie soft drinks in Argentina that addressed local preferences for carbonated drinks and local flavors, along with an emphasis on health consciousness.[43]

Danone paid close attention to its customer target countries. For example, in Indonesia Danone introduced a yogurt beverage, named Milkuat, that was tailored to local tastes, while offering nutrition in the form of vitamins and added calcium. Noting that 60 percent of people in Indonesia earn less than $3 per day, the company introduced a drinkable yogurt at a low price; the company charged about 1,000 rupiah for a 100 ml bottle. To keep costs down, Danone used the resources of its own beverage unit in Indonesia, Danone Aqua. Recognizing geographic limitations (4,000 islands and 2 million small points of sale), the Danone Aqua unit contracted with seventy distributors so that it had 10,000 trucks with Aqua logos serving 1.3 million points of sale. The distribution of the yogurt drink piggybacked on the water distribution network. The drinkable yogurt was highly successful, selling 10 million bottles within 90 days of its introduction.[44]

In the wake of the Tsunami in South-east Asia, Groupe Danone distributed its local products free of charge to victims of the disaster: "The Group's 3 Indonesian subsidiaries, acting with the help of their local product distributor Pak Yunus and the armed forces, had already transported around 2 million bottles of Aqua water, 2 million packets of Biskuat biscuits and 800,000 bottles of Milkuat milk drinks."[45]

Danone's operations in Asia, particularly in China, were largely production and distribution through FDI without production for export. Danone's Asia-Pacific operations were almost two-thirds in China, with the rest distributed in Australia, India, Indonesia, Malaysia, and New Zealand.

In its many markets, Danone pursued a strategy of continual product innovation. Another of its competitive weapons was its extensive product lines.[46] In many developed markets, Danone followed a premium brand product differentiation strategy, which was subject to challenges from competing premium brands as well as cost-cutting entrants. In addition, it developed strong relationships with local and international distributors, such as Carrefour.[47] The company faced many challenges to its dominant position – for example, the German multinational dairy company Müller challenged Danone in Spain with a premium Yogurt line.[48]

Carrying out product innovation required organizational coordination. New products developed in one geographic area would need to be made known to parts of the company operating in other geographic areas where they might appeal to customers. To achieve this objective Danone brought together its R&D teams to their joint research center in Palaiseau, France. The research facility, known as the Danone Vitapole Centre de Recherche Daniel Carasso, comprised "600 people from 25 different nationalities, of which near to 500 are researchers, developers and Quality engineers."[49]

Overview

The Danone Group had achieved the leading position in the world in both fresh dairy products and biscuits, and second place in bottled waters. The company was focused on key brands and innovative healthy products and had begun to overcome its dependence on European markets. Danone was well diversified geographically but faced the many challenges of operating around the world. As one of the largest global food companies, Danone faced challenges from large diversified competitors and many local rivals.

The company had achieved significant growth in its target countries – China, Indonesia, Mexico, Russia, and the US and Franck Riboud identified new frontiers for business in North Africa and the Middle East. The company continued to seek "geographic balance," having achieved a global profile with 80 percent of its business outside its home country and half of its business outside Western Europe.[50]

The organizational structure that Franck Riboud had established would help the company maintain its competitive advantages in international markets. The company's organizational transformation provided important lessons for global business managers. The company's divisions reflected the global markets that it served; these allowed division managers responsibilities for business that crossed international borders. The company could operate at the scale needed to serve global markets.

The global market divisions also allowed the company to be market responsive, tailoring its offerings to customer needs within countries. The organizational structure favored decentralized decision making. Franck Riboud emphasized that:

our organizations are structured to allow decisions to be taken at local level as often as possible, making local management teams responsible for their revenues and income and for their own business functions, including marketing, sales, logistics and production.

The decentralized structure allowed the company to pursue partnerships and JVs as a means of entering target markets.

For Riboud:

our approach to markets supposes local presence and close relationships with local people. Food is very much a matter of culture, so understanding different cultures is essential to our business . . . Similarly, in our distribution strategy, we are building increasingly close ties to traditional retailing to ensure that our products are accessible in all the places where people live, commute, work, and play.[51]

Danone's organizational structure, with its basis on global markets, enabled the company to face global competitive challenges.

Conclusion

Global competition is fierce, and intensifies every day. New market leaders are springing up around the world, including champions from emerging markets. Companies must be prepared for competition from firms with world-class products, cutting-edge technologies, and drastic cost efficiencies.

Trade barriers are falling continually, although national borders remain "sticky." Each small decline in barriers to trade opens new opportunities for international transactions, and falling trade barriers are changing business methods in a growing number of industries. Local businesses are finding it to be increasingly difficult to maintain a protected niche in a local market. To be successful, more and more companies discover that they must have a global competitive strategy.

The continued expansion of world trade affects all aspects of our daily lives, at work and at home. Residents of developed economies have long benefited from low-cost imports. Now they are being joined by residents of many emerging economies, with consumption of housing, cars, and electronics, spreading across the world. The number of nations that embraces world trade forms a growing consensus.

Billions of new consumers have entered the global market place, as developing countries participate in world trade. An expanding middle class in emerging markets is driving increased consumption and an expansion of global business.[1] In many countries, driven by gains from trade and the forces of economic specialization, workers are shifting to more productive sectors of their economies.

Globalization is making management strategy into a common language. Countries are connected as never before. Advances in communications, IT, and transportation are shrinking the planet. Familiarity and trust are uniting distant trading partners. Businesses are gaining knowledge and experience operating in multiple countries and coordinating global organizations.

Yet, we live in a bumpy world. Globalization is a powerful trend, but it has lots of ups and downs. Countries tear down barriers to trade and erect new ones – the playing field is far from being level. National borders continue to matter. The evidence for this is the persistent differences in wages and incomes. Moreover, there continue to be significant differences in wealth, health, education, and technology. Prices and products are very different across countries.

Managers must learn to read the world's economic contours. Today's barriers to trade are tomorrow's business opportunities. Companies benefit by arbitraging between different national economies. They address the staggering size of global markets by offering world-class products and services, and by tailoring their product offerings to the amazing diversity of national markets.

This book sets out a method for strategy making that is geared to the needs of the international business manager. The "Star Analysis" provides the manager with a means of gathering, processing, and organizing geographic and national economic data. The analysis yields data that can be applied to generating a strategy that takes into account the features of the company's home country, supplier countries, partner countries, and customer countries.

The "Star Analysis" is also used to evaluate competitors. By performing an analysis of the competitor's home, supplier, partner, and customer countries, the manager can identify critical differences. The manager can determine whether the competitor's supplier countries offer higher quality, better technology, lower cost, better proximity to customers, or better trade regulations. The manager should consider whether the competitor's partner countries offer better access to manufacturing locations, distribution systems, and technology, that complement the competitor's activities. The manager should further examine whether the competitor's footprint of customer countries is national, regional, or global, and the pattern of countries where the company and its rival compete directly. The critical differences revealed by this analysis can be the basis for the company's competitive advantage.

The global firm seeks competitive advantage by activities and transactions that connect its home, supplier, and partner countries with its target customer countries. This book introduced the concept of the *global value connection* to provide a tool for analyzing production, distribution, and transaction processes that cross national borders. The international business manager cannot choose supplier or customer markets in isolation. The country markets that are linked by the company much be chosen together so as to create the greatest net gains from trade.

International business is no longer a set of unconnected foreign-country operations. The key word in global business is *coordination*. Managers make the best use of the global factory by coordinating across their home country, supplier countries, and partner countries. Managers make the best use of the global store by coordinating distribution and sales across their customer countries. Most significantly, they seek to create value from critical country pairs by connecting countries across the globe. The firm's global value connection is an important source of competitive advantage.

World trade has begun to shift from a regional focus to global connections. Transactions span the Americas, Europe, Asia, Africa, and Latin America. Companies are developing global factories in which design, production, and assembly connect continents. The global store offers logistics and distribution between regions of the world.

The international business manager must get the direction of trade just right, linking supplier markets with the right customer markets. Value for the international business rides the wave of gains from trade between countries. These sources of value are balanced against the costs of trade: transactions, tariffs, transportation, and time. By structuring cross-border transactions in an innovative fashion, the international business gains a global competitive advantage.

Specific global advantages tend to be temporary. The sources of gains from trade are constantly changing in response to technological advances, worker training, demographic shifts, and varying customer demands. The manager must be vigilant in identifying new sources of supply and flexible in relocating operations, opening new facilities, and developing new relationships with suppliers and partners.

The world's economic contours are constantly shifting, as well. The falling costs of trade continue to drive globalization. Technological change drastically impacts "the four Ts." Transportation costs are declining with advances in logistics and transportation technology. The *Emma Maersk*, at over 1,300 ft in length, heralds the arrival of the super-container ships capable of carrying 11,000 standard containers.[2] The super-container ships offer substantial economies of scale and cost reductions in ocean shipping. Advances in telecommunications, from increased use of the Internet to ubiquitous mobile devices, lower the costs of transactions.

International transaction costs are falling as executives become familiar with distant markets through increased business interaction. With experience, businesses are developing ways to reduce the time consumed by international transactions, lowering time to market and the time required to develop contracts across borders.

The pressure of business opportunities drives changes in public policy. Businesses find ways around trade regulations and create political pressure for relaxing barriers. National governments have additional incentives to reduce barriers in order to attract FDI. Although borders remain highly "sticky," countries increasingly try to demonstrate that they are "open for business."

The global firm faces the dual challenge of achieving world-class scale economies while responding to the imperative of local customer differences. The forces calling for *standardization* include:

- Convergence in customer preferences and income across target countries with economic development and trade
- Competition from successful global products
- Growing customer awareness of international brands in many countries
- Economies of scale and other cost benefits from standardization
- Falling costs of trade with greater globalization
- Cultural exchange and business interactions between countries.

The competitive forces calling for *customization* for local markets include:

- Persistent differences in customer preferences resulting from country differences in social organization, culture, history, traditions, and politics
- Persistent differences in customer incomes across target countries
- The need to build local brand recognition
- Competition from successful and innovative domestic companies
- Variations in the costs of trade across countries
- Regulatory requirements (quality, safety, technical specifications, domestic content).

Business managers need competitive strategies to address this dual challenge.

The book has introduced five generic strategies for coping with the two sides of the global challenge, the "G5 strategies":

- Create global platforms
- Develop global networks
- Become a global intermediary between buyers and sellers across borders
- Achieve entrepreneurial entry into new markets
- Manage a global investment strategy by making the right combination of contracts and vertical integration.

The "G5 strategies" help the manager to make the best strategic mix of standardization and customization. They allow the business to extend its global reach to serve the huge global market place. They also allow the business to tailor its offering to target countries.

These strategies are not exhaustive. Rather, they suggest the greater complexity in business strategies required to build a global value connection. Achieving global competitive advantage requires greater skills, capabilities, and knowledge than ever before. For global business managers, the journey is only just beginning.

Glossary

ABB	Asea Brown Boveri
ADR	American Depositary Receipt
ADS	American Depositary Shares
AG	Aktiengesellschaft
BA	Business Area (ABB)
BSN	Boussois Souchon Neuvesel
CAS	Chinese Academy of Sciences
CEO	chief executive officer
COO	chief operating officer
CRL	China Research Laboratory
EBITDA	earnings before interest, tax, depreciation, and amortization
FDI	foreign direct investment
fob	freight-on-board
GATT	General Agreement on Tariffs and Trade
GDP	gross domestic product
GE	General Electric
GM	General Motors
GPS	Global Positioning Satellite

HP	Hewlett-Packard
IMF	International Monetary Fund
IP	intellectual property
IT	information technology
JIT	just-in-time
JV	joint venture
LBO	leveraged-buyout
LCD	liquid crystal display
LSE	London Stock Exchange
LTL	less-than-truckload
M&A	mergers and acquisitions
MDO	Market Development Organization (P&G)
MFA	Multifiber Agreement
MFN	most-favored nation (trading status)
MNC	multinational corporation
mt	metric tons
NAFTA	North American Free Trade Agreement
NASDAQ	National Association of Securities Dealers Automated Quotation
NPV	net present value
NYSE	New York Stock Exchange
OECD	Organization for Economic Cooperation and Development
OEM	original equipment manufacturer
OTC	over-the-counter

P&G	Procter & Gamble
P&O	Peninsular & Oriental Steam Navigation
PC	personal computer
PLC	public limited company
PPF	production possibility frontier
PPP	purchasing power parity
PRC	People's Republic of China
QDI	Quantum Design International Corp. (Legend)
R&D	research and development
SA	Société Anonyme
SBU	strategic business unit
SEC	Securities and Exchange Commission
SUV	Sport Utility Vehicle
TRIPS	Trade Related Aspects of Intellectual Property Rights
UAE	United Arab Emirates
UN	United Nations
UNCTAD	United Nations Conference on Trade and Development
VAT	value added tax
WTO	World Trade Organization

Notes and references

Introduction: the global challenge

1 Jeffrey McCracken, "Reassembling Delphi," *Wall Street Journal*, October 17, 2005, p. B1.

2 Brock Yates, "What's Good for General Motors," *Wall Street Journal*, May 24, 2005.

3 Thomas Friedman argues that the international market place is already a level playing field because of the Internet and other factors, but misses many of the complexities of international business. See Thomas L. Friedman, 2005, *The World is Flat: A Brief History of the Twenty-First Century*, New York: Farrar, Straus & Giroux.

4 United Nations Conference on Trade and Development (UNCTAD), "Efficient Trade Facilitation and Transport to Improve Participation by Developing Countries in International Trade," Geneva, January 2004.

5 See David Hummels, Jun Ishii, and Yi Kei-Mu, 2001, "The Nature and Growth of Vertical Specialization in World Trade," *Journal of International Economics*, 54 (1), June, pp. 75–96.

6 David S. Landes, 1998, *The Wealth and Poverty of Nations*, New York: Norton, p. xx.

7 Transparency International Policy and Research Department, "Report on the Transparency International Global Corruption Barometer 2005," 2005, Berlin, Germany, transparencyinternational.org.

8 Sarah Rundell, 2004, "Lapping Up Luxury," *Africa Investor*, October–December, pp. 10–13.

1 The global mosaic

1 On historical and geographic factors that affect the wealth of countries, see David S. Landes, 1998, *The Wealth and Poverty of Nations*, New York: Norton.

2 Adam Smith, 1998 [1776], *An Inquiry into the Nature and Causes of the Wealth of Nations*, Washington, DC: Regnery Publishing, p. 10.

3 See J. Anderson and E. van Wincoop, 2004, "Trade Costs," *Journal of Economic Literature*, 42, pp. 691–751. They estimate the combined effects of transportation, border-related trade barriers, and wholesale and retail trade.

4 Daniel F. Spulber, 1996, "Market Microstructure and Intermediation," *Journal of Economic Perspectives*, 10, Summer, pp. 135–152.

5 This is according to a UPS case study, see http://ups-scs.com/solutions/case_studies/cs_adidas.pdf.

6 See the UPS case study http://ups-scs.com/solutions/case_studies/cs_adidas.pdf.

7 The World Bank and the International Finance Corporation, 2006, *Doing Business in 2006: Creating Jobs*, Washington, DC: World Bank, p. 53. This publication is hereafter referred to as *Doing Business 2006*.

8 *Doing Business 2006*, p. 54.

9 A. T. Kearney, 2006, "Emerging Market Priorities for Global Retailers: The 2006 Global Retail Development Index," p. 4

10 Mei Fong, "Chinese Rules May Tie Up Foreign Retailers," *Wall Street Journal*, July 17, 2006, p. A6.

11 Quoted by James J. Cramer, "Behind the Euronext Deal," *Wall Street Journal*, May 26, 2006, p. A10.

12 Quoted in Jenny Anderson and Heather Timmons, "Big Board Bids for Exchanges Across Europe," *New York Times*, May 23, 2006, p. A1.

13 Quoted in Jeremy Grant, "SEC and Euronext in NYSE Merger Plan Talks," *Financial Times*, August 3, 2006.

14 Ohmae argues that in a borderless world what counts are "economic zones" such as Silicon Valley, rather than nation-states, Kenichi Ohmae, 1995, *The End of the Nation State: The Rise of Regional Economies*, New York: Free Press. Kindleberger states that as an economic unit, "the state is just about through," Charles P. Kindleberger, 1969, *American Business Abroad*, New Haven: Yale University Press.

15 A. C. Nielsen, 2000, *A Report into International Price Comparisons*, February 13, prepared for the UK Department of Trade and Industry.

16 The Economist Intelligence Unit, 2001, *International Price Comparisons*, A Report Prepared for the UK Department of Trade and Industry and the Swedish Ministry for Foreign Affairs, London: DTI.

17 The Economist Intelligence Unit, *ibid.*, pp. 15–16.

18 "A $2,200 Car in 2008," *Red Herring*, August 7, 2006, www.redherring.com.

19 See O. Ashenfelter and S. Jurajda, 2001, "Cross-Country Comparisons of Wage Rates: The Big Mac Index," Princeton University Working Paper, October.

20 T. L. Friedman, 2005, *The World Is Flat: A Brief History of the Twenty-First Century*, New York: Farrar, Straus & Giroux.

21 Ashenfelter and Jurajda, "Cross-Country Comparisons," *ibid.*, assume that productivity levels are similar and interpret the ratio of the wage rate to the price of a "Big Mac" as adjusting for PPP. They argue that PPP-adjusted real wages in the US, Japan, and Western Europe were four or five times higher than in Eastern Europe, Korea, or Brazil and ten times higher than in China, India, or Columbia.

22 Friedman, *The World Is Flat*, *ibid.*, p. 182.

23 Richard Florida, 2005, "The World is Spiky," *The Atlantic Monthly*, October, pp. 48–51. See also Richard Florida, 2003, *The Rise of the Creative Class*, New York: Basic Books, and Richard Florida, 2005, *The Flight of the Creative Class*, New York: HarperBusiness.

2 Global strategic analysis

1 The present analysis differs from that of Michael E. Porter, 1990, *The Competitive Advantage of Nations*, New York: Free Press. Porter's important analysis provides a method for evaluating a country's competitiveness and helps public policy makers choose the best

conditions for businesses from their country, such as the development of "clusters" of firms in a Silicon Valley setting. Porter discusses the home country of a firm and points out that: "The strongest competitive advantages often emerge from clusters that are geographically localized" (p. 580). My framework looks at how a company uses its international connections in many countries to achieve competitive advantage. In my framework, the home country is one aspect of many in the business' global strategy and it can transcend its immediate geography by international transactions.

2 In the US, a company is incorporated in a specific state, with the corporate charter specifying the company's name, purpose, shares, and other details of its corporate governance, although the company's incorporation is recognized nationally.

3 P. N. Doremus, W. W. Keller, L. W. Pauly, and S. Reich, 1998, *The Myth of the Global Corporation*, Princeton, NJ: Princeton University Press, p. 52. See their work generally for a comparison of corporate governance in the US, Germany, and Japan.

4 See Bernardo Kosacoff, Jorge Forteza, H. Inéz Barbero, F. Porta, and E. Alejandro Stengel, 2002, *Going Global From Latin America: The Arcor Case*, Buenos Aires: McGraw-Hill Interamerican.

5 R. H. Coase, 1937, "The Nature of the Firm," *Economica*, 4, pp. 386–405.

6 The mode of entry choice also applies to entry into a customer country. For a discussion of modes of entry, see F. R. Root, 1994, *Entry Strategies for International Markets*, San Francisco: Lexington Books.

7 The elasticity of demand E is the percentage change in the quantity sold Q caused by percentage change in the price P, that is,

$$E = -(\Delta Q/Q)/(\Delta P/P) = -(\Delta Q/\Delta P)(P/Q).$$

Since demand is decreasing in the price, a price increase causes a reduction in quantity sold. For convenience, it is useful to think of the elasticity of demand as a positive number, so that a minus sign is included to make the term positive.

8 The company's revenue equals price times output, $R = PQ$. Marginal revenue due to a change in output is

$$MR = P + Q\Delta P/\Delta Q = P(1 + (Q/\Delta Q)(\Delta P/P)) = P(1 - 1/E).$$

9 With pricing to market, the company's price in each country i satisfies

$$P_i(1 - 1/E_i) = MC_i.$$

The price will vary across countries, depending on variations in elasticity of demand and variations in marginal cost. With the same marginal cost across countries, the international business will generally choose a lower price in a country with a greater price elasticity of demand.

10 Oliver Wild, www.ess.uci.edu/~oliver/silk.html. See also Frances Wood, 2004, *The Silk Road: Two Thousand Years in the Heart of Asia*, Berkeley: University of California Press.

11 Phred Dvorak and Evan Ramstad, "Behind Sony–Samsung Rivalry, An Unlikely Alliance Develops," *Wall Street Journal*, January 3, 2006, p. A1.

12 Dvorak and Ramstad, *ibid.*

13 The partnership was called S-LCD. See Ed Frauenheim, "Sony–Samsung Complete LCD Plant," *ZDNet News*, July 15, 2004, http://news.zdnet.com/2100-9584-22-5271407.html.

14 "Sony, Samsung Bolster Alliance, Agree to Share 24,000 Patents," *Japan Times*, December 15, 2004, www.japantimes.co.jp.

15 *Japan Times, ibid.*

16 "IBM, Sony, Toshiba in Alliance," *Red Herring*, January 13, 2006, www.redherring.com.

17 See Andrew S. Grove, 1996, *Only the Paranoid Survive*, New York: Doubleday.

18 Michael Y. Yoshino and U. Srinivasa Rangan, 1995, *Strategic Alliances*, Boston, MA: Harvard Business School Press, p. 21.

19 Yoshino and Rangan, *ibid.*, 109.

20 Yoshino and Rangan, *ibid.*, chapter 6. See also Bettina Büchel, Christianne Prange, Gilbert Probst, and Charles-Clemens Rüling, 1998, *International Joint Venture Management*, New York: John Wiley & Sons.

21 Airbus is 80 percent owned by EADS and 20 percent owned by the British BAE Systems PLC. EADS was founded on July 10, 2000, the result of a merger between Aerospatiale Matra SA of France, Construcciones Aeronáuticas SA of Spain, and DaimlerChrysler Aerospace AG of Germany. According to the two CEOs of EADS, Philippe Camus and Rainer Hertrich: "The new integrated structure is as important for a transparent and efficient industrial organization as for its new projects like the super Airbus A3XX," www.eads-nv.com/eads/en/index.htm.

22 John Tagliabue, "Airbus Clears Plans to Build Long-Range Jumbo Jet," *New York Times*, December 20, 2000, p. W1.

23 "The cabin interior is produced in Buxtehde and Laupheim in Germany. Plants for the fuselage (forward and aft) are spread across Germany in Hamburg, Nordenham, Bremen and Varel. Cockpit and center fuselage come from sites in France at Meaulte, Saint Nazaire and Nantes. The wings are made in Filton and Broughton, UK and assembled in Broughton. The tailplane and landing door gears are made in Spain at Puerto Real, Getafe and Illescas." See Phil Bishop, "Aerospace, Raising the A380," October 19, 2005, www.hoistmagazine.com/story.asp?sectioncode=109&storyCode=2031887.

24 Airbus was 20 percent minority-owned by the British BAE Systems PLC, which subsequently sold its shares to EADS which became the full owner of Airbus. EADS was publicly traded.

25 Neil Fligstein, 2006, "Sense Making and the Emergence of a New Form of Market Governance: The Case of the European Defense Industry," *American Behavioral Scientist*, 49 (7), March, pp. 949–960.

26 Fligstein, *ibid.*, p. 959.

27 Mark Landler and Keith Bradsher, "Raising the Bar in the Aircraft Wars," *New York Times*, March 15, 2006, p. C1.

28 Alex Taylor, III, "Lord of the Air: What's Left for Airbus After Overtaking Boeing in the Commercial Aircraft Market? Building a Really Big Plane," *Fortune Magazine*, November 10, 2003, p. 34.

29 Mark Landler, "Politics Joins Production as Problem for Airbus," *New York Times*, July 4, 2006, p. C1. On political control, see also Holman Jenkins, Jr., "How Airbus Lost Its Bearings," *Wall Street Journal*, May 24, 2006, p. A15.

30 "Thank you, Singapore," *The Economist*, September 30, 2000, p. 63.

31 To increase the range of the plane, the wing was widened near the fuselage to boost the amount of fuel-storage space, and a trailing-edge wedge was added to increase the lift of

the wings, see Jeff Cole, "Wing Commander: At Boeing, an Old Hand Provides New Tricks in Battle with Airbus," *Wall Street Journal*, January 10, 2001, p. A1. Boeing also added a variety of more powerful, fuel-efficient engines for customers to choose from. The updated aircraft, which Boeing called the 747-400, would transport between 416 to 524 passengers with an extended range and is available in four models. In addition to the basic 747-400, Boeing offered a high-capacity domestic version that could carry up to 568 passengers, a combination aircraft with passengers in the front and cargo in the back, and an all-cargo freighter. See Boeing home page, http://boeing.com/commercial/747family/index.html, for 747-400.

32 *Boeing Current Market Outlook*, http://boeing.com/commercial/cmo/4da05.html.

33 Laurence Zuckerman, "Boeing's Planned Jetliner to Be Almost Supersonic," *New York Times*, March 30, 2001, p. C1.

34 www.boeing.com/commercial/777family/background.html.

35 Richard Aboulafia, "The Airbus Debacle," *Wall Street Journal*, June 20, 2006, p. A20.

36 Jiangsu Longliqi Group Co. Ltd, www.longliqi.com/llqenglish/llqenglish.asp.

37 See "About Us" on the C-BONS website, www.cbons.com/index.html.

38 Phelps and Fuller examine competition between corporate affiliates within multinational corporations, and point out that there is considerable geographic inertia, see N. A. Phelps and C. Fuller, 2000, "Multinationals, Intracorporate Competition, and Regional Development," *Economic Geography*, 76 (3), July, pp. 224–243.

39 Willie Chen, Stan Shih, and Po-Young Chu, 2005, *Business Growth Strategies for Asia Pacific*, Singapore: Wiley.

3 Global competitive advantage

1 www.nokia.com/A4149133.

2 Andy Reinhardt, "Nokia's Magnificent Mobile-Phone Manufacturing Machine," August 3, 2006, businessweek.com, www.businessweek.com/globalbiz/content/aug2006/gb20060803_618811.htm.

3 www.lifung.com/business/index.html.

4 The principles of value creation can be illustrated with a basic example. A single customer representing a specific market segment has a willingness to pay of $200. Therefore, the most value that the company could create is $200. In serving the customer, the company employs some of its own assets, that are valued at $80. The company also purchases inputs from a supplier, who has costs of $50. The value created by the company's buy-and-sell transactions is the customer's benefit net of the cost of using the firm's assets and net of the supplier's costs: $200 − $80 − $50 = $70.

5 For a discussion of the concept of added value based on game theory, see Adam M. Brandenburger and Harborne W. Stuart, Jr., 1996, "Value-based Business Strategy," *Journal of Economics & Management Strategy*, 5, Spring, pp. 5–24. The notion that value is the additional contribution of a player to a coalition in a game is familiar to students of cooperative game theory; see, for example, Richard Aumann, 1987, "Game Theory," in J. Eatwell, M. Milgate, and P. Newman, eds., *The New Palgrave: A Dictionary of Economics*, London: Macmillan, pp. 460–482. See also the discussion in E. Davis and J. Kay, 1990, "Assessing Corporate Performance," *Business Strategy Review*, 1, 1990, pp. 1–16.

6 Michael Dell, Address to The Executives' Club of Chicago, "Netspeed: The Supercharged Effect of the Internet," October 23, 1998, www.executivesclub.org/static/News98-99/ Michael%20Dell.htm.

7 For 2000, it was estimated that Dell Computer had a cost of goods sold equal to 78.8 percent of operating revenue and selling, general, and administrative cost of goods sold of 10.9 percent. See Lori Calabro and Gunn Partners, "Cost Management Survey: Bend and Stretch, Why the Best Companies Remain Focused on Cost Cutting – Whatever the Business Cycle," *CFO Magazine*, 26 February, 2002, cfo.com.

8 See also Robert C. Feenstra, 1998, "Integration of Trade and Disintegration of Production in the Global Economy," *Journal of Economic Perspectives*, 12, Fall, pp. 31–50.

9 Porter explains that each firm's internal value chain is embedded in an external value system of activities composed of supplier value chains upstream and distribution channel and buyer value chains downstream. Porter defines the firm's value chain as its internal processes: "Every firm is a collection of activities that are performed to design, produce, market, deliver and support its product." See Michael E. Porter, 1985, *Competitive Advantage: Creating and Sustaining Superior Performance*, New York: Free Press.

10 See Christian Broda and David E. Weinstein, 2004, "Globalization and the Gains From Variety," NBER Working Paper 10314, February, Cambridge, MA, National Bureau of Economic Research.

11 Adam Smith, 1998 [1776], *An Inquiry into the Nature and Causes of the Wealth of Nations*, Washington, DC: Regnery Publishing.

12 David Ricardo, 1911 [1817], *Principles of Political Economy and Taxation*, London: Dent & Sons.

13 Suppose that there are two countries A and B, and a set of goods indexed by j. The wage rates in the two countries are denoted W_A and W_B. The productivities of a unit of labor for good j are denoted g_{Aj} and g_{Bj}. The wage rates adjust to market forces given the productivity parameters and each country's consumption patterns. Country A will export good 1 if it has a lower unit labor cost than Country B – that is, $W_A/g_{A1} < W_B/g_{B1}$.

Rearranging the fraction, Country A will export good 1 to Country B if the relative productivity of labor in Country A as compared to Country B is greater than the ratio of the wage in Country A to the wage in Country B, $W_A/W_B < g_{A1}/g_{B1}$.

For a given set of goods, those with relative productivities greater than the wage ratio are exported from Country A to Country B, and those with relative productivities less than the wage ratio are exported in the other direction. Economists will doubtless recognize this multi-product adaptation of the Ricardian model of comparative advantage, see Rudiger Dornbusch, Stanley Fischer, and Paul A. Samuelson, 1977, "Comparative Advantage, Trade, and Payments in a Ricardian Model with a Continuum of Goods," *American Economic Review*, 67, December, pp. 823–839.

14 This type of gains from trade is associated with the Heckscher–Ohlin–Vanek model of international trade.

15 A country's production possibilities frontier is a schedule of the various mixes of goods that it can produce given that it efficiently uses its resources and technologies.

16 These types of gains from trade are those represented by the Edgeworth–Bowley box. At the initial endowments of goods, the two countries have different marginal rates of substitution between the goods. This means that the two countries are off the contract curve

representing the best possible allocation of endowments. By exchanging some properly chosen amounts of the goods, the countries' marginal rates of substitution move closer together and the countries approach the contract curve, making both countries strictly better off than they were without trade.

17 For a development of the theory of international technology markets, see Daniel F. Spulber, 2005, "Innovation, Technology Transfer and International Trade," Northwestern University, Working Paper.

18 Consider the following numerical example of value creation. Suppose that customer's willingness to pay for the firm's product or service is 200 and the ask price of the firm's product or service is 110. Then, the value received by the firm's customer is $200 - 110 = 90$. Next, suppose that the supplier costs are 15 and the bid price offered to the firm's supplier is 70. Then, the value obtained by the supplier is $70 - 15 = 55$. Suppose further that the cost of using the firm's assets is 10. The total value captured by the firm is Ask price $-$ bid price $-$ cost of the firm's assets, which equals $110 - 70 - 10 = 30$. The value created by the firm equals Customer value $+$ supplier value $+$ value of the firm, which comes to $90 + 55 + 30 = 175$. Notice that the customer willingness to pay minus supplier costs minus cost of the firm's assets equals $200 - 15 - 10 = 175$. These two methods of calculating value creation are equivalent.

19 There can be market frictions that permit firms to deliver less value than competitors and still attract customers. If competitors face capacity constraints and entry barriers, the firm will be able to attract customers without necessarily outperforming competitors. If customers are not well informed about alternatives or face costs of switching to another firm's products, a firm may continue serving customers while delivering lower value. However, such advantages are temporary, and likely to be quickly eroded by competition.

20 Michael Porter offers three well-known generic strategies for attracting customers: product differentiation, cost leadership, and focus, where the firm offers both better products and lower costs to a customer niche, see Michael E. Porter, 1980, *Competitive Strategy: Techniques for Analyzing Industries and Competitors*, New York: Free Press.

21 To attract investment capital, managers maximize the value of the firm. Maximizing the firm's present value of expected cash flows assures that the firm is maximizing the owner's equity since the shares represent ownership of the firm's future stream of expected cash flows net of debt costs. Shareholder value is the market value of owner's equity. Since shareholders claim the residual earnings of the company, shareholder value is the NPV of expected cash flows net of debt costs.

22 See Gary Lilien, Philip Kotler, and K. Sridhar Moorthy, 1992, *Marketing Models*, Englewood Cliffs, NJ: Prentice Hall, pp. 512–517.

23 Timothy Bresnahan and Daniel F. G. Raff, 1991, "Intra-Industry Heterogeneity and the Great Depression: The American Motor Vehicles Industry, 1929–1935," *Journal of Economic History*, 51, June, pp. 317–331.

24 Joseph A. Schumpeter, 1997, *The Theory of Economic Development*, New Brunswick, NJ: Transaction Publishers, p. 229.

4   Global competitive strategy

1 Paul Ingrassia and John Stoll, "The Weekend Interview with Carlos Ghosn, Hottest Car Guy on Earth," *Wall Street Journal*, January 14–15, 2006, p. A8.

2 Ingrassia and Stoll, *ibid.*

3 Gary S. Vasilash, "Nissan: How to Achieve Shift," *Automotive Design and Production*, 2005, www.autofieldguide.com.

4 Information regarding the platforms comes from the *Renault–Nissan Alliance Renault–Nissan Handbook*, September 2005.

5 *Renault–Nissan Alliance*, *ibid.*

6 A firm's technology has multi-product economies of scale if the sum of the firm's marginal costs of each good times the quantity of each good is less than total costs.

7 Micheline Maynard, "Ford Eliminating Up To 30,000 Jobs and 14 Factories," *New York Times*, January 24, 2006, p. A1.

8 "Got 5,000 Euros? Need a New Car?," *BusinessWeek*, July 4, 2005.

9 "The Acer Group's China Manufacturing Decision," Richard Ivey School of Business, Case 1999-08-25.

10 Kevin P. Hopkins, "Value Opportunity Nine: Improving Asset Utilization," *BusinessWeek Online*, January 20, 2006, www.businessweek.com.

11 "Building a Global Loyal Following," *Appliance*, April 2003, pp. W1–W4.

12 Joan Magretta, 1998, "Fast, Global and Entrepreneurial: Supply Chain Management, Hong Kong Style, An Interview with Victor Fung," *Harvard Business Review*, September–October, pp. 102–114.

13 Magretta, *ibid.*, p. 111.

14 Magretta, *ibid.*, pp. 102–114.

15 Andrew Tanzer, 1999, "Stitches in Time," *Forbes Magazine*, September 6, www.forbes.com.

16 David Birnbaum, 2000, *Birnbaum's Global Guide to Winning the Great Garment War*, Hong Kong: Third Horizon Press, pp. 265, 269. According to Birnbaum, the Hong Kong and Chinese industries were integrated before the return of Hong Kong to Chinese sovereignty in 1997.

17 Tanzer, "Stitches in Time," *ibid.*

18 Tanzer, "Stitches in Time," *ibid.*

19 Tanzer, "Stitches in Time," *ibid.*

20 "Gap International ended its relationship with Li & Fung in the late 1980s," see Joanna Slater with Eriko Amaha, 1999, "Masters of the Trade," *Far Eastern Economic Review*, July 22, www.feer.com.

21 "Asia's Largest Textile Market: Shaoxing," December 18, 2003, www.tdctrade.com.

22 China Council for the Promotion of International Trade, Ningbo Sub-Council, Chairman's Message, www.ccpitnb.org/eng/nb02.htm.

23 www.solectron.com.

24 This is as of July 1, 2005, according to the company, www.7-Eleven.com.

25 www.cendant.com/franchising/real_estate.html.

26 "Franchising Industry in China," 2006, BuyUSAinfo, US Commercial Service, US Department of Commerce, www.buyusainfo.net/.

27 Jeremy Rivkin, 2000, *The Age of Access*, New York: Tarcher Putnam.

28 http://pages.ebay.com/aboutebay/the company/company overview.html, 2006.

29 See Saul Hansell, "Meg Whitman and eBay, Net Survivors," *New York Times*, Section 3, May 5, 2002, p. 17, and Saul Hansell, "Google's Toughest Search is for a Business Model," *New York Times*, April 8, 2002, p. C1.

30 Paul Meller, "Europeans Not Entrepreneurial? Yes They Are eBay's Chief Says," *New York Times*, February 8, 2006, p. C6.

31 Some of this discussion is adapted from chapter 3 of Daniel F. Spulber, 1998, *The Market Makers: How Leading Companies Create and Win Markets*, New York: McGraw-Hill/BusinessWeek Books.

32 Dealers play a prominent role in financial markets. Individual investors buy and sell securities through dealers in the over-the-counter (OTC) market. Operated by the trade group for major securities dealers, the NASDAQ service provides a record of current prices of individual stock transactions as well as posting median prices. These prices reflect the bid and ask prices and completed transactions of many individual dealers and their customers. The NASDAQ market competes for listings and for investors with auction markets for securities such as the NYSE or the American Stock Exchange. Also, *within* the NYSE and other auction markets, there are dealers known as *specialists* who buy and sell particular stocks by matching buy and sell orders and trading on their own account, subject to rules made by the exchange. These types of dealers are referred to as "market makers."

33 Armen Alchian observed that specialists provide information at a lower cost than search, see Armen Alchian, 1969, "Information Costs, Pricing, and Resource Unemployment," *Western Economic Journal*, pp. 109–127. Immediacy in financial markets is discussed by Harold Demsetz, 1978, "The Cost of Transacting," *Quarterly Journal of Economics*, 82, pp. 33–53.

34 This is quoted in George Stalk, Jr. and T. M. Hout, 1990, *Competing Against Time*, New York: Free Press, p. 69.

35 "Wi-Fi" refers to *wireless fidelity*, which is a technical standard for wireless transmission of digital signals, mostly between computers and the Internet.

36 Paul Otellini, President and CEO of Intel, Keynote Address to the International Consumer Electronics Show, Las Vegas, Nevada, January 5, 2006.

37 Otellini, *ibid.*

38 Anand Lal Shimpi, "Intel's Centrino CPU (Pentium-M): Revolutionizing the Mobile World," AnandTech, March 12, 2003, www.anandtech.com.

39 Anand, *ibid.*

40 John Markoff, "Intel's Big Shift After Hitting Technical Wall," *New York Times*, May 17, 2004, p. C1.

41 Don Clark, "Big Bet Behind Intel Comeback: In Chips, Speed Isn't Everything," *Wall Street Journal*," November 18, 2003, p. A1.

42 Clark, *ibid.*

43 Clark, *ibid.*

44 S. Rai, "In India, a High-Tech Outpost for US Patents," *New York Times*, December 15, 2003, p. C4.

45 D. Altman, "China: Partner, Rival or Both?," *New York Times*, Section 3, March 2, 2003, p. 11.

46 United Nations Conference on Trade and Development (UNCTAD), 2005, *World Investment Report 2005*, New York: United Nations, p. A-18.

47 P. Landers and J. S. Lublin, "Merck's Big Bet on Research by its Scientists Comes Up Short," *Wall Street Journal*, November 28, 2003, p. A1.

48 OECD, 2003, *Science, Technology and Industry Scoreboard*, Paris: Organization for Economic Cooperation and Development, oecd.org/statisticsdata.

49 Smith noted that innovations, in particular improvements in machinery, have been made not only by those who use the machines or make the machines, but also by these "men of speculation." Adam Smith, 1998 [1776], *An Inquiry into the Nature and Causes of the Wealth of Nations*, Washington, DC: Regnery Publishing, p. 8.

50 See International Bank for Reconstruction and Development, 2005, *Doing Business in 2005*, Washington, DC: World Bank and Oxford University Press.

51 World Bank, *ibid.*, p. 19.

52 World Bank, *ibid.*, p. 18.

53 Joseph A. Schumpeter, 1961 [1934], *The Theory of Economic Development*, New York: Oxford University Press.

54 On the role of companies as knowledge brokers, see Andrew B. Hargadon, 1998, "Firms as Knowledge Brokers: Lessons in Pursuing Continuous Innovation," *California Management Review*, 40, Spring, pp. 209–227.

55 See Christopher A. Bartlett and Sumantra Ghoshal, 1989, *Managing Across Borders: The Transnational Solution*, Boston: Harvard Business School Press, and Gunnar Hedlund and D. Rolander, 1990, "Action in Heterarchies – New Approaches to Managing the MNC," in C. A. Bartlett, Y. L. Doz, and G. Hedlund, eds., *Managing the Global Firm*, London: Routledge.

56 Julian Birkinshaw, 2000, *Entrepreneurship in the Global Firm*, London: Sage.

5 Global investment strategy: choosing the best mix of transactions and investment

1 Paul Glader and Jason Singer, "Mittal & Son, Steelmakers," *Wall Street Journal*, February 13, 2006, p. B1.

2 Company profile, www.mittalsteel.com.

3 Heather Timmons, "Finding the Future in an Old Industry," *New York Times*, October 28, 2004, p. W1.

4 All data in this paragraph are from *Mittal Steel Fact Book 2004*, Mittal Steel, www.acelormittal.com.

5 *Mittal Steel Fact Book, ibid.*

6 *Mittal Steel Fact Book, ibid.*, p. 5.

7 *Mittal Steel Fact Book, ibid.*, p. 5.

8 James Kanter, "Politicians and Unions Weigh In on Mittal's Hostile Bid," *New York Times*, January 31, 2006, p. C4.

9 Kanter, *ibid.*

10 Matthew Kominski, "The Weekend Interview with Lakshmi Mittal: The Richest Man Americans Have Never Heard Of," *Wall Street Journal*, February 4–5, 2006, p. A8.

11 See www.acelormittal.com.

12 United Nations Conference on Trade and Development (UNCTAD), 2005, *World Investment Report 2005*, New York: United Nations. The rankings of companies based on foreign assets uses data from 2003.

13 All data on FDI in this section are sourced and adapted from the United Nations Conference on Trade and Development (UNCTAD), 2005, *World Investment Report 2005*, New York: United Nations. The data are for the year 2004 unless otherwise indicated.

14 UNCTAD, *ibid.*

15 "The Birth of BP," www.bp.com.

16 www.bp.com, *ibid.*

17 The Anglo-Persian Oil Company, renamed the Anglo Iranian Oil Company, became British Petroleum (BP) in 1954.

18 Statement of John Browne, www.bp.com.

19 www.bp.com, *ibid.*

20 Matt Murray, "Critical Mass: As Huge Companies Keep Growing, CEOs Struggle to Keep Pace," *Wall Street Journal*, February 8, 2001, p. A1.

21 See the discussion in chapter 10.

22 Franklin R. Root, 1994, *Entry Strategies for International Markets*, San Francisco: Lexington Books. Root compares entry modes extensively and points out the need for managers to compare entry modes in terms of their profitability for each target market, see Root, *ibid.*, chapter 6.

23 See Root, *ibid.*, for further discussion.

24 See Root, *ibid.*, for additional discussion.

25 The account relies on company information about the JV, see www.tbg.co.uk. On Anda, see also http://china-window.com/Shenzhen_w/business/company/sz2/ad/ad.html.

26 Quoted from Intellectual Property and Licensing, ibm.com.

27 Shawn Tully, "The Modular Corporation," *Fortune Magazine*, February 8, 1993, pp. 106–113.

6 The global business organization

1 See Louis Sullivan, 1924, *The Autobiography of an Idea*, New York: AIA Press.

2 The strategic business unit (SBU) was first associated with GE and emerged in the 1970s as companies began to take competitive strategy into account in designing organizational divisions.

3 Jay R. Galbraith suggests that many of the headquarters functions should be distributed to country or regional divisions to handle political and regulatory bodies such as the EU, giving the divisions greater autonomy and flexibility, see Jay R. Galbraith, 2000, *Designing the Global Corporation*, San Francisco: Jossey Bass, p. 11.

4 The information on the Ingram Micro divisions is provided on their website at www.ingrammicro.com under the heading of specialized divisions. Some of the descriptions of the divisions are based upon or paraphrased from the company descriptions of its divisions.

5 Ingram Micro was selected as the preferred distributor for five years straight by a *Computer Reseller News* survey and named the preferred distributor by a *VARBusiness* poll, see the discussion at www.ingrammicro.com under the heading of specialized divisions.

6 N. Fligstein, 1990, *The Transformation of Corporate Control*, Cambridge, MA: Harvard University Press.

7 See Richard Whittington and Michael Mayer, 2001, "Economics, Politics and Nations: Resistance to the Multidivisional Form in France, Germany and the United Kingdom, 1983–1993," Oxford University Working Paper; and Michael Mayer and Richard Whittington, 1999, "Strategy, Structure and 'Systemness': National Institutions and Corporate Change in France, Germany and the United Kingdom, 1950–1993," *Organizational Studies*, 20, pp. 933–960.

8 Theodore Levitt, 1975, "Marketing Myopia," *Harvard Business Review*, September–October, pp. 2–14.

9 Quoted in *The Economist*, October 1998.

10 GM's *Annual Report* for 1998, Letter to Shareholders.

11 GM's *Annual Report* for 1999.

12 This paragraph draws upon an ABB Company Press Release, "ABB Realigns Business Segments to Tap Market Trends, Names New Group Executive Committee," August 12, 1988, www.abbgroup.com.

13 This paragraph draws upon an ABB Company Press Release, *ibid.*

14 Information about ABB is mostly drawn from abb.com/global.

15 Although country managers still play a strong role in single-business and multiple business companies, Galbraith, *Designing the Global Corporation, ibid.*, p. 92 notes that: "with the emergence of freer trade, deregulation and privatization the power in diversified companies has swung away from country managers to the managers of business units." As Galbraith observes: "It is difficult today to find a multibusiness company with a pure geographical structure; most are a balance of business and geography." See Galbraith, *ibid.*, p. 92.

16 Andrew Ross Sorkin, "Procter & Gamble Agrees to Acquire Clairol for $4.95 Billion," *New York Times*, May 22, 2001, p. C4.

17 Emily Nelson, "P&G Seeks to Shed Crisco and Jif Brands," *Wall Street Journal*, April 26, 2001, p. B9; and Julian E. Barnes, "Procter & Gambles Says it Wants to Jettison Jif and Crisco Brands," *New York Times*, April 26, 2001, p. C1.

18 Julian E. Barnes, "P.&G. Reports Net Loss After Cost of Revamping," *New York Times*, August 8, 2001, p. C8.

19 "The Death of the Geneen Machine: ITT," *The Economist*, 335, June 17, 1995, p. 70.

20 Claudia H. Deutsch, "G.E. is Selling Off Most of Electronic Commerce Business," *New York Times*, June 25, 2002, p. C10.

21 http://investors.tycoint.com/news/.

22 Tarun Khanna and Krishna Palepu, 1997, "Why Focused Strategies May Be Wrong for Emerging Markets," *Harvard Business Review*, July–August. They also observe that the industrial groups recruit, train, and allocate labor services in economies that do not have well-developed labor markets.

23 Khanna and Palepu, *ibid.*

24 Tarun Khanna and Krishna Palepu, 1998, "House of Tata, 1995: The Next Generation (A)," Cambridge, MA: Harvard Business School Case Study N9-798-037, April 28.

25 www.samsung.com/about/index.html.

26 Robert A. Guth, "Electronics Giants of Japan Undergo Wrenching Change," *Wall Street Journal*, June 20, 2002, p. A1.

7 Lenovo: entering global competition

Daniel F. Spulber prepared this case study to illustrate an issue in management strategy for the purpose of class discussion. Aaron M. Spulber provided valuable research assistance.

1 David Barbosa, "An Unknown Giant Flexes Its Muscles," *New York Times*, December 4, 2004, p. B1.

2 Chairman's Message, Legend Group, 2003, www.legendgrp.com/cgi-bin/main. cgi?section=about&sub_section=chair_message.

3 Dexter Roberts, with Joyce Barnathan and Bruce Einhorn, "How Legend Lives Up to Its Name," *BusinessWeek*, February 15, 1999, pp. 75–76. See also Tony Jordan, 1999, "Mastering the Market," *Asian Business*, February; © Far East Trade Press Ltd.

4 Tony Jordan, "In the Beginning," *Asian Business*, February 1999.

5 Bill Powell, "The Legend of Legend," *Fortune Magazine*, September 16, 2002, p. 34.

6 According to Mary Ma, chief financial officer and senior vice president of the publicly traded unit, "the Chinese government owns 65 percent of the parent company, which in turn owns 57 percent of the Hong Kong operations," see Keith Bradsher, "Chinese Computer Maker Plans a Push Overseas," *New York Times*, February 22, 2003, p. B1.

7 Jordan, "In the Beginning," *ibid.*

8 Jordan, *ibid.*

9 Ariel Tam, "Yang Yuanqing – The PC Mogul," *ZD Net India*, April 2, 2001, www.zdnetindia.com/biztech/people/columnists.

10 Tam, *ibid.*

11 Roberts, "How Legend Lives Up," *ibid.*

12 Kenneth L. Kraemer and Jason Dedrick, 2002, "Enter the Dragon: China's Computer Industry, *IEEE Computer*, 35, February, pp. 28–36.

13 Roberts, "How Legend Lives Up," *ibid.*

14 Bruce Einhorn, "Legend's Home-Field Advantage," *BusinessWeek Online*, June 10, 2001, www.businessweek.com.

15 Based on data from the *Customs Import and Export Tariffs of the People's Republic of China*, 1998 edn., from Peggy Lim and Ivan Trinh, 1999, "Personal Computers & Peripherals," US & Foreign Commercial Service, US Department of State.

16 White House Fact Sheet on US-China WTO Accession Deal, March 1, 2000, www. usconsulate.org.hk/uscn/wh/2000/030102.htm.

17 See White House Fact Sheet, *ibid.* However, according to US complaints before the WTO, China's 17 percent VAT on semiconductor sales in China created competitive advantages for Chinese companies because the Chinese government gave rebates to Chinese semi-conductor producers of up to 14 percent for an effective tax rate of 3 percent. The case was resolved in July 2004, with China agreeing to stop providing tax refunds to domestic pro-ducers. See Office of the US Trade Representative, "US and China Resolve WTO Dispute Regarding China's Tax on Semiconductors," July 8, 2004.

18 "China has traditionally restricted imports through high tariffs and taxes, quotas and other non-tariff measures, and restrictions on trading rights. As part of its first year in the WTO, China significantly reduced tariff rates on many products and the number of goods subject to import quotas, expanded trading rights for Chinese enterprises, and increased the transparency of its licensing procedures. However, during China's second year of WTO membership, while China continued to reduce tariff rates on schedule and made other implementation progress, bureaucratic inertia and a desire to protect sensitive industries contributed to a significant loss of the momentum created in the first year of China's WTO membership." See Office of the US Trade Representative, *Foreign Trade Barriers*, March 30, 2004. www.ustr.gov/assets/Document_Library/Reports_Publications/2004/2004_ National_Trade_Estimate/2004_NTE_Report/asset_upload_file231_4191.pdf.

19 See Powell, "The Legend of Legend," *ibid.*

20 Chairman's Message, *Annual Report*, Legend Group Ltd., www.legend-holdings.com, 2002.

21 Wang Chuandong, "Legend Initiates Strategic Merger," *China Daily*, May 10, 1999, North American edn., p. 5.

22 Bruce Einhorn and Dexter Roberts, "A New Twist in Legend's Tale," *BusinessWeek*, June 23, 2003, p. 50.

23 Bruce Einhorn, "Foreign Rivals vs. the Chinese: If You Can't Beat 'Em . . .," *BusinessWeek*, February 15, 1999, p. 78.

24 Jordan, "Mastering the Market," *ibid.*

25 Roberts, "How Legend Lives Up," *ibid.*

26 Jordan, "Mastering the Market," *ibid.*

27 Bradsher, "Chinese Computer Maker," *ibid.*

28 World Information Technology and Services Alliance, "Background Paper on the World Trade Organization's Negotiations and Issues Regarding Information and Communications Technology (ICT)," December 2002.

29 Roger Roxin Chen, 2004, "Corporate Reputation: Pricing and Competing in Chinese Markets – Strategies for Multinationals," *Journal of Business Strategy*, 25, pp. 45–50.

30 This phenomenon was not unique to computers but also occurred in household appliances and electronics generally, see Chen "Corporate Reputation," *ibid.*

31 Roberts, "How Legend Lives Up," *ibid.*

32 Charles Bickers, 1999, "Sharing the Pie," *Far Eastern Economic Review*, 162, June 17, pp. 54-56; © Dow Jones & Company, Inc.

33 Bickers, *ibid.*

34 *Legend Annual Report*, 2000–2001, p. 19.

35 Lily Wu, head of Salomon Smith-Barney's regional technology research, notes that distribution is Legend's main advantage, see T. Jordan, "Mastering the Market," *ibid.*

36 Corporate News, *2002/2003 Annual Results*, www.legendgrp.com and company information.

37 Company Press Release, August 9, 1999, www.legend-holdings.com.

38 Powell, "The Legend of Legend," *ibid.*

39 Karen Cohn, "Extending Legendary Success," *Electronic Business*, May 15, 2003, p. 52.

40 Powell, "The Legend of Legend," *ibid.*

41 Powell, *ibid.*

42 "Legend Announces 2002/03 Annual Results," Press Release, Legend Group, www.legendgrp.com/.

43 Yadong Luo, 2000, *How to Enter China: Choices and Lessons*, Ann Arbor; University of Michigan Press, p. 13.

44 Bureau of Economic Analysis, www.bea.gov.

45 Einhorn, "Legend's Home-Field Advantage," *ibid.*

46 Rebecca Buckman, "Hewlett Reports Jump in Deliveries of PCs to China," *Wall Street Journal* (Eastern edn.), December 4, 2003, p. B1.

47 Bloomberg, "Legend's Q4 Net Falls as Rivals Erode Market Share," *Taipei Times*, May 29, 2003, p. 11.

48 Bickers, "Sharing the Pie," *ibid.*, pp. 54–56.

49 Bickers, *ibid.*

50 Powell, "The Legend of Legend," *ibid.*

51 Bickers, "Sharing the Pie," *ibid.*

52 Einhorn, "Foreign Rivals," *ibid.*, p. 78.

53 Einhorn, *ibid.*

54 Bickers, "Sharing the Pie," *ibid.*

55 Rebecca Buckman, "Computer Giant in China Sets Sights on US," *Wall Street Journal*, June 19, 2003, p. B1.

56 "HP Breaking into Home PC Market with Low Prices," *SinoCast China Business Daily News*, June 12, 2003, p. 35

57 Bien Perez, "Buoyant HP Steps Up Sales Drive in Asia," *South China Morning Post*, March 4, 2003.

58 "HP Breaking into Home PC Market," *ibid.*, p. 35.

59 Perez, "Buoyant HP," *ibid.*

60 Perez, *ibid.*

61 *Source*: Li Weitao, "HP Back in Home PC Market," *China Business Weekly*, June 10, 2003, www1.chinadaily.com.cn.

62 Luo, *How to Enter China, ibid.*

63 Luo, *ibid.*

64 Bien Perez, "Career Path Traces the Rise of Big Blue," *South China Morning Post*, March 25, 2003.

65 Luo, *How to Enter China, ibid.*, pp. 200–210.

66 Luo, *ibid.*, pp. 200–210.

67 www.research.ibm.com/beijing.

68 "IBM Ranked No. 1 in Chinese Software Market," *AsiaPort Daily News*, July 9, 2002, p. 5.

69 Andrew Batson, "Interview: IBM Focuses On Software, Services in China," *Dow Jones International News*, February 24, 2003.

70 Bradsher, "Chinese Computer Maker," *ibid.*

71 Daffyd Roderick "For Whom the Dell Tolls: Can Legend Computer Save China from the World's Biggest Boxmaker?," *Time International*, March 25, 2002, p. 44.

72 Roderick, *ibid.*

73 "Legend Announces 2002/03 Annual Results," Press Release, Legend Group, www.legendgrp.com/.

74 Rebecca Buckman, Ben Dolvenin, and Susan V. Lawrence, 2003, "Legend Goes for the Big League," *Far Eastern Economic Review*, June 19, p. 32.

75 Buckman *et al.*, *ibid.*

76 Powell, "The Legend of Legend," *ibid.*

77 Legend Group, Press Release, April 2003.

78 Einhorn and Roberts, "A New Twist in Legend's Tale," *ibid.*

79 Einhorn and Roberts, *ibid.* See also Powell, "The Legend of Legend," *ibid.*

80 Buckman *et al.*, "Legend Goes for the Big League," *ibid.*

81 Bradsher, "Chinese Computer Maker," *ibid.*

82 Bradsher, *ibid.*

83 Company information provided for this case study.

84 Buckman, "Computer, Giant in China," *ibid.*

85 The information and quotations in this paragraph are drawn from "Legend Opens Factory in City," Shanghai Foreign Investment Service Center, July 29, 2003, www.sfisc.com/news/0308a02.htm.

86 "Legend Holdings Cooperates with Local Notebook Makers," *Computex Online*, June 8, 2001, www.computex.com.tw/comp2001/news0608.asp.

87 Li Weitao, "Matsushita to Tap Local PC Market," *Business Weekly*, March 4, 2003, http://www1.chinadaily.com.

88 Michelle Levander, "A Great Leap Forward? Legend's Innovative Partnership with AOL May Signal the Direction of China's Internet Market," *Time International*, June 25, 2001, p. 28.

89 "Legend Launches the First Innovative Technology Convention: Legend World 2002," Company Press Release, Beijing, December 3, 2002.

90 "Legend Technologies Selling Microsoft Products," *Asiainfo Daily China News*, Dallas; © Asia Intelligence Wire from FT Information, April 14, 1999.

91 Bickers, "Sharing the Pie," *ibid*.

92 "Legend–Toshiba Marketing College Opened," *Asiainfo Daily China News*, Dallas; © Asia Intelligence Wire from FT Information, July 6, 1999.

93 *China Daily*, June 1, 1999.

94 Kraemer and Dedrick, "Enter the Dragon," *ibid*.

95 *New York Times*, December 31, 2004, p. C4.

96 Barbosa, "An Unknown Giant," *ibid*.

97 Steve Lohr, "IBM Sought a China Partnership, Not Just a Sale," *New York Times*, December 13, 2004, p. C1.

98 Lenovo Press Release, "Lenovo Appoints William J. Amelio CEO and President to Succeed Stephen M. Ward, Jr.," Purchase, NY, December 20, 2005, www.lenovo.com/news/us/en/2005/12/ceo.html.

99 Lenovo Press Release, *ibid*.

100 Glenn Rifkin and Jenna Smith, "Quickly Erasing 'I' and 'B' and 'M'," *New York Times*, April 12, 2006, p. C9.

8   Cemex: making global markets

This case was written jointly with Alberto Salvo at the Kellogg School of Management, Northwestern University. The authors prepared this case study to illustrate an issue in management strategy for the purpose of class discussion. A substantially different earlier version received research assistance from John Baker, Jennifer Bracale, and Adrian Diazgonsen.

1 "Cemex: Solid as Mexico Sinks," *BusinessWeek*, February 27, 1995, pp. 58–59.

2 "Survey: World's Most Respected Companies: Deliveries in Pizza-Style, Complex Computer Systems Keep the Mexican Cement Company's Tricks Close to Customers," *Financial Times*, November 30, 1998.

3 "Survey: World's Most Respected Companies," *ibid*.

4 Lorenzo H. Zambrano, Letter to Shareholders, Cemex *Annual Report*, 1998.

5 See Donald R. Lessard and Rafel Lucea, 2006, "Embracing Risk as a Core Competence," in *Cemex 100th Anniversary Volume*, MIT Sloan School of Management. Lessard and Lucea explain that strategic risk management is a core competence for Cemex.

6 The company has been widely studied. Other case studies with an emphasis or approach that differs from the present study include David P. Baron and Justin Adams, 1994, Joel Podolny, John Roberts, Joon Han, and Andrea Hodge, 1999, Pankaj Ghemawat and Jamie L. Matthews, 2000, Donald A. Marchand, Katarina Paddack, and Rebecca Chung, 2002, and R. Sarathy and D. T. A. Wesley, 2003, "Cemex and Antidumping,", Stanford University Case Study, January 1; "The Globalization of Cemex," Harvard Business School, 701017, September 8; "Cemex: The Southdown Offer," Northeastern University and Richard Ivey School of Business, University of Western Ontario, Case 9B03M013, March. "Cemex: Global Growth Through Superior Information Capabilities," IMD084, January 1; "Cemex, SA de CV: Global Competition in a Local Business," IB17, July 9.

7 The company acquired Cementos Maya in 1966, a plant in León in 1972, Cementos Guadalajara in 1976, and Cementos Anahuac in 1987.

8 In the late 1980s and early 1990s, Mexico adhered to the GATT, joined the OECD, and entered NAFTA.

9 Cement is used in the form of concrete, which results from the hardening of a mixture of cement, sand, gravel, and water. Customers can acquire cement and mix concrete on site (typically for small- or large-scale construction) or they can acquire already mixed concrete from ready-mix concrete firms (typically mid-sized construction operations).

10 Peter Fritsch, "Hard Profits: A Cement Titan in Mexico Thrives by Selling Cement to Mexico's Poor," *Wall Street Journal*, April 22, 2002, p. A1.

11 The Mexican antitrust agency, the Federal Competition Commission, was created in 1993. Commission officials pointed out to the *Wall Street Journal* (Fritsch, "Hard Profits," April 22, 2002) that much of the consolidation of the Mexican cement market had taken place before the Commission was set up.

12 John Moody, "A Mexican Cement Maker With a Worldview," *New York Times*, April 15, 2004, p. W7.

13 Cemex *Annual Report* 1998, online.

14 Several sources: Cemex Historical Development, www.cemex.com, accessed in 1998; authors' computations; 2004 *Annual Report*.

15 Marco Morell, "Cemex Leads the Way Towards Globalization," *Handelsblatt, Wirtschafts- und Finanzzeitung*, June 13, 1999.

16 Sarathy and Wesley, "Cemex: The Southdown Offer," 2003, *ibid*.

17 "Cemex Cements Its Position With Agreement to Buy RMC," *Wall Street Journal*, September 28, 2004, p. A7.

18 See J. N. Bhagwati, E. Dinopoulos, and K. Y. Wong, 1992, "Quid Pro Quo Foreign Investment," *American Economic Review*, 82, papers and proceedings of the American Economic Association, pp. 186–190.

19 From 1991 to 1999, the Brazilian cement industry consolidated from nineteen to eleven producers.

20 Though limestone is abundant in many regions, obtaining the right to explore reserves can be costly for environmental reasons, or because such rights already lie in the hands of incumbents.

21 H. Dumez and A. Jeunemaître, 2000, *Understanding and Regulating the Market at a Time of Globalization: The Case of the Cement Industry*, London: Macmillan.

22 As mentioned, the cement industry is a major consumer of energy. In addition, the production of clinker directly releases vast quantities of greenhouse gases into the atmosphere. According to the US Department of Energy, around 60 percent of the carbon dioxide emissions from industrial processes in the US are from cement manufacture alone. Source: *Emissions of Greenhouse Gases Report*, Energy Information Administration, Washington, DC, 2004.

23 Plant production costs depended on plant characteristics such as the technology, scale, age, and capacity utilization of the equipment, as well as the type of fuel employed in the kiln (i.e. fuel oil, natural gas, pet coke, etc.). Unit production costs for plants *with similar characteristics* thus tended to be similar, regardless of the characteristics of the owner, such as whether the owner operated many or few plants (assuming that input prices, such as the price of fuel, were similar).

24 Examples of governments that had sold cement-producing assets were those of France, the Philippines, Portugal, Spain, and Turkey.

25 Based on several issues of the industry trade journals *World Cement* and *International Cement Review*.

26 Asked about Cemex's debt pile of $6 billion in 2002, following the acquisition of Southdown, investment fund managers and large investors stated that they were not worried, in view of Cemex's Mexican operations which were expected to generate $1.2 billion in free cash flow that year. Fritsch, "Hard Profits," *ibid.*, p. A1.

27 See "History" of Lafarge at Lafarge.com.

28 See "History" of Lafarge, *ibid.*

29 See "Lafarge at a Glance" at Lafarge.com.

30 See holcim.com.

31 Medard Meier, "Cemex Emerges as the Real Dynamo of the Cement Industry," *Bilanz*, June 14, 1999, www.cemex.com/en/news/en/19990614.asp.

32 See holcim.com.

33 See holcim.com.

34 Moody, "A Mexican Cement Maker," *ibid.*

35 This account draws on Dumez and Jeunemaître, *Understanding and Regulating*, *ibid.*

36 *World Cement*, January 2000.

37 *International Cement Review*, December 2000.

38 Source: Cemex Fact Sheet, "Building the Future," posted online.

39 *International Cement Review*, December 1999.

40 For further discussion of market making, see Daniel F. Spulber, 1998, *The Market Makers: How Leading Companies Create and Win Markets*, New York: McGraw-Hill/Business Week Books and Daniel F. Spulber, 1999, *Market Microstructure: Intermediaries and the Theory of the Firm*, New York: Cambridge University Press.

41 Cemex, *Annual Report* 1998, online: "Trading Market Highlights."

42 Morell, "Cemex Leads the Way," *ibid.*

43 Cemex Fact Sheet, *ibid.*

44 Cemex webpage, www.cemex.com/en/ir/ar/1998/html/en331005.asp.

45 Company presentation delivered in Norwalk, CT, on July 1, 2004, entitled "Value Creation at CEMEX."

46 Cemex webpage, *ibid.*

47 Cemex webpage, www.cemex.com/en/ir/ar/1998/html/en331010.asp.

48 Company documents.

49 "Concrete Benefits from a Plunge into Cyberspace," *BusinessWeek*, April 20, 1999, online.

50 "In Search of the New World," *Fast Company*, April 1999, p. 218.

51 Jose Garces, Senior Analyst, Select-IDC, Mexico City, as quoted in "Concrete Benefits from a Plunge into Cyberspace," *ibid.*

52 *ibid.*

53 "Survey: World's Most Respected Companies," *ibid.*, p. 7.

54 "In Search of the New World," *Fast Company*, April 1999, p. 218.

55 "Survey: World's Most Respected Companies," *ibid.*

56 "Concrete Benefits from a Plunge into Cyberspace," *ibid.*

57 Cemex, *Annual Report* 1998, online, *ibid.*

58 "Survey: World's Most Respected Companies," *ibid.*

59 Cemex: Investors Relations Center.

60 Cemex, *Annual Report* 2004, online, *ibid.*

61 Cemex webpage, www.cemex.com/en/ir/ar/1998/html/en331008.asp.

62 "Expensive Energy? Burn Other Stuff, One Firm Decides. Mexico's Cemex Feeds Kilns a Cheap Refinery Leftover Called Petroleum Coke," *Wall Street Journal*, September 1, 2004.

63 "Concrete Benefits from a Plunge into Cyberspace," *ibid.*

64 *Ibid.*

65 Interview with Francisco Aguilera, Cemex, May 15, 1999.

9   Dairy Farm: regional retail strategy

Dairy Farm International Holdings Ltd is hereafter designated simply as Dairy Farm. Daniel F. Spulber prepared this case study for the purposes of class discussion. Scott Paul H. Davis provided research assistance on an earlier version of the case study.

1 See Thomas Reardon, Peter Timmer, and Julio Berdegue, 2004, "The Rapid Rise of Supermarkets in Developing Countries: Induced Organizational, Institutional, and Technological Change in Agrifood Systems," *electronic Journal of Agricultural and Development Economics*, Agricultural and Development Economics Division (ESA), FAO, www.fao.org/es/esa/eJADE, 1 (2), pp. 168–183; and Andrew W. Shepherd, 2005, "The Implications of Supermarket Development for Horticultural Farmers and Traditional Marketing Systems in Asia," Agricultural Management Marketing, and Finance Service, FAO, Rome, Working Paper.

2 Louie Lucas, "Fruitful Outlook for HK's Dairy Farm," *Financial Times*, September 25, 1998.

3 Incorporated in Bermuda, Dairy Farm International Holdings Ltd had its primary share listing on the London Stock Exchange (LSE) and the majority of its shares traded in Singapore.

4 Historical information and quoted excerpts are from Nigel Cameron, 1986, *The Milky Way: The History of Dairy Farm*, Hong Kong: Windsor House.

5 Subsequent years produced a profit, although the size of the profit dropped from HK$90,000 in 1914 to HK$55,000 in 1915, then rose to HK$125,000 in 1916; Cameron, *The Milky Way, ibid.*

6 Dairy Farm International Holdings Ltd, *Outline of Operations*, 1997, p. 7.

7 Cameron, *The Milky Way, ibid.*, p. 211.

8 *Ibid.*, p. 246.

9 "The Jardine Matheson Group – Still at Home in Causeway Bay after 160 Years," *Thistle: The Magazine of Jardine Matheson*, 1, 2005, pp. 16–21.

10 www.jcclgroup.com/group/astra/index.html.

11 Cameron, *The Milky Way, ibid.*, p. 287.

12 Information and excerpts, Cameron, *ibid.*

13 Source: Dairy Farm International Holdings Ltd.

14 Dairy Farm International Holdings Ltd, *Outline of Operations 1997, ibid.*, pp. 24–25.

15 "Franklins Supermarkets Australia," The Professional Assignments Group, June 2001, www.pag.com.au/articles/franklins.htm.

16 "Franklins Supermarkets Australia," *ibid.*

17 Dairy Farm, *Annual Report* 1998. See also www.dairyfarmgroup.com/dfarm_graphic/default.html.

18 Dairy Farm International Holdings Ltd, *Annual Report* 2004.

19 Dairy Farm International Holdings Ltd, *Annual Report, ibid.*

20 Store data from Dairy Farm International Holdings Ltd, *Interim Report*, 2005.

21 Data on sales and stores from "Doing Business in Hong Kong & Macau: A Country Commercial Guide for US Companies," Washington, DC: US & Foreign Commercial Service and US Department of State, 2005.

22 Information about Park N Shop from www.aswatson.com.

23 Dairy Farm International Holdings Ltd, www.irasia.com/listco/sg/dairyfarm/press/.

24 Shri Kamal Nath, Minister for Commerce & Industry, Government of India, Seminar on "Retailing in India: FDI and Policy Options for Growth," New Delhi, February 23, 2005.

25 The information on India's retail industry and its population is from "Doing Business in India: A Country Commercial Guide for US Companies," Washington, DC: US & Foreign Commercial Service and US Department of State, 2004.

26 Eric Bellman and Kris Hudson, "Wal-Mart Stakes India Claim," *Wall Street Journal*, January 18, 2006, p. A9.

27 Bellman and Hudson, *ibid.*

28 "Doing Business In (Indonesia): A Country Commercial Guide for US Companies," Washington, DC: US & Foreign Commercial Service and US Department of State, 2005.

29 *Ibid.*

30 Dairy Farm International Holdings Ltd, www.irasia.com/listco/sg/dairyfarm/press/p980217.htm.

31 Dairy Farm International Holdings, *Interim Report* 2005, Store data as of June 30, 2005.

32 Wayne Arnold, "Indonesia's Grocery Revolution," *New York Times*, November 18, 1999, p. C1.

33 Arnold, *ibid.*

34 Quoted in "Time to Deliver," *The Economist*, December 9, 2004.

35 www.aswatson.com.

36 Howard W. French, "New Boomtowns Change Path of China's Growth," *New York Times*, July 28, 2004, p. A1.

37 Morgan Stanley Consumer Team, "China: Not the Same Golden Opportunity Across Staples," *Industry Report, Global Consumer Staples*, June 21, 2005.

38 The information in this paragraph is from China Forum, *Thistle: The Magazine of Jardine Matheson*, 1, 2005, pp. 6–7.

39 Andrew W. Shepherd, 2005, "The Implications of Supermarket Development for Horticultural Farmers and Traditional Marketing Systems in Asia," Agricultural Management, Marketing and Finance Service, FAO, Working Paper, Rome.

40 Dairy Farm International Holdings Ltd, www.irasia.com/listco/sg/dairyfarm/press/p990813.htm. In 1994, Dairy Farm established a 50/50 JV to establish supermarkets with Cold Storage, Malaysia, see History, www.dairyfarmgroup.com/global/home.htm.

41 Amy Hsueh, 2004, "Taiwan Retail Food Sector Report 2004," USDA Foreign Agricultural Service, Global Agriculture Information Report TW4052, December.

42 Hsueh, *ibid*.

43 Hsueh, *ibid*.

44 Carrefour *Annual Report* 2004.

45 The information in this paragraph relies on Hsueh, *ibid*.

46 Wal-Mart Fact Sheets for the fiscal year ending January 31, 2005, http://walmartstores.com.

47 Mark Landler and Michael Barbaro, "No, Not Always, Wal-Mart Discovers That Its Formula Doesn't Fit Every Culture," *New York Times*, August 2, 2006, p. C1.

48 Landler and Barbaro, *ibid*.

49 Landler and Barbaro, *ibid*.

50 The information on the Trust-Mart Acquisition and the hiring of Ed Chan is from Loretta Chao, "Wal-Mart Appoints an Outsider From Region to Lead China Unit," *Wall Street Journal*, October 23, 2006, p. B11.

51 Information from www.carrefour.com, as of December 2004 unless otherwise indicated.

52 The hypermarket is a large-scale store that combines a department store and a supermarket.

53 Carrefour *Annual Report* 2004, *ibid*. The number of stores includes fully-owned stores, JVs, and franchised units. Carrefour's entry dates are as follows: Taiwan (1989), Malaysia (1994), China (1995), Republic of Korea (1996), Thailand (1996), Singapore (1997), Indonesia (1998), and Japan (2000).

54 Carrefour *Annual Report* 2004, *ibid*.

55 Information about the company is from www.tescocorporate.com.

56 Jackie Lin, "Carrefour to Take Over Tesco's Shops," *Taipei Times*, Saturday, October 1, 2005, p. 10.

57 www.tescocorporate.com.

58 Reardon, Timmer and Berdegue, "The Rapid Rise of Supermarkets," *ibid*.

59 Reardon, Timmer and Berdegue, "The Rapid Rise of Supermarkets," *ibid*.

10   Danone: organizing for global competition

Scott Paul H. Davis provided research assistance on an earlier version of the case. Much of the company data is drawn from Form 20-F, April 15, 2005, as filed with the US Securities and Exchange Commission.

1 Janet Guyon, "Europe's New Capitalists," *Fortune Magazine*, February 15, 1999.

2 Guyon, *ibid*.

3 Danone Group, *Annual Report* 1998.

4 John Tagliabue, "A Corporate Son Remakes Danone," *New York Times*. April 1, 1998, p. C1.

5 www.danonegroup.com/meet_the _danone_group/danone_group_history/1966.html.

6 www.danonegroup.com, *ibid.*

7 Tagliabue, "A Corporate Son," *ibid.*

8 www.danonegroup.com, *ibid.*

9 Tagliabue, "A Corporate Son," *ibid.*

10 www.danonegroup.com, *ibid.*

11 *New York Times*, June 24, 1981.

12 www.danonegroup.com/meet_the_danone_group/brands_and_activities/index.html.

13 Danone Group, *Annual Report* 1998, *ibid.*

14 John Sutton, 1991, *Sunk Costs and Market Structure*, Cambridge, MA: MIT Press.

15 www.danonegroup.com, *ibid.*

16 www.danonegroup.com, *ibid.*

17 Tagliabue, "A Corporate Son," *ibid.*

18 *Ibid.*

19 *Ibid.*

20 www.danone.com, *ibid.*

21 Danone Press Release, 1999, "Danone Sells Off Remaining Pasta Interests," www.danonegroup.com.

22 Danone Press Release, *ibid.*

23 Danone Group, *Annual Report* 1988.

24 *Ibid.*

25 *Ibid.*

26 Bruce Barnard, 1999, "The Corporate Food Chain," *Europe*, 389, Washington, DC, September, p. 13.

27 Danone Group, *Annual Report* 1998, *ibid.*

28 *Ibid.*

29 Barnard, "The Corporate Food Chain," *ibid.*, p. 13.

30 Danone Group, *Annual Report* 1998, *ibid.*

31 *Ibid.*

32 *Ibid.*

33 The Danone Adventure, Groupe Danone 2004, www.danone.com.

34 *Ibid.*

35 www.danone.com/wps/portal/jump/DanoneCorporateIntl.Company.Strategy.

36 *Ibid.*

37 *Ibid.*

38 *Ibid.*

39 *Ibid.*

40 *Ibid.*

41 *Ibid.*

42 *Ibid.*

43 *Ibid.*

44 *Ibid.*

45 Danone Press Release, "Danone Solidarity for Asia," February 28, 2005,

www.danone.com/wps/portal/jump/DanoneCorporateIntl.Press.Commun2004Press
Releases/ref/CMS.DanoneCorporateIntl.Press.2004PressReleases.Trimestre4.CP_021705.

46 Michaela Draganska and Dipak C. Jain, 2005, "Product Line Length as a Competitive Tool," *Journal of Economics & Management Strategy*, 14, Spring, pp. 1–28.

47 Francisco Redruello, "Müller Enters the Spanish Yoghurt Market to the Ire of Danone," *Euromonitor*, November 18, 2003, www.euromonitor.com/article.asp?id=2181.

48 Redruello, *ibid*.

49 www.danone.com/wps/portal/jump/DanoneCorporateIntl.Company.Strategy.

50 www.danone.com.

51 *Ibid*.

Conclusion

1 *Forbes'* list of billionaires has become a global club: "Notable newcomers include Tulsi Tanti, a former textile trader whose alternative energy company owns Asia's largest wind-farm; Vijay Mallya, the liquor tycoon behind Kingfisher beer; Kushal Pal Singh, India's biggest real estate developer; and Anurag Dikshit . . . another online gaming mogul . . . Russia . . . benefited from strong gains in commodities prices. The surge swelled the fortunes of its 33 billionaires, including 7 newcomers who join the list. China now has 8 billionaires." "The World's Billionaires, Billionaire Bacchanalia," eds. Luisa Kroll and Allison Fass, March 27, 2006, Forbes.com.

2 Daniel Machalara and Bruce Stanley, "Giants of the Sea," *Wall Street Journal*, October 10, 2006, p. B1.

Index